DEFINING A DISCIPLINE

DEFINING A DISCIPLINE

Archival Research and Practice in the Twenty-First Century

Essays in Honor of Richard J. Cox

Edited by
Jeannette A. Bastian & Elizabeth Yakel

SOCIETY OF
American
Archivists

CHICAGO

Society of American Archivists
www.archivists.org

© 2020 by the Society of American Archivists

Printed in the United States of America.

Library of Congress Cataloging-in-Publication Data

Names: Cox, Richard J., honouree. | Bastian, Jeannette A., editor. | Yakel,
  Elizabeth, editor. | Society of American Archivists, issuing body.
Title: Defining a discipline : archival research and practice in the
  twenty-first century : essays in honor of Richard J. Cox / edited by
  Jeannette A. Bastian & Elizabeth Yakel.
Description: Chicago : Society of American Archivists, [2020] | Includes
  bibliographical references and index. | Summary: "Fourteen archivists
  present a mosaic of the research that represents the current state of
  archival science and introduces themes that will carry the profession
  into the future as a complex academic discipline. As the archival
  profession in the United States continues to evolve, the book honors one
  of its most prolific and influential thinkers and writers, Richard J.
  Cox, who retired from the profession in 2017 after a 45-year career. The
  book addresses the archival themes of accountability and evidence,
  ethics and education, archival history, and memory. Defining a
  Discipline demonstrates the importance of the role of archivists,
  archives, and archival institutions in communities, organizations, and
  the digital environment. It looks forward-a direction that the
  pioneering Cox promoted throughout his career"-- Provided by publisher.
Identifiers: LCCN 2020000063 | ISBN 9781945246272 (paperback) | ISBN
  9781945246289 (epub) | ISBN 9781945246296 (pdf)
Subjects: LCSH: Archives--Research--Methodology.
Classification: LCC CD931 .D44 2020 | DDC 027.0072--dc23
LC record available at https://lccn.loc.gov/2020000063

Book design by Tyler Crumrine

ISBN: 978-1-945246-27-2 (print)
eISBN: 978-1-945246-28-9 (epub)
eISBN: 978-1-945246-29-6 (pdf)

On the cover: Richard J. Cox, *Distant Lighthouse*, Oil on Canvas, 2012.

TABLE OF CONTENTS

Introduction

Jeannette A. Bastian and Elizabeth Yakel

What makes a discipline, how is it professionalized, and how do we know when it has matured and been integrated into the wider society? There are many ways to chart this progress, such as establishing professional organizations, drafting ethical codes, designing educational curricula, and creating standards and norms in practice, just to name a few. But the outstanding hallmark of a discipline's maturity may be in the recognition and honoring of its own distinguished scholars. This collection of essays honors archival educator Richard J. Cox, a prolific author, a diligent researcher, a prescient thinker, a conscientious teacher, and, above all, a foremost contributor to the development of the archival discipline in the United States. Through fifteen books and more than a hundred articles and reviews, blogs, countless presentations both at conferences and in classrooms, and participation in the archival profession at the highest levels, Cox has championed the archival discipline. He has done this not only by addressing myriad aspects of archival theory and practice but also, and in particular, by focusing our attention outward on the importance of records in contemporary society.

Honoring Richard Cox

Richard Cox began his career in the 1970s as a practicing historian and archivist at the Maryland Historical Society (1972–1978). He went on to work for the City of Baltimore (1978–1983), the Alabama Department of Archives and History (1983–1986), and the New York State Archives and Records Administration (1986–1988). In 1988 he joined the faculty at the University of Pittsburgh's School of Information as a lecturer, and, after receiving his doctorate in 1992, he became part of the faculty as a tenure-track professor. He went on to establish a premier archives program that became a model and exemplar for graduate archival education.

Active in the archival profession at the national level, Cox joined the Society of American Archivists (SAA) in 1972. He went on to chair the SAA committee that drafted the first graduate archival education guidelines in 1988, and as a result he served on the new Committee on Education and Professional Development. In 1986, Cox was elected to the SAA Council. He was the editor of the *American Archivist* from 1991 to 1995; editor, from 2001 to 2007, of the *Records & Information Management Report* published by M. E. Sharpe; and the publications editor for SAA from 2004 to 2007. In 1989 his service to the profession was recognized when he was elected a Fellow of the SAA.

Cox began his career in academia as a doctoral student. His was one of the first doctoral dissertations that problematized the archives, diverging from the previous norm of candidates writing dissertations using historical methods and archival sources.[1] Through qualitative methodology that entailed gathering data from various segments of the archival community to gauge the readiness of the profession to manage electronic records, Cox concluded that, despite several decades of activity, archivists were not yet doing well in this critical records area. His early accomplishment signaled his intellectual focus on validating archives as its own distinct discipline. Cox maintained that an emphasis on the need for archival research, combined with the need for individuals with doctorates to focus on archives, was essential to the furtherance of graduate archival education. This conviction spurred him to build a highly successful and productive doctoral program at Pittsburgh. Richard Cox retired as professor emeritus in 2017.

Cox was not only an educator at Pittsburgh; he was a mentor, guide, and advisor to the entire archival discipline. Mentorship occurred through discussions (sometimes heated) at professional meetings and through blog postings. Perhaps his most widely read effort was his blog, *Reading Archives* (http://readingarchives .blogspot.com/). Between 2006 and 2009, Cox regaled us with his frequent posts about scholarship concerning archives and archival issues (broadly defined). Cox's commitment to dialoging with the wider archival community continued between 2015 and 2017 with his second blog, *Reading Archives and the Academy* (https:// readingarchivestheacademy.wordpress.com/), where he discussed an even broader range of scholarship. His voracious reading, ability to identify archival issues in diverse literature, and in-depth reviews were gifts to the profession.

Although this book honors Cox, the essays are not about him; rather, they seek to carry his vision of an archival discipline and the transformational power of scholarship forward. At the same time they push this vision into new, related directions.

Scholarship

How to explain in this short introduction the tremendous impact that Cox has had on the archives profession? One way may be to briefly look at the breadth and depth of his scholarship through his own writings. Of his fifteen books, three received the Waldo Gifford Leland Award—an annual award given by the Society of American Archivists for a monograph that "encourages and rewards writing of superior excellence and usefulness in the field of archival history, theory, or practice."[2]

Cox's first book—and first award winner—was *American Archival Analysis: The Recent Development of the Archival Profession in the United States*, which announced the focus that he pursued throughout his career: the growth of the archives profession as a discipline in its own right rather than as an accessory to history. In advocating that growth, he explored and encouraged research and theoretical development in a range of archival areas, including appraisal (*Documenting Localities: A Practical Model for American Archivists and Manuscripts Curators* 1996), and *No Innocent Deposits: Forming Archives by Rethinking Appraisal*, 2004); evidence, accountability, and ethics (*Managing*

Records as Evidence and Information, 2001, and *Ethics, Accountability, and Recordkeeping in a Dangerous World,* 2006); and professionalization and education (*Closing an Era: Historical Perspectives on Modern Archives and Records Management,* 2000, and *Archives and Archivists in the Information Age,* 2005).

Importantly, Cox also placed archival issues within a wider context, seeing records both as personal expressions (*Personal Archives and a New Archival Calling: Readings, Reflections and Ruminations,* 2008) and critical components of larger societal issues, as demonstrated in *Archives and the Public Good: Accountability and Records in Modern Society,* which he co-edited with David A. Wallace (2002), and *Flowers After the Funeral: Reflections on the Post-9/11 Digital Age* (2003). By continually making connections between archives and contemporary concerns in his writings and his presentations and by placing records within a broader civic context, Cox has been a leader in promoting an understanding of the centrality of records to contemporary ethical and social justice concerns.

Teaching

His writings alone do not explain the influence of Richard Cox on the archives discipline. He has always put a premium on teaching and mentoring, and indeed, both of these activities have been critical elements of his impact. Throughout his long teaching career, in addition to educating hundreds of master's students, Cox mentored and supervised eighteen completed doctoral dissertations, a record for archival educators. His doctoral graduates went on to teach in such universities as the University of Toronto, the University of Michigan, Simmons University, SUNY Albany, the University of Puerto Rico, the University of South Carolina, and the University of Iowa, where they are now teaching a new generation of archivists. At the time of this writing, several of these professors have themselves guided doctoral students to completion, making Cox's intellectual genealogy one of the longest in the profession.

For those who know Richard Cox or have been his students, it would be remiss not to reference his personal impact as well. At meetings, at conferences, in the classroom, or over a glass of wine, Cox is outspoken, expressive, forthright and knowledgeable. A person with strong convictions and an immediate grasp of a discussion and its implications, he convinces not just by force of personality but because he keeps the core values of the archival endeavor at the center of his vision. Although you might disagree with him, you will always respect him and learn from him.

The Writing of This Book

This book was initiated in discussions between Cox's former doctoral students and other archival educator colleagues who wanted to honor his many significant contributions to the discipline. As a group, they determined that a collection of essays focusing on the continuing development of the themes that Cox himself championed and fostered would both recognize and contribute to realizing his vision. Defining and furthering the archival discipline was Cox's mission throughout his career. These essays carry that mission forward.

The essays are organized around themes that are of enduring importance to archivists: accountability and evidence, ethics and education, archival history, and memory. While these are not the only issues of significance, they are ones that Cox consistently explored in his research and writing. Former doctoral students as well as his educator colleagues were invited to submit essays in these categories. To involve as many former doctoral students as possible, the editors also invited commentaries on the essays.

"Accountability and Evidence," the first section of the book, includes essays by two of Cox's former doctoral students who are now professors, David Wallace and Wendy Duff (writing with Jefferson Sporn), and by fellow educators Luciana Duranti and Michelle Caswell (writing with Joyce Gabiola, Gracen Brilmyer, and Jimmy Zavala). In the introduction to *Archives and the Public Good*, Cox and Wallace write that "it is our contention that the chief value of records is, in fact, a broad accountability binding individuals with each other and with governments, organizations, and society across space and time."[3] Wallace explores that accountability through the government records of the Vietnam War. Duff and Sporn, also concerned with accountability, look at the validity of "witnessing" as archival evidence. Caswell and her UCLA colleagues report on the results of focus groups with users of community archives and their understanding of evidence and records. Duranti analyzes concepts of evidence from both an archival and a legal perspective. Heather Soyka, another former doctoral student and current archival educator, offers an extended commentary on all four essays.

In the second section of the book, "Ethics and Education," educator Heather MacNeil examines the concept of integrity as it relates both to ethics and to the archival profession, while Cox's former doctoral student Eleanor Mattern examines ethics through the case of Hillary Clinton's emails and the role of the US National Archives. These timely approaches echo Cox's own concern expressed in 2013 that "Ethical issues in the archival profession have become a much more significant topic than anyone could have ever predicted, even just a decade or two ago. It is also a topic that has outraced professional structures and the complexities of dealing with information and recordkeeping technologies."[4] In the final essay in this section, educators Anne Gilliland and Kathy Carbone look at archival education that crosses disciplinary areas, distance, and diasporas. Alison Langmead, Cox's Pittsburgh colleague, ties ethics and education together in her commentary.

The three essays in this book's third section deal with archival history, an area of abiding concern to Cox, who continually encouraged archivists to engage with their own history. He set his own example through extensive writings on Lester Cappon, presidential libraries, and archival history in the United States.[5] Cox's former doctoral student, Donghee Sinn, who is now an educator, recounts and examines the conflicting historical memories of No Gun Ri, a mass killing incident during the Korean War, while another former doctoral student and current educator, Lindsay Kistler Mattock, explores records creation from Sir Hilary Jenkinson to MakerSpaces. Educator Patricia Galloway recalls Camp Pitt, an early electronic records education project that Cox helped to sponsor, and its impact on digital recordkeeping. Robert Riter, another former doctoral student, who is now an archival educator, offers commentary on these essays in light of Cox's own writings on archival history.

In the last section, "Memory," the writers of the three essays have vastly different perspectives. All are former doctoral students of Cox's, and all are now archival educators. Each draws inspiration from Cox's own writings on memory.[6] Janet Ceja Alcalá takes Cox's discussions of documentation strategy beyond the textual to document the living social memory of a Mexican religious ritual. Tonia Sutherland builds on Cox's discussions of culture wars to examine contested oral memories around property and the African American community. Jeannette Bastian explores the changing role of memory in archival work. Joel Blanco-Rivera, also a former doctoral student, offers commentary as well as his own perspectives on memory.

The last essay in the book is by James O'Toole, an archival colleague and co-author with Cox of the second edition of SAA's Archives Fundamental Series, *Understanding Archives and Manuscripts* (2006). O'Toole brings personal insights not only about Cox but about the archival generation that both represent.

Although each section has a specific focus, a number of ideas emerge that cut across all of the essays: community and engagement, moving the profession away from perceptions of neutrality and objectivity, urging archivists toward agency, advocating for archivists to engage with current events, and making archivists question not only how we relate to the records and evidence of those events but also to the events themselves. Many of these threads represent both the logical and evolutionary developments of the basic themes—and they are certainly further steps toward Cox's vision of an independent archival discipline.

The paintings on the front cover and throughout the text are by Cox, who started painting in the mid 2000s. Cox notes that he was "inspired by the beauty of mid-coast Maine and the aesthetics of the Arts and Crafts movement where land- and seascape painting went hand-in-hand with its furniture, pottery, and architecture designs." Although he has principally pursued painting as a hobby, he has also exhibited and sold some of his work through local galleries. When asked about his motivations, he further notes that, "the therapeutic act of experimenting with color and design remains his main pursuit, especially as he settles into his retirement years." One of his pleasures continues to be giving paintings to friends and colleagues.[7]

As always, Richard Cox would like the last word. In this case, it is fitting. Cox was a founding partner of the Archival Education and Research Initiative (AERI), a project led by Anne Gilliland at UCLA and originally funded by the Institute for Museum and Library Services to foster community and strengthen doctoral-level education and scholarship in the archival profession. Cox attended all of these events before his retirement. At the AERI meeting immediately before his retirement, Cox presented a paper, "A New Landscape? The Archival Mission in the Post-Truth Era," which he also posted on his *Reading Archives and the Academy* blog. In that presentation, Cox urged archivists—specifically, prospective archival educators—to transform advocacy to deal with political issues, emphasize the role of archives in democratic regimes, embrace the notion of evidence and truth, revisit archival ethics, and develop graduate curriculum and a research agenda that better prepares the next generation of archivists. In closing, he implored the audience,

> We need new ideas and efforts, and these need to come from you, not my generation. . . . Personally, I am not concerned about being remembered. But I am concerned that we have a vigorous, relevant mission and people who are committed to it. . . . We need leadership, creativity, and light in the profession. And maybe nonviolent gadflies as well. . . . We need to create tension in our profession that enables the archival profession to speak more forcibly, be more visible, and carry more weight. We can accomplish this through our teaching, writing, presenting, and other activities.[8]

This volume seeks to answer Cox's call for new ideas, original scholarship, and creative tension as the archival discipline continues to develop and define itself.

Notes

[1]   Richard J. Cox, "Archivists, Electronic Records, and the Modern Information Age: Re-examining Archival Institutions and Education in the United States, with Special Attention to State Archives and State Archivists" (PhD diss., University of Pittsburgh, 1992).

[2]   Society of American Archivists, "Waldo Gifford Leland Award," https://www2 .archivists.org/governance/handbook/section12-leland, captured at https://perma .cc/N8AX-ZF5E.

[3]   Richard J. Cox and David A. Wallace, eds., *Archives and the Public Good: Accountability and Records in Modern Society* (Westport, CT: Quorum Books, 2002).

[4]   Richard J. Cox, "Rethinking Archival Ethics," *Journal of Information Ethics* 22, no. 2 (Fall 2013): 13–20.

[5]   See, for example, Richard J. Cox, ed., *Lester J. Cappon and the Relationship of History, Archives and Scholarship in the Golden Age of Archival Theory* (Chicago: Society of American Archivists, 2004); "Lester J. Cappon and the Idea of the Public Scholar," *Libraries: Culture, History, and Society* 1, no. 1 (2017): 126–151; "On the Value of Archival History in the United States," *Libraries & Culture*, 23, no. 2 (Spring 1983): 135–151; and "The Failure or Future of American Archival History: A Somewhat Unorthodox View," *Libraries & Culture,* 35, no. 1 (Winter 2000):141–154.

[6]   See, for example, "War, Memory, and Archives: Building a Framework," *Library and Archival Security*, 25, no. 1 (2012): 21–57.

[7]   Cox, Richard. "Questions About the Book." Email, 2019.

[8]   Richard Cox, "A New Landscape? The Archival Mission in the Post-Truth Era" (paper, AERI 2017, July 10–14, 2017, Toronto, Ontario, Canada).

THEME ONE
Accountability and Evidence

Richard J. Cox, *Breakers Atlantic Shore*, Oil on Canvas, 2016.

1

A Reservoir of No Viability?

The Documentary Politics of US Atrocities and War Crimes in Vietnam

David A. Wallace

> . . . all wars are fought twice,
> the first time on the battlefield,
> the second time in memory.
>
> — Viet Thanh Nguyen,
> *Nothing Ever Dies: Vietnam and*
> *the Memory of the War*

Introduction

In 2002, Richard Cox and I edited a book on accountability that advocated the role records can play for administrative, governance, social, and historical accountability. Several contributors complicated this assertion with chapters demonstrating accountability's problematic nature, where powerful actors compromise recordmaking and recordkeeping to their advantage.[1] While I still—as, I am sure, does Richard—see records and archives as potent instruments of accountability, over the years we have been equally drawn to their shortcomings and failures to live up to their promise of ensuring answerability as unassailable evidence of actions and decisions. It is increasingly being recognized that recordmaking and recordkeeping are embedded in complex sociopolitical processes that can be deceitful and manipulated to slant perceptions of "reality" and subsequent historical narratives. This is nowhere more evident than in contemporaneous and more recent attempts to rehabilitate the actions of the US armed forces during the war in Vietnam (1955–1975) and especially so in the painful arena of atrocities and war crimes committed by US forces against Vietnamese civilians.

This essay traces the limits and possibilities of records as objects of accountability by charting the manipulation and control of the documentary record of US military atrocities and war crimes against civilians during the Vietnam War. As a standard operating practice, these acts often went unrecorded, misrecorded, and falsified to deny, obfuscate, cover up, and rationalize them. When accurately recorded, not only were these accounts unwelcome, there were severe efforts to control access to the records of these crimes. These dynamics continue to this day. These features complicate assurances of records as trustworthy mechanisms of accountability and remembrance by locating them within deeper contexts of political power, organizational malfeasance, national remembrance, and military lionization. They also contribute enduring false narratives that have been largely successful in writing these crimes "out of history."[2]

This chapter's motivations align with Viet Thanh Nguyen's call for "just memory"[3] and Barbara A. Mizstal's promotion of "cosmopolitan memory"[4]; both writers oppose nationalistic memory. They seek to ensure that the politically weak, the dominated, and the silenced are not written out of history and memory but are instead foregrounded as objects of attention as much as the excessively celebrated and commemorated—in this case, the US warrior and the political-military invasion of Southeast Asia. This essay demonstrates how nationalistic remembering merges with antecedent recordmaking and recordkeeping processes that not only biased the record but continue to ensure that the vast scope of US war crimes against Vietnamese civilians remain muted and deeply unacknowledgeable. This approach centers on an ethics of remembering that rejects nationalistic calls that "urge . . . citizens to remember their own and to forget . . . others."[5] It counters structures of information authority that shape what is representable through government, media, and other public discourse channels that offer a simplified world of good versus evil, of "our boys" versus an inhuman enemy, thereby manipulating citizen empathy, emotions, and understanding.

The Nature and Scope of
US Atrocities and War Crimes

It is far too simplistic to refer to the 1955–1975 period—the "Vietnam War" to Americans and the "American War" to the Vietnamese—as a war between two nations' opposing militaries. Vietnam itself was embroiled in an internecine struggle between North and South. The war had wider import to the region, resulting in devastating consequences for Laos and Cambodia. Other nations that felt an impact were US allies (including Australia, New Zealand, South Korea, Philippines, and Thailand) and North Vietnamese allies (China, North Korea, and the Soviet Union), which usually sit in the shadows of remembrance and commemoration.[6] Likewise sitting in the shadows are the civilian inhabitants of Southeast Asia for whom the effects were shattering and staggering in scope. Through its overwhelming superiority and extensive application, the effects of the actions of the US military were decidedly catastrophic, evidenced by the widespread killing of civilians, destruction of villages, ecocide, rural depopulation, forced urbanization, refugee crises, and sexual crimes and exploitation. These actions violated with impunity the Geneva Conventions of 1949 to which members of the US military were bound,[7] especially those clauses on the "protection of civilian persons in time of war," which barred:

> the deportation of individuals or groups, the taking of hostages, torture, collective punishment, offenses that constitute "outrages upon personal dignity," the imposition of judicial sentences (including executions) without due process guarantees, and discriminatory treatment on the basis of race, religion, nationality or political beliefs.[8]

Files in the US National Archives from the War Crimes Working Group, a secret military body set up after the infamous My Lai massacre,[9] "demonstrated that atrocities were committed by members of . . . every major army unit in Vietnam."[10]

Loss of Life

According to a 1995 Vietnamese government study, South and North Vietnam together experienced 3.35 million dead as well as millions of nonfatal casualties. The US bombing campaigns and civil wars in the "sideshows" of Laos and Cambodia killed an additional 1 million. A disturbing majority of those killed were civilians of all ages. Of the approximately 3.35 million Vietnamese deaths, 2 million (or 60%) were civilian, 1.1 million were North Vietnamese military and allied South Vietnamese Viet Cong forces, and 200,000 to 250,000 were South Vietnamese military allied with the United States. The United States experienced more than 58,000 military deaths while its other military allies experienced roughly 4,900 deaths.[11] Although absolute factual numbers are impossible to arrive at—a 2008 joint Harvard Medical School and University of Washington study exceeded Vietnam's own estimate and counted upward of 3.8 million military and civilian war-related Vietnamese deaths—the rough contours hold.[12] Proportionately, based on the 3.35 million estimate, for every US military death, there were 34.4 Vietnamese civilian deaths, 18.9 North Vietnamese and Viet Cong military deaths, and 4.3 South Vietnamese military deaths. Hence, not only did the Vietnamese bear the overwhelming brunt of fatal encounters, it was civilians who died, by far, most frequently. This disproportionate loss can be seen as the most serious marker of the destructiveness and recklessness of the war, in a country that is 1/30th the geographical size of the United States. The war's impacts continue to have substantial health and psychological effects on surviving Vietnamese and US military veterans.[13]

Killing of Civilians

Contrary to the conventionally promoted view in the United States that civilians were unintentionally and tragically killed by rogue elements, poorly executed operations, or by accident, the blunt reality is that the killing of unarmed Vietnamese civilians by US forces was overwhelmingly intentional and widely covered up, implicated the entire chain of command, and resulted from the standard operating procedures used by the United States to conduct the war.[14] Racism and dehumanization, ideologies of American exceptionalism, war-induced frustration and anger, meeting killed in action (KIA) quotas and pressures to show battlefield success, disincentives to reprimand and hold personnel accountable for violations, and sociopathy and trauma all played a part in atrocities and war crimes and their cover-up and denial. All were facilitated by the United States' vastly superior and overwhelmingly abundant warfare technologies—air-, sea- and river-craft, ground vehicles, weaponry and munitions, communications and targeting, chemical weapons, and more—against an enemy considerably less well equipped and a mostly poor, agrarian-based civilian population. Tactics and operational policies—such as "search and destroy," "free-fire" and "free-strike" zones, "harassment and interdiction," "application of massive firepower," and "carpet"/"saturation" bombing—created a system of "overkill" based on disproportionate response and reprisal that inevitably and intentionally killed civilians. However, the United States did not officially count civilian casualties but counted only "enemy" killed in action, a category that often conflated civilian deaths to meet heightened pressures for "body count" as the measure of military success.[15]

A 1972 *Newsweek* article reported that upward of 5,000 civilians were "killed deliberately" during Operation Speedy Express in 1968. Although the military reported nearly 11,000 enemy killed in action, only 748 weapons were found.[16] Command structure offered rewards to those units who could demonstrate the highest body counts, initiating corrosive incentives to supply counts irrespective of their source, no questions asked.[17] A retired brigadier general who served on the Vietnam War Crimes Working Group at the Pentagon said he believed that tens of thousands of Vietnamese civilians were killed under classifiable war crimes but had not been acknowledged or scrutinized and that the very nature of wars like Vietnam made such war crimes inevitable.[18] Beyond the formalistic and legalistic claims of respect for the human rights of the Vietnamese, institutionalized racism and racist language were often in play on the ground, dehumanizing both the Vietnamese as targets and US military personnel as assailants. Telford Taylor, who was the chief US prosecutor during the Nazi war crimes trials at Nuremburg and later a critic of the US policy in Vietnam, noted the progression of debasement: "The trouble is no one sees the Vietnamese as people. . . . Therefore it doesn't matter what you do to them."[19]

Defoliation

Between 1962 and 1971, the United States sprayed approximately eighteen million gallons of toxic herbicides, colloquially grouped together as "Agent Orange," on nearly six million acres, including 20 percent of South Vietnamese jungles and 36 percent of its mangrove forests. While this ecocide was justified to "deny cover and concealment to the enemy" and to eradicate their food supply,[20] a 2003 study using census data reported a far wider impact. Between 2.1 and 4.8 million people in more than 4,500 hamlets were sprayed.[21] Despite a long and painful campaign by US veterans and their advocates to obtain official government acknowledgement and compensation for exposure—the US Department of Veterans Affairs now recognizes birth defects; a range of cancers; Hodgkin's, Parkinson's, and heart diseases; and other health complications—to this day the United States continues to deny any similar effects on or provide support to exposed Vietnamese who suffered in far greater numbers.[22]

Bombing: Airstrikes and Ground-based Artillery

In North and South Vietnam, Laos, and Cambodia, the United States conducted the largest aerial bombing campaign in history. Between 1964 and 1973, the US Air Force, Navy, and Marine Corps dropped approximately 7.6 million tons (or 15.2 billion pounds),[23] equivalent to several hundreds of pounds per capita and approximately a hundred times the firepower of the atomic weapons dropped on Hiroshima and Nagasaki.[24] Between 1965 and 1968, the United States dropped an average of 64,000 pounds of bombs on North Vietnam *per hour.*[25] Beyond standard aerial weapons, antipersonnel munitions such as napalm (800 million pounds), white phosphorous (3 million rockets purchased), and cluster bombs (hundreds of millions purchased) were also fired from aircraft. In terms of scale, a single sortie payload of six B-52s could destroy an area equivalent to two miles long and five-eighths of a mile wide, the size of the National Mall in Washington, DC.[26] A "guava" cluster bomb, made up of up to 670 bomblets, could, when dropped by a B-52, cover almost an entire square mile with more than 7.5 million steel ball bearings. This level of bombing, by a far margin, caused most of the civilian deaths and resulted in destroyed villages and communities, flattening of hospitals, religious structures, and schools; caused abandonment and destruction of cultivated land and irrigation systems; and displaced large swaths of the rural population. By the early 1970s, the South Vietnamese landscape had more than twenty-one million craters. Some twenty-one million acres of forest underwent "saturation bombing." In the Quang Tri province, one of the most intensively bombed areas in South Vietnam, only 11 of its 3,500 villages were spared bombing.[27]

In addition to the destruction discussed above, US forces and their allies engaged in widespread torture, sexual violence and exploitation, corpse mutilation, and forced removals, which created enormous refugee crises—all forbidden by the laws of war and largely unacknowledged and unpunished, resulting in widespread social and economic disintegration.

Recordmaking and Recordkeeping

Vietnam's 11,000 hamlets, 260 districts, and 44 provinces, when weighed alongside 3,500 enemy actions and 35,000 air assaults per month at the height of the war, presented enormous information creation, use, and management challenges for the US military and their civilian counterparts. Massive amounts of data and records were generated and fed into computers to quantify and analyze the effectiveness of the war effort, from the number of enemies killed to social, political, and economic conditions. Detailed instructions for report writing and the pressing desire to demonstrate "progress" in light of an increasingly controversial and contested war created enormous stresses and burdens on US military forces around records production. At the mid-point of the war, province advisory teams were creating up to 50 reports per month; by 1971, when report production was diminishing, it was estimated that military headquarters and its commands were spending 500,000 hours annually on report creation.[28]

Records creators at the ground level experienced design and redesign efforts of reports for conciseness and timeliness while superiors were striving to measure and understand a deeply complex social and military situation to satisfy the strategic demands of the war managers sitting at the top of the information food chain. In such circumstances, even understanding what was occurring became overwhelming and contingent on data quality from the point of collection onward. As Eliot Wilczek writes, documents like province reports, "attempted to normalize the war into understandable concepts whose notions of success were . . . measurable."[29] Such dynamics undermined comprehending the insurgency as a social and economic movement by instead probing it solely as a military problem. This conceptual framework fundamentally shaped how documentation was ideated and promulgated and how "success" was framed. Such dynamics found expression in two of the most controversial recordkeeping issues of the war: "skewing the content of reports to give a positive account of the war and skewing reports to give a favorable gloss to one's own performance."[30]

It was not just creating records that was challenging and compromised. Managing and using them was onerous, and, at times, their deficiencies were exposed. A military inquiry into the My Lai massacre uncovered so many records management shortcomings that the Inquiry's investigating team added an appendix on them into its official report and recommended follow-up remedial actions. In its efforts to locate pertinent records, the team found a "minimal, generally unsatisfactory" documentary trail characterized by "incomplete permanent records" and "a tendency among units to destroy records rather than to retire them in accordance with established procedures." Files designated for more formal lifecycle management were found to be "poorly selected, poorly organized and, in some cases, inaccurately identified. . . ."[31] The irony of engaging in a war largely directed through information gathering and analysis but which failed to effectively create and manage the necessary information was not lost on many throughout the military and civilian bureaucracies who were skeptical not only of data quality but also of the hubris and omnipotence implied through the control and mobilization of data and information.

It is within this larger context that recordmaking and record-keeping processes played instrumental roles in misrepresenting, covering up, and historically burying documentation of the vast scope of US atrocities and war crimes against Vietnamese civilians. Simultaneously, and ironically, these dynamics also seeded the groundwork for the eventual recovery of those records. The former highest-ranking officer overseeing war crimes files reported that he had been told that, in the wake of the publicity surrounding My Lai,

President Nixon (1969–1974) wanted to "get the army off the front page" and that "the only way to get them off the front page is to say that [war crimes violations] are founded and appropriate action was taken, or that they are unfounded and propaganda tools."[32] Despite all the evidence to the contrary, this officer was still claiming decades later that they were "probably planted by North Vietnam and Hanoi." When asked why the military was so remiss in prosecuting confirmed perpetrators, he responded:

> We . . . tried to follow as nearly as we could what President Nixon said or directed not only for respecting the reputation of the army but the reputation of the United States to not be in continuing violation of the Geneva conventions. And we succeeded. . . . What happened to the files then? I suppose they ended up in the reservoir of official documents that no longer have viability.[33]

These documents-based currents evidence the disquieting dialectic of records as both concrete evidence charting disturbing events and as manipulation and silencing of unwanted and un-faced realities. We want to and need to rely on records for factuality and accountability, but their embeddedness in contested, complex, and power-laden social dynamics vacates simple analyses and direct lines linking records to events. Partiality in recording, the univocality and seeming authoritativeness of official records, and their contradiction by informal personal records, as well as the power undercurrents in which they are situated, makes definitive reliance on them exceedingly tentative.[34]

The larger social issue of what is validated and seen as legitimate and reliable information also plays a determinative role. James William Gibson, pointing to the "warrior's knowledge as expressed in memoirs, novels, poems and plays by . . . soldiers" and their oral histories, notes that they challenged the success and lawfulness of the war's conduct "at virtually every level."[35] He attributes variance in legitimacy to social stratification about whose knowledge counts in the broader culture of authority, characterized as belief in the "scientific" knowledge of institutions and the promotion of "facts" over meaning. He also alludes to Foucault's notion of "subjugated knowledges," whereby the lowest-ranked soldiers relay versions of their experiences that "do not follow the social and intellectual rules governing who can be a serious thinker and the correct form for serious ideas and important facts." Gibson underscores how we tend to see institutional bureaucracies as "legitimate sites of knowledge." Those that are highly placed have more information and more sophisticated and technologically advanced information to sift through to make sense of the war, thus lending them greater social weight and influence. Those later analyzing the war place greater emphasis on these official and formerly secret sources and become discourse dominant because they are seen as beacons of insight and accuracy. These source material biases and obfuscations are ill-considered and not meaningfully interrogated. In these contexts, lower-level accounts are much less valued, because they offer a narrower view, the opposite of the presumed "big picture" from official sources and more highly placed actors. The differential treatment of these "inside" and "outside" perspectives and their associated legitimacy result also in part from the discourses employed in foot soldiers' writings. These are replete with vulgarity, obscenity, and more intense descriptions of and experiences with violence that are unsettling and dismissible as too emotionally driven.[36]

The interplays between the official and unofficial, the written and oral, the recorded and unrecorded, the legalistic and experiential, the bureaucratic and individual, the open and hidden, what can be said close to events and what can be said decades later, and what seemingly can't be remembered by some but can't be forgotten by others, all combine in a multifaceted documentary archipelago. This documentary complex reflects how recordmaking and recordkeeping serve both as smokescreen and explanation in a contest over social memory that promotes and challenges nationalistically driven false narratives. We especially see these dynamics in nonrecording and misrecording of events, outright falsification, resistance and counternarrative building, the decades-long roles played by archives, and the undermining role that secrecy plays across all of these.

Nonrecording and Misrecording

Despite the US military's absolute obsession with quantification to promote "success," it never systematically or officially recorded Vietnamese civilian deaths. This is especially true for aerial bombing, which was responsible for the greatest loss of civilian life. The sporadic attempts to record civilian losses dramatically misrepresented their actual scope and were primarily kept secret when they ran counter to the success narrative or the laws of war. The conscious nondocumentation of war crimes by both lower-level soldiers on the ground and their higher-ups who did not pursue accusations created a compact of silence that made the majority of war crimes officially invisible and thus readily deniable. The documents that did record these war crimes were the exception and were "unusual only in that they were reported in some form or recounted by witnesses instead of vanishing entirely from the historical record."[37] Some soldiers who tried to report war crimes stated that their accounts were suppressed by both higher-ups and those responsible for investigating atrocities. In other cases, investigations were perfunctory and "misleading classifications [such as legally unproven confirmed allegations] contributed to the false perception that many reports of abuse had been wholly fabricated," making it easy to discard deeper probing, especially in regards to officer culpability. In one case, a military investigation spent "hours" with a veteran who gave many details on what he witnessed, including "names, dates, details." However, this witnessing ended up in the official record as a "two-line synopsis."[38] These currents continue to play out decades after the war ended. One infantry website where veterans posted their recollections avoided all mention of a massacre reported in investigatory files,[39] making such episodes publicly invisible by locking them away in the closed "memory box."[40] The memory box silences and buries the past through social and tacit agreement not to openly discuss certain memories—such as participation in human rights violations. The box can sometimes be opened among like-minded comrades in arms but not beyond that and certainly not for larger public consumption.

Falsification

Although there was no shortage of official "directives, regulations … [and] codes of conduct" that gave the US military a "paper trail of deniability,"[41] there were very real pressures on how records were produced to ensure that they reinforced an arc of inevitable success. As described by one military report writer:

> The first [report] was from the facts at hand, from the information we had collected, as objective as could be. Then we sent it in, and

always it came back, doctored. This was . . . standard operating procedure . . . for the time I spent as . . . [brigade] historian. The result is that the battle news is edited and revised until it is acceptable to higher-ups. I've been ordered to write open lies on our civil aid programs. . . . I've been ordered to raise the figures for food distribution in refugee villages. I've also had to retype battle reports . . . [where] the whole time sequence was destroyed . . . and vital facts omitted by the commanding general . . . thereby turning an NVA victory over superior American forces into a U.S. victory.[42]

Positive reports "affirmed the reality of official policy" and were welcomed.[43] Adverse reports, on the other hand, were seen as "an act of disloyalty, or dissent from official goals and disrespect for superiors."[44] As a result, the further the recipients up the chain of command were from the source event of a misrepresentative report, the easier it was to confuse the misrepresentation, filtering through as "words and numbers," with actuality.[45] As one major noted, such duplicitous records "became the ultimate reality."[46] A general quoted by one researcher noted that the "immensity of the false reporting [was] a blot on the honor of the Army. . . ."[47]

Pressure on producing "body counts" of enemy combatants killed in action—the sine qua non for success—all too often resulted in a substantially larger number of bodies than of weapons, problematizing the notion that those killed were other than unarmed civilians. Realizing this, one notorious unit, Tiger Force, began to officially report only estimates so as not to raise concern. A military investigator using army radio logs to plot the movement of Tiger Force noticed patterns in the standard phrasings of engagements, such as "V[iet] C[ong] running from hut, resulting in VC killed." By his own count, this happened nearly 50 times over 11 days, and at no time were any weapons recovered. The investigator surmised that even commanders must have realized that soldiers were shooting unarmed people. This investigator came to realize that this recordkeeping was not only erroneous but that it unintentionally demonstrated that hundreds of unarmed civilians were being killed as standard operating procedure. One soldier, who alone counted 120 murders, stated, "We'll never know how many were killed."[48]

The earlier noted 1972 *Newsweek* article, which reported that 5,000 civilians were "killed deliberately" during Operation Speedy

Express in 1968, is another case in point. A research staffer for the publication started compiling statistics from US military records connected to daily press briefings and concluded that something was deeply amiss in regards to the number of purported enemy killed. The paucity of recovered weapons was glaring in "kills-to-weapons" ratios, especially when combined with local hospital records of civilian casualties. The number arrived at by *Newsweek* matched an estimate given to them by a seasoned American official. A lengthy and detailed article resulting from this research implicated not only ground troops but the entire chain of command. Editors deemed its message—that these atrocities were standard operating procedure—too hot to publish and instead ran a deeply watered-down version. A contemporaneous military inspector general's report that confirmed *Newsweek's* deeper findings was not shared publicly and languished in the "army's secret archives" for decades.[49]

Initial official reports and records about the My Lai massacre lauded the operation as a military success that killed many Viet Cong enemy and, unintentionally, 20 civilians. The only US casualty shot himself in the foot. In reality, it was a slaughter of more than 500 unarmed civilians that included rapes, corpse mutilation, and destruction of domiciles. At one point, up to 150 civilians were executed in an irrigation ditch.[50] Seen as a reprisal for the dozens of US casualties suffered while seeking engagement with an elusive Viet Cong battalion, the massacre and the initial cover-up surrounding it prompted a military investigation that found "widespread killing" of civilians "almost exclusively of old men, women, and children." Further, the report noted "deliberate suppression or withholding of information . . . at every command level . . ." and indicated the creation of fake reports to whitewash the massacre. These key conclusions were only released years later.[51]

Deborah Nelson reports similar instances: a massacre of unarmed women and children falsified as "enemy kills," other massacres that were not filed and thus remained officially invisible; members of one unit who reported that three civilian villagers were executed and their identification cards confiscated so they could be set up to look like guerillas; and a report of ten North Vietnamese soldiers killed in action who were actually unarmed civilians, including three women and two children.[52] A South Vietnamese former director of police told a US adviser how he would falsify documents stating that enemy prisoners were killed while attempting to escape when, in reality, they were executed in a premeditated fashion. The falsified records were used as effective cover in the event of oversight visits.[53] Although these revelations of falsification can be seen as episodic and nonrepresentative, they signify a broader information pathology that was in sync with the success metric pressures and groupthink elucidated above. As information deception became systematic and structural to the conduct of the war, records-related deception regarding the killing of civilians was a logical outcome.

Resistance and Counternarratives

Despite the difficulties with official records noted above—their oversights, strikeouts, and biases—and intense disagreements within the US military over culpability for Vietnamese civilian deaths, the broader documentary universe and contours of memory were not as easily controlled or manipulated. Soldiers' letters home were one venue in which they could confide what they had witnessed. However, going public with such experiences opened one to state harassment and social sanction, as well as having to navigate internal investigatory follow-through and the huge gulf to be traversed between credible allegations and legal evidence.

A military photographer on-site at the My Lai massacre used two cameras—one for official records that showed nothing untoward and certainly no evidence of war crimes and a second that he used to document the massacre and which he kept out of the military's reach. These latter, graphic images were later published to accompany a Pulitzer Prize–winning exposé.[54] One soldier—who was transferred from his unit for trying to prevent the killing of civilians—tape recorded his experiences before he died so that some trace of the event would survive. Another soldier serving as a military journalist who had witnessed war crimes, including the killing of unarmed civilians and the gang-rape and execution of a woman, knew he could not report on such actions in the military press—and in fact was deterred from even reporting such by an army chaplain— decided that he would create his own unofficial record of what he had seen and who he served with, even keeping the identity cards of executed civilians. After returning to the United States, he held a press

conference that initiated an official internal investigation. Within two
years, the investigation, which made good use of his remembrances
and led to onerous searches of military records to locate still active
personnel, was terminated with no charges filed.[55] The US Army's
Criminal Investigation Command (CID) assembled numerous files
of reported war crimes by members of the US military. By 1972 they
were struggling with a backlog of unexamined cases and reluctance by
some to pursue allegations against fellow servicemen:

> Scores of soldiers were stepping forward with allegations, sometimes
> after their military discharges a year or two later, and often with
> infractions that could never be proven. Potential witnesses were
> scared to talk, and in the end, hundreds of investigations went
> nowhere fast. . . . these investigations were often seen by the troops
> as unpatriotic, attacking soldiers who had to carry out impossible
> orders.[56]

A powerful counternarrative challenging unrecorded events, denials,
and unpursued cases was built by returning veterans who refused
to stay silent on what they witnessed. The 1971 Vietnam Veterans
Against the War's "Winter Soldier Investigation" saw testimony from
more than a hundred veterans demonstrating that war crimes were
not one-off occurrences by a solitary few. There were reports from
"almost every major combat unit from all periods of the war."[57] This
counternarrative, however, was aggressively challenged, infiltrated,
and discredited just enough to sow larger public doubts and discourage
other veterans from coming forward.[58] In other instances, army
investigators "intimidated potential witnesses and whistle-blowers,
plied them with alcohol during interviews, entreated them to lie, and
carried out overt surveillance meant to bully them into silence." At
one point the legal adviser to the military's war crimes investigatory
unit admitted that the process was in fact consciously working
against its stated mission.[59] By the early 1970s there existed a slew of
publications, including "hundreds of antiwar newspapers created by
returning veterans" relaying disturbing accounts of US atrocities and
war crimes that were not so easily dismissed.[60] Over time, though,
the military was able to retake control of the narrative. Key to that
effort was its ability to control and keep secret critical information
from its own investigations that confirmed widespread atrocities

and war crimes as well as its refusal to give an official imprimatur to veteran allegations. As a result, the mainstream news media was reluctant to pursue the story.[61] Records associated with war crimes investigations that were disseminated to military and political leaders at the highest levels would seemingly ensure that recipients could not deny knowledge of such investigations. Yet President Gerald R. Ford (1974–1977), Defense Secretary James Schlesinger and his successor Donald Rumsfeld, and Secretary of the Army Howard Calloway would all later claim ignorance of war crimes allegations. Their privileged access further provided them the advantage to forestall investigatory depth and undertake damage control by publicly and falsely promoting reports of war crimes as isolated, and not structural, events. Failing that, they could also use their positions to cover up those reports.[62]

Archives as Inert and Activated Resources

One of the most interesting threads to emerge in the research for this essay was the role that archives played as repositories of documentation awaiting activation.[63] Secrecy and information control across decades permeates the entire issue of the killing of Vietnamese civilians, and it is archives that offer a potent arena for reopening this story and seeding the development of new oral sources. Many of the military's own investigatory reports confirmed cases of torture, murder, sexual assault, and corpse mutilation by its own members, yet those cases were neither prosecuted nor publicly divulged.[64] Even when internal studies concluded that the devastation against the civilian population and infrastructure as reported by independent sources was accurate, the confirming studies were kept secret. Many thousands of documents remained suppressed or secret or laid dormant in official archives for many years, such as a Pentagon review of US troops' comprehension of the Geneva Conventions on the conduct of war that found low levels of understanding.[65]

Archives were substantial also for contemporaneous investigatory efforts. One military investigator, eager to locate potential witnesses to war crimes, turned to the records repository in Suitland, Maryland, for critical "morning reports" that listed all unit personnel on certain dates. However, many of these reports "no longer existed. . . . Some had been deliberately destroyed" and others had yet to be deposited.

A key problem with the unit identified with specific war crimes allegations—Tiger Force—was that they, on face value, didn't exist on paper. A deeper search at Suitland, however, yielded records under the unit's more formal Battalion and Infantry number, which provided a pathway to locate witnesses and confirm accounts.[66]

After exposure of the war's most publicly notorious war crime— My Lai—the army very publicly investigated and confirmed the massacre. Afterward it created a nonpublic war crimes investigatory body that spent five years examining additional claims and compiled a 9,000-page record. A monthly report was disseminated to the highest levels, yet, at the time, its findings were never shared publicly as there was no appetite for confronting the grim reality that US troops from "every major division," with command knowledge, had a hand in a range of war crimes. Nearly forty years later, journalists accessed this archive. Nick Turse, who is largely responsible for resurfacing and supplementing the vast scope of US atrocities and war crimes, recounts how an offhand comment from an archivist on the relationship between war crimes witnessing and post-traumatic stress disorder soon found him pouring over

> box after box of criminal investigation reports and day-to-day paperwork long buried away and almost totally forgotten. . . . document[ing] a nightmare war that is essentially missing from our understanding of the Vietnam conflict . . . [some] 300 allegations of massacres, murders, rapes, torture, assaults, mutilations, and other atrocities that were substantiated by army investigators.[67]

Once he started reviewing these documents decades later with living veteran participants, he could see "just how incomplete" they were, "even though [they] detailed hundreds of atrocity allegations."[68] An additional 500 allegations from the files "couldn't be proven or weren't fully investigated." In the minds of the original military investigators, these numbers barely touched on the actual scale of the problem. The Pentagon not only buried these findings, they "stonewalled" reporters' requests for documents on a particular investigation.[69]

On leaving the service, Lt. Henry Tufts, one-time commander of the army's Criminal Investigation Command, took 25,000 pages— 6 linear feet, including classified documents—related to Tiger Force's war crimes that the army, despite overwhelming evidence, decided not to prosecute. He deposited them in his basement, where they stayed until he died in 2002. To ensure that these documents became public, he left them to a friend, who sent them to the University of Michigan Library,[70] where they became the foundation for a Pulitzer Prize–winning series in the *Toledo Blade* on Tiger Force's war crimes against civilians.[71] Using one key file of damning allegations and testimony, the reporters submitted Freedom of Information Act requests and visited the US National Archives in Maryland, where archivists found a much larger incriminating file. Efforts to probe the archival record more deeply were squashed by the army, who sealed the records. Despite this, the reporters were able to trace names to still-living veterans to piece together the story.[72] Another use of Tufts's files was made by Nelson and Turse, who found files related to a torture investigation. Alongside other files they pieced together, they documented "more than one hundred allegations of torture and cover-up between March 1968 and October 1969."[73]

Conclusion

Control over memory and forgetting are unequally distributed, both within and between societies. The irony is that the United States—although, in reality, it lost the Vietnam War—has emerged victorious in social memory through its cultural and commemorative dominance across the world via movies, books, news media, official memorialization, and even the "production of historical archives."[74] These limited and limiting efforts on how to fully remember the costs of war in terms of life, property, community, culture, and morality mandates a neglected "ethics of remembering"[75] that supports advocacy to impose uncomfortable memories on the unwilling.[76]

The United States, in similar fashion to most every nation-state, reveals and promotes substantial blind spots in how it remembers its actions, roles, and responsibilities by centering on its own real and perceived losses at the expense of those of its enemies and others. This follows a traditional script in which

> how to remember war is central to the identity of the nation, itself almost always founded on the violent conquest of territory and the subjugation of people [and where] citizens garlands of euphemism and a fog of glorious myth shroud its bloody past. The battles that

shaped the nation are most often remembered by the citizenry
as defending the country, usually in the service of peace, justice,
freedom, or other noble ideas.[77]

Despite the astounding loss of Vietnamese civilian lives, US
memorialization almost completely erases them from Vietnam War
remembrance. It ignores that the United States was directly culpable
for the substantial loss of civilian life in violation of the laws of war.
The default US position that civilians were not targeted or killed as
a matter of standard operating procedure is not only untenable but
can be legitimately characterized as outright deception about the
nature and effect of the war and how the United States conducted it.
The recent raft of official fiftieth-anniversary commemorative events
solidifies this nationalist position by noting *only* US losses.[78] Excluded
is any meaningful opportunity for reflection or probing of US intents
and effect on the Vietnamese, for whom there can be no allusion to
mutual loss.

However, as previously noted, the US military atrocities and
war crimes are part of a large documentary universe that, despite its
shortcomings, presents an undeniable case that Vietnamese civilian loss
of life was standard operating procedure. This reality was both ignored
and subjected to attempts, largely successful, to consciously erase the
atrocities and war crimes through contemporaneous nonrecording,
misrecording, and falsification of documents. This obscuring was
also the result of ongoing official secrecy and a society that refuses to
honestly confront this painful past. However, traces survive in closed
and open archives formally accessioned into governmental and other
institutionalized repositories, in informal personal collections such as
letters and diaries and scrapbooks, as living witness interviews and
oral history, and in mass media newspapers and the underground
press. These tell the fuller story of US atrocities and war crimes
against civilians. These traces further survive in the individuals
who witnessed and participated and were subjected to them. Salleh
and Weiss's relaying of story after story of US veterans and Turse's
conversations with hundreds of rural Vietnamese demonstrate that
many remain unable to expunge such painful memories and continue
to be deeply affected.[79] On a visit to Vietnam to understand massacres
from the Vietnamese perspective, Nelson and Turse encountered

multiple shrines and inscribed monuments and memorial sites to civilian victims of US and South Korean militaries.[80] As was evident from the interviews they conducted there, the still vivid memories of survivors remain deeply traumatizing and are haunting to read.[81] These explorations further demonstrate how insufficient official military records are in conveying the horrors of war.

As is evident from the above discussion, accountability through recordmaking and recordkeeping is a complex and untidy arena. Despite explicit rules and processes in place presuming records-based accountability, we have seen that these are easily manipulated and elided. Time and again, records were sculpted to serve the interests of those creating them to avoid accountability. Incriminating records were easily concealed and their unwanted contents undisclosed. Many were kept secret through the "legitimate" system for classifying information, both during the war's conduct and for decades afterward. Yet, this is not the entire story. Many official records that confirmed atrocities and war crimes against Vietnamese civilians became objects of contestation, and they continue to trickle out of government archives. Despite these maskings, suppressions, and access struggles, it is important to understand that the official does not exist in isolation. It is powerfully counteracted by the unofficial, unsanctioned, and maligned, as contained in personal documents, oral testimonies and witnessing, public fora, mainstream and radical journalism, and visual representations. These result, by and large, from the actions of individuals seeking accountability not renderable through official channels. Paradoxically, it is the unofficial, informal, unsanctioned, and maligned that frequently offer a truer image than that documented and promoted through authority structures.

This undeniable reality raises fundamental and difficult questions for archivists who place so much professional weight behind and trust in official institutions as purveyors of accurate and reliable records and whose history as a profession is so deeply tied to the founding of official state memory institutions. Archivists need to more meaningfully grapple with concepts of social, political, bureaucratic, and state power and their potential for deeply malicious, antidemocratic, and deadly consequences. Conventional recordmaking, recordkeeping, and access-control regimes serve as powerful reality-shaping devices for unaccountable social control. Up to the present, the United States has never fully wrestled morally or pragmatically with the vast scope of its atrocities and war crimes in Southeast Asia. Its citizens have never had to hear or be exposed to the Vietnamese version of their devastation. They have never had to analyze it or make sense of it or confront how nationalistic loyalty fostered ignorance and partiality.[82] It is an absolute ethical and moral obligation of memory workers such as archivists to live up to their much-lauded and self-touted responsibilities to the past, especially to a nation that does not want such pasts ventilated or even acknowledged. This is especially salient in regards to developing more affinity to the unofficial and the unwelcome. It is only by doing justice to the past as a moral responsibility that memory workers can have any hope of contributing to the necessary struggle against unaccountable power that has become an omnipresent and destructive centerpiece of US society.

Notes

[1] Richard J. Cox and David A. Wallace, eds., *Archives and the Public Good: Accountability and Records in Modern Society* (Westport, CT: Quorum Books, 2002).

[2] Nick Turse, *Kill Anything That Moves: The Real American War in Vietnam* (New York: Metropolitan Books, 2013), 191.

[3] Viet Thanh Nguyen, *Nothing Ever Dies: Vietnam and the Memory of the War* (Cambridge, MA: Harvard University Press, 2016), 16–19.

[4] Barbara A. Mizstal, "Collective Memory in a Global Age: Learning How and What to Remember," *Current Sociology* 58, no. 1 (January 2010): 24–44.

[5] Nguyen, *Nothing Ever Dies*, 11.

[6] Nguyen, *Nothing Ever Dies*, 7–8.

[7] The US Army gave its soldiers less than 2 hours of training on the Conventions and combat rules of engagement, supplementing that training with a card listing eighteen forbidden war crimes. See Michael Sallah and Mitch Weiss, *Tiger Force: A True Story of Men and War* (New York: Little, Brown, 2006), 39.

[8] Malcolm Shaw, "Geneva Conventions 1864–1977," *Encyclopaedia Britannica,* https://www.britannica.com/event/Geneva-Conventions, captured at https://perma.cc/ZBM4-UHH6.

[9] The most well-known and publicized US military massacre of Vietnamese civilians occurred on March 16, 1968, when Charlie Company (1st Battalion, 20th Infantry Regiment, 11th Infantry Brigade) murdered up to 500 unarmed inhabitants of My Lai, a section of the village of Son My. See Michael Ray, "My Lai Massacre," *Encyclopaedia Britannica,* https://www.britannica.com/event/My-Lai-Massacre,

captured at https://perma.cc/8TWV-6XBF.

[10] Turse, *Kill Anything That Moves*, 21 (emphasis added).

[11] Ronald H. Spector, "Vietnam War 1954–1975," *Encyclopaedia Britannica*, updated May 23, 2019, https://www.britannica.com/event/Vietnam-War, captured at https://perma.cc/V2R3-BMNN.

[12] Turse, *Kill Anything That Moves*, 13.

[13] In 2000, the US Department of Veterans Affairs reported that one-sixth of Vietnam veterans were struggling with post-traumatic stress disorder, characterized by flashbacks, nightmares, and depression. See Salleh and Weiss, *Tiger Force*, 252. And 40 years after service, 11 percent of male and 7 percent of female Vietnam veterans still experienced PTSD, which doesn't account for those veterans who had passed away and who may have suffered. According to one earlier study, "Veterans who had PTSD in 1987 were nearly twice as likely to have died compared to those who did not have PTSD." US Department of Veterans Affairs, "PTSD and Vietnam Veterans: A Lasting Issue 40 Years Later," *Agent Orange Newsletter*, Summer 2015, https://www.publichealth.va.gov/exposures/publications/agent-orange/agent -orange-summer-2015/nvvls.asp, captured at https://perma.cc/D2B2-PFUP. The substantial psychological costs to some soldiers involved in the killing of civilians is documented in Salleh and Weiss, *Tiger Force*, 313–314, 321–322.

[14] Turse, *Kill Anything That Moves*, 22–23.

[15] James William Gibson, *The Perfect War: Technowar in Vietnam* (New York: Atlantic Monthly Press, 1986), 102–110, 135, 186, 230; Turse, *Kill Anything That Moves*, 51–53, 59–64, 77–93, 77–79, 233; Salleh and Weiss, *Tiger Force*, 54–67, 77–80, 98–102, 108–113, 150–157, 197–214, 277–278; and Deborah Nelson, *The War Behind Me: Vietnam Veterans Confront the Truth About U.S. War Crimes* (New York: Basic Books, 2008), 165.

[16] Kevin Buckley, "Pacification's Deadly Price," *Newsweek*, June 17, 1972, quoted in Nelson, *War Behind Me*, 89–90.

[17] Nelson, *War Behind Me*, 74–76.

[18] Nelson, *War Behind Me*, 177–179.

[19] Telford Taylor, *Nuremburg and Vietnam: An American Tragedy* (Chicago: Quadrangle Books, 1970), 171, quoted in Gary D. Solis, *Son Thang: An American War Crime* (Annapolis, MD: Naval Institute Press, 1997), 103.

[20] William A. Buckingham Jr., *Operation Ranch Hand: The Air Force and Herbicides in Southeast Asia 1961–1971* (Washington, DC: United States Government Printing Office, 1982), iii, 199–200.

[21] Jeanne M. Stellman, Steven D. Stellman, Richard Christian, Tracy Weber, and Carrie Tomasallo, "The Extent and Patterns of Usage of Agent Orange and Other Herbicides in Vietnam," *Nature* 422 (April 2003): 684–686.

[22] US Department of Veterans Affairs, "Veterans' Diseases Associated with Agent Orange," https://www.publichealth.va.gov/PUBLICHEALTH/exposures /agentorange/conditions/index.asp, captured at https://perma.cc/3AB6-CRVP; Viet Thanh Nguyen and Richard Hughes, "The Forgotten Victims of Agent Orange," *New*

York Times, September 15, 2017, https://www.nytimes.com/2017/09/15/opinion/agent-orange-vietnam-effects.html, captured at https://perma.cc/BBE7-RMMD.

[23] Michael Clodfelter, *Vietnam in Military Statistics: A History of the Indochina Wars, 1772–1991* (Jefferson, NC: McFarland, 1995).

[24] Edward Miguel and Gérard Roland, "The Long-run Impact of Bombing Vietnam," *Journal of Development Economics* 96, no. 1 (2011): 1–15, http://emiguel.econ.berkeley.edu/research/the-long-run-impact-of-bombing-vietnam, captured at https://perma.cc/7B7E-ES6W.

[25] Turse, *Kill Anything That Moves,* 79 (emphasis added).

[26] Neil Sheehan, *A Bright Shining Lie: John Paul Vann and America in Vietnam* (New York: Vintage Books, 1988), 618.

[27] Turse, *Kill Anything That Moves,* 80–85, 93–94.

[28] Donald Fisher Harrison, "Computers, Electronic Data, and the Vietnam War," *Archivaria* 26 (Summer 1988): 18–31; Eliot Wilczek, "The Wicked Problem of Documenting Counterinsurgencies: A Case Study of US Province Reports Written During the Vietnam War" (PhD diss., Simmons College, 2017), 229–231.

[29] Wilczek, "Wicked Problem," 130.

[30] Wilczek, "Wicked Problem," 195, 222. See also Harrison, "Computers, Electronic Data, and the Vietnam War."

[31] US Department of the Army, "Report of the Department of the Army Review of the Preliminary Investigations into the My Lai Incident, Volume I: The Report of the Investigation," March 14, 1970, B-1-2, https://www.loc.gov/rr/frd/Military_Law/pdf/RDAR-Vol-I.pdf, captured at https://perma.cc/C38U-YBKG.

[32] Nelson, *War Behind Me,* 174.

[33] Nelson, *War Behind Me,* 175.

[34] See Jarrett M. Drake, "Insurgent Citizens: The Manufacture of Police Records in Post-Katrina New Orleans and Its Implications for Human Rights," *Archival Science* 14 (2014): 365–380; Patricia Garcia, "Documenting and Classifying Labor: The Effect of Legal Discourse on the Treatment of H-2A Workers," *Archival Science* 14 (2014): 345–363; James M. O'Toole, "Cortes's Notary: The Symbolic Power of Records," *Archival Science* 2, no. 1–2 (2002): 45–61; Ann Laura Stoler, *Along the Archival Grain: Epistemic Anxieties and Colonial Common Sense* (Princeton, NJ: Princeton University Press, 2009); Ciaran B. Trace, "What Is Recorded Is Never Simply 'What Happened': Record Keeping in Modern Organizational Culture," *Archival Science* 2, no. 1–2 (2002): 137–159; John Van Maanen and Brian Pentland, "Cops and Auditors: The Rhetoric of Records," in *The Legalistic Organization,* ed. Sim B. Sitkin and Robert J. Bies (Thousand Oaks, CA: Sage Publications, 1994), 53–90.

[35] Gibson, *Perfect War,* 461.

[36] Gibson, *Perfect War,* 461–467.

[37] Turse, *Kill Anything That Moves,* 12, 22, 143.

[38] Nelson, *War Behind Me,* 60–61, 140–142.

[39] Nelson, *War Behind Me*, 24.

[40] Steve Stern, *Remembering Pinochet's Chile: On the Eve of London 1998. Book One of the Trilogy: The Memory Box of Pinochet's Chile* (Durham, NC: Duke University Press, 2006), 111–112.

[41] Turse, *Kill Anything That Moves*, 55.

[42] Murray Polner, *No Victory Parades: The Return of the Vietnam Veteran* (New York: Holt, Rinehart and Winston, 1971), 55–56, quoted in Gibson, *Perfect War*, 152.

[43] Gibson, *Perfect War*, 152.

[44] Gibson, *Perfect War*, 152.

[45] Gibson, *Perfect War*, 152.

[46] Cincinnatus, *Self-Destruction: The Disintegration and Decay of the United States Army During the Vietnam Era* (New York: W. W. Norton, 1981), 57, quoted in Gibson, *Perfect War*, 152. See similar dynamics reported in Frances Fitzgerald, *Fire in the Lake: The Vietnamese and Americans in Vietnam in Vietnam* (New York: Atlantic–Little Brown, 1972), 366.

[47] Harrison, "Computers, Electronic Data, and the Vietnam War," 22.

[48] Salleh and Weiss, *Tiger Force*, 212, 279.

[49] Turse, *Kill Anything That Moves*, 249–257.

[50] Ray, "My Lai Massacre."

[51] Joseph Goldstein, Burke Marshall, and Jack Schwartz, *The My Lai Massacre and Its Cover-Up: Beyond the Reach of Law? The Peers Commission Report with a Supplement and Introductory Essay on the Limits of Law* (New York: Free Press, 1976), 45, 52, quoted in Turse, *Kill Anything That Moves*, 228–230. Investigations into the massacre resulted in a single conviction of one lieutenant—William Calley— whose life sentence was later commuted after he had served roughly three years. Other defendants were able to successfully invoke that they were merely following orders, a rebuke to the principles established by the Nuremburg Nazi War Crimes Trials held after World War II.

[52] Nelson, *War Behind Me*, 42, 59, 95.

[53] Turse, *Kill Anything That Moves*, 188–189.

[54] Ray, "My Lai Massacre."

[55] Salleh and Weiss, *Tiger Force*, 75–82, 129–130, 223–224, 229, 317, photographs section.

[56] Salleh and Weiss, *Tiger Force*, 216–220.

[57] Turse, *Kill Anything That Moves*, 239.

[58] Nelson, *War Behind Me*, 16–17.

[59] Turse, *Kill Anything That Moves*, 243.

[60] Turse, *Kill Anything That Moves*, 5–6, 231–241.

[61] Turse, *Kill Anything That Moves*, 247.

[62] Salleh and Weiss, *Tiger Force*, 246–247, 263, 319.

[63] To their credit, staff at the US National Archives fulfilled FOIA requests, made open records available, provided reference services, and offered leads to researchers.

[64] In one instance, exposure to such cases and how they implicated the chain of command led to the suicide of one military investigator, whose home was raided for files after he killed himself. Nelson, *War Behind Me*, 156–157.

[65] Nelson, *War Behind Me*, 154–157, 168–169; Turse, *Kill Anything That Moves*, 17, 105, 137–138, 187, 192, 223–224, 233.

[66] Salleh and Weiss, *Tiger Force*, 221–222.

[67] Turse, *Kill Anything That Moves*, 14

[68] Turse, *Kill Anything That Moves*, 17.

[69] Nelson, *War Behind Me*, 3, 26.

[70] Colonel Henry Tufts Papers, Joseph A. Labadie Collection, University of Michigan Library Special Collections Research Center, https://quod.lib.umich.edu/s/sclead/umich-scl-tufts.

[71] The series on Tiger Force, published October 19–22, 2003, in the *Toledo Blade* included "THE SERIES: Elite unit savaged civilians in Vietnam," http://www4.toledoblade.com/special-tiger-force/2003/10/19/THE-SERIES-Elite-unit-savaged-civilians-in-Vietnam.html, captured at https://perma.cc/YL6H-S679; "DAY 1: Rogue GIs unleashed wave of terror in Central Highlands," https://www.toledoblade.com/special-tiger-force/2003/10/19/day-1-rogue-gis-unleashed-wave-of-terror-in-central-highlands.html, captured at https://perma.cc/QA7Y-DNVG; "DAY 2: Inquiry ended without justice," https://www.toledoblade.com/special-tiger-force/2003/10/20/DAY-2-Inquiry-ended-without-justice.html, captured at https://perma.cc/N63Y-WN53; "DAY 3: Pain lingers 36 years after deadly rampage," https://www.toledoblade.com/special-tiger-force/2003/10/21/DAY-3-Pain-lingers-36-years-after-deadly-rampage/stories/201105180179, captured at https://perma.cc/6YVZ-7ZUZ; "DAY 4: Demons of past stalk Tiger Force veterans," https://www.toledoblade.com/special-tiger-force/2003/10/22/DAY-4-Demons-of-past-stalk-Tiger-Force-veterans/stories/201105180182, captured at https://perma.cc/7AFV-ZL43.

[72] In one instance, an oversight of unredacted social security numbers enabled researchers using an open war crimes collection at the National Archives to trace still-living veterans to confirm the files' contents. Nelson, *War Behind Me*, 8–9.

[73] Salleh and Weiss, *Tiger Force*, 222, 273, 279, 306, 309–311; Nelson, *War Behind Me*, 61–62.

[74] Nguyen, *Nothing Ever Dies*, 15.

[75] Nguyen, *Nothing Ever Dies*, 9–15.

[76] Avishai Margalit, *The Ethics of Memory* (Cambridge, MA: Harvard University Press, 2002); David A. Wallace, "Locating Agency: Interdisciplinary Perspectives on Professional Ethics and Archival Morality," *Journal of Information Ethics* 19 no. 1 (Spring 2010): 172–189.

[77] Nguyen, *Nothing Ever Dies*, 5.

[78] For examples, see President Obama's proclamation to commemorate the fiftieth anniversary of the war. Executive Office of the President, Office of the Press Secretary, "Presidential Proclamation—Commemoration of the 50th Anniversary of the Vietnam War," May 25, 2012, http://www.whitehouse.gov/the-press -office/2012/05/25/presidential-proclamation-commemoration-50th-anniversary -vietnam-war, captured at https://perma.cc/D7PL-GLER; and the commemorative website of the Department of Defense (http://www .vietnamwar50th.com/) and that of the National Archives and Records Administration's "nonprofit partner," the National Archives Foundation (https://www.archivesfoundation.org/vietnam/). For convincing pushback on these representations, see Sheryl Gay Stolberg, "Paying Respects, Pentagon Revives Vietnam, and War Over Truth," *New York Times*, October 9, 2014, https://www.nytimes.com/2014/10/10/us/pentagons-web-timeline-brings -back-vietnam-and-protesters-.html, captured at https://perma.cc/R5B2-K5CL; and Arnold Isaacs, "Fact-Checking the Pentagon's Vietnam War Commemoration," Modern War Institute at West Point, November 14, 2017, https://mwi.usma.edu/fact -checking-pentagons-vietnam-war-commemoration, captured at https://perma.cc /EN82-2SNU.

[79] Salleh and Weiss, *Tiger Force*; Nick Turse, "The Ken Burns Vietnam War Documentary Glosses Over Devastating Civilian Toll," *The Intercept*, September 28, 2017, https://theintercept.com/2017/09/28/the-ken-burns-vietnam -war-documentary-glosses-over-devastating-civilian-toll, captured at https://perma .cc/92Q7-VENU.

[80] The site of the My Lai massacre was reconstituted as a museum and commemorative memorial site that identified mass graves and listed the victims. See Ray, "My Lai Massacre." These village-funded memorials were initially dissuaded by the Vietnamese government as they countered the nationalistic preference for heroic revolutionary resistance.

[81] Nelson, *War Behind Me*, 119–136; Turse, *Kill Anything That Moves*, 20–21, 115– 133.

[82] Nguyen, *Nothing Ever Dies*, 112–114.

2

The Question of Oral Testimony in the Archival Concept of Evidence

Wendy Duff and Jefferson Sporn

Introduction

In a career spanning almost 50 years, Richard Cox has always looked outside his own discipline for knowledge and inspiration. As a professor and doctoral supervisor, he encouraged his students to read widely and search beyond the archival literature for inspiration and insights, as one of the authors experienced firsthand. In the spirit of Richard's ceaselessly interdisciplinary career, in this essay we will draw on a wide range of sources and consider the evidentiary value of oral testimony acquired by archives.

Evidence and the Archives

For most of its nineteenth- and twentieth-century history, proponents of archival theory accepted ideas of an immediately accessible and positivist past, guarded by the neutral, passive objective archivist.[1] Though coming rather later than other disciplines, archival theory's "postmodern turn" saw sustained attacks on previous notions of archives as neutral repositories of documents and archivists as "moral defenders" of the archives. Drawing on the writing of Michel Foucault, Jean-François Lyotard, and Jacques Derrida, archival scholars now acknowledge that archives are "contested sites of power"[2] that profoundly affect how society understands the past and, by extension, the present. Archival decisions contribute to the meaning and making of archival records and leave an indelible mark on records of the past.[3]

The once-assumed relationship between record and evidence is now being questioned as well. Archival scholars investigating previously unstated assumptions of the record–evidence relationship in archival discourse have laid excellent groundwork.[4] These writers hope to move away from what Heather MacNeil calls the "assumption that a unitary and stable relationship exists between a representation (that is, a record) and its referent (i.e., a pre-existent reality)"[5] and toward a relationship based on the analysis of relationships and contexts, from which the record can be viewed as having multiple, even conflicting, meanings. Instead of looking at records solely as evidence of past actions, archivists might instead look at the contingencies that make the record trustworthy or evidentiary. As MacNeil goes on to say, "The criteria [that records] establish for determining what counts as true are themselves the product of historical, cultural, and political choices and do not exhaust all the possible ways of looking at the world or at the relationship between records and the world."[6]

In this light, Jennifer Meehan builds off previous discussions and interrogates the association between records and evidence. Like other authors before her, Meehan rejects the notion of a neutral or one-way relationship between records and evidence, taking issue with conceptions of evidence that posit it as inherent within the record itself. Instead, she posits that evidence is a "relationship that can be associated with a record, but that is not, and cannot be, contained within a record."[7] Further, she avers that the relationship between record and evidence is steeped in contextualities, impressed upon by provenance, relationships with other records, arrangement and description, and much more: "Neither containing evidence, nor facts per se, a record merely refers to events (or facts) outside itself. The process of arriving at an understanding of the events to which the record refers is one of inference."[8] In reconstituting the record–evidence relationship, "space opens up for considering different types of records and archival activities that are usually excluded from discussions of evidence that rely too heavily on legal concepts and the rules of evidence."[9]

Testimony

Oral testimony has always been a fundamental part of legal proceedings. The *Oxford English Dictionary* defines *testimony* as "personal or documentary evidence or attestation in support of a fact or statement; hence, any form of evidence or proof."[10] To "bear witness" links testimony to facts or statements that provide evidence or proof, a key element of any court case. But this relatively straightforward definition connecting testimony to any form of evidence ignores the complexities of the ways in which testimonies are created or used. Camila Loew suggests that "to produce one's own speech as a material evidence for truth—is to accomplish a speech act rather than to simply formulate a statement."[11] Derrida reminds us that witnessing involves an act of faith, and he argues that unlike a statement or a straightforward transmission of knowledge, testimony involves someone *committing* "*himself* in regard to someone, by an oath that is at least implicit."[12] Testimonies are speech acts, statements that implicitly perform an action, in this case an oath by one person made to another or others. Testimonies are not passive statements of facts or proof, actively created by a witness and an examiner or an interviewee and an interviewer.[13]

Some have questioned the authenticity of testimonies or oral sources gathered by archives, judging these sources to be an unreliable and inauthentic form of records.[14] Despite its privileged and ubiquitous role in contemporary discourses surrounding human rights and other responses to global issues, oral testimony still faces problems with strongly held archival ideas of authenticity and trustworthiness.[15] Theorists like Richard Cox have attempted to move away from such traditions, toward greater inclusivity and a diversity of form in the historical record, but archivists have yet to establish how one might examine oral testimony records as evidence within contemporary formulations of archival theory. Following Meehan's discussion of evidence and record, evidence in testimony is found in the relationships and contingencies surrounding and between a record and an event. Evidence is found not just in what is said but in ways in which the testimony emanates from the historical, cultural, institutional, and mediating milieus that surround and contextualize it. Michal Givoni, however, links the increased interest in testimony to a neo-liberal agenda that has transformed government "from an interventionist apparatus that shapes and inculcates normal behaviours to a much more restrained and allusive regulation that propels individuals to act responsibly and adopt socially desirable attitudes of their own initiative." In doing so, contemporary witnessing "transfers responsibility to private individuals in matters pertaining to both global and social injustice."[16] Givoni notes that both the rise of neo-liberal government and the increased interest in testimony date from the 1970s.

This essay is organized into four sections. First is a review of the literature on which we will build an understanding of the meditating and contingent elements surrounding testimony. Second, we will examine the authenticity of oral testimony, where personal stories and historical narratives converge and diverge in meaningful ways, and then we will look at the genre of video testimony, and the ways in which the video medium contributes its own set of meaning and significance to the way that testimony is created and used. Finally, we describe the novel use of testimony in the Living Archives on Eugenics in Western Canada project, which brings together many of the elements of testimony to powerful effect and demonstrates the ways in which the contexts and mediation of testimony can act as evidence.[17]

Review of the Literature

While the Western court system has always relied on testimony, the scholarly or public spheres have only relatively recently accepted testimonies as reliable historical sources.[18] Until the 1980s, memory, and by extension, personal testimony, were both seen as unreliable and capricious, and historians treated them as "an undisciplined activity that troubles the clear waters of historiography."[19] Annette Wieviorka identifies the 1961 trial of Adolf Eichmann, at which 117 Holocaust survivors recited their testimonies, as the beginning of the rise of the era of testimony. Although Holocaust survivors had previously recounted their experiences, the Eichmann trial provided a mechanism for the public to observe the testimony via radio and television. The idea of the witness began to coalesce into an identifiable social figure (e.g., "survivors"), and ushered in the era of witness testimony.[20] Hannah Arendt has taken issue with the witness testimony presented at the trial, finding the testimonies of the Holocaust survivors to be a distraction from the judgment of Eichmann and his crimes. She has argued that only one witness possessed the proper credentials—"a purity of soul, an unmirrored, unreflected innocence of heart and mind that only the righteous possess"[21]—to bear witness to the horrors of the Holocaust. Despite her criticisms, the Eichmann trial provided a space for a collective account of the Holocaust to emerge from the individual testimonies of survivors, imbuing each story with an authority previously reserved only for the written historical record.

It is worth asking what exactly makes testimony such a compelling and fascinating phenomenon. What is it that makes the witness what Annette Wieviorka calls a "bearer of history" and an "embodiment of memory attesting to the past and to the continuing presence of the past"?[22] Witnessing and testimony place the listener in direct relation to the testifier, conveying information about an event in question while also reasserting the human experience of the event. As Geoffrey Hartman writes, "Each testimony places us in the presence of an individual, communicates something of the original impact of what was experienced, retrieves in the spontaneous flow of the interview forgotten episodes, and is generally unafraid of the emotional aura."[23] The nature of testimony is deeply personal and, Wievorka writes, "appeals to the heart and not to the mind. It elicits compassion, pity, indignation, even rebellion. The one who testifies signs a 'compassionate pact' with the one who receives the testimony."[24] By directly engaging the human elements of history, first-person accounts burn through what Hartman calls the "cold storage of history" and give "texture to memory or to images that otherwise would have only sentimental or informational impact."[25] In short, Hartman says, "survivor testimonies . . . can be a source for historical information or confirmation, yet their real strength lies in recording the psychological and emotional milieu of the struggle for survival, not only then *but also now.*"[26]

The Eichmann trial created what Wievorka calls "a social demand for testimony," and concomitantly, historians began to incorporate testimonies into histories "from below," to give voice to the "excluded, the unimportant, the voiceless."[27] The interest in firsthand accounts has given rise to the creation of major testimony archives, such as the Yale Fortunoff Video Archive, founded in 1974, and the USC Shoah Foundation Institute for Visual History and Education, founded in 1994, to record and to preserve the stories of the Holocaust for posterity through interviews with survivors. More recently, community archives and organizations documenting the marginalized and historically forgotten have begun collecting testimonies as a vital part of their mandate.[28] As Wievorka writes, "The mission that has devolved to testimony is no longer to bear witness to inadequately known events, but to keep them before our eyes. Testimony is to be a means of transmission to future generations."[29]

Fuyuki Kurasawa writes that in addition to asserting a presence or transmitting memory across generations, "testimonial appeals are also increasingly being addressed to a global imagined community composed of diasporic cultural groups, overseas governments, NGOs, social movements, multilateral organizations, media outlets and concerned citizens around the planet."[30] These organizations use testimony as a way to remember and preserve past events, acknowledging and publicizing atrocities, and, at the same time, using these testimonies to initiate "judicial procedures on behalf of victims and survivors who are geographically distant."[31]

Within this framework, some scholars[32] almost completely reject notions of use value for testimony. As one such scholar, Tony Kushner, writes, "Survivor testimony, whether in written, oral, or video form, has to be taken seriously on its own terms. It becomes distorted or manipulated if used crudely as a weapon against denial or simply as a provider of 'color' or texture to educational, museum, or artistic representations of the Holocaust."[33] Proponents of testimony collections insist that listeners or viewers of testimony must consider the totality of a witness's life. Survivor testimony, they argue, is so much more than just the event. It is the life before and after, the ways stories are influenced and change over time, the ways humans cope and grow with their stories. Conflating use value for testimonial merit obscures the whole for the part, the life lived for the stories told. Furthermore, Kushner posits that "using insights gained from psychology and literary and cultural studies, the construction of life story has become increasingly sophisticated," allowing for complex and insightful explorations of human memory, identity, and creation of self.[34] Testimony has a special place in contemporary social and historical milieus, whether tied to its scholarly use value or simply as a means of remembering the past.

The Interview

As with all archival material, an understanding of a specific testimony recording depends on knowledge of the circumstances and contexts of its creation. Over the last few decades, scholars have begun to study the role of the interviewer and the institutional context in testimony creation. According to Alexander Freund, testimony is not a "neutral tool used for emancipatory purposes that confronts the oral historian simply with problems of interpretation."[35] As previously noted, the postmodern-turn in cultural and archival theory reminds us that the production of knowledge never occurs in a vacuum. The interviewer plays an inseparable role in testimony because every interview is inherently dialogic, contextually grounded, created by *both* interviewer and interviewee, shaped by the questions asked and the agenda set beforehand. In recent decades, theorists in feminist, queer, and postmodern epistemology have written about the interview process as a site of power and meaning-making.[36] Such writers recognize that the interpersonal and contextual factors of the interview are a profound influence on what is said and how it is interpreted. They posit that a "shift of focus from data gathering to interactive process affects what the researcher regards as valuable information. As such, an interview should center both interviewer and subject in the creation of testimony."[37]

Holocaust survivors who have been interviewed numerous times have been shown to differentiate between what they deem to be "real interviews" and ones in which they are merely expected to recite stories and narratives expected of them.[38] From this, Holocaust scholar Henry Greenspan has developed the concept of "knowing with," one of the clearest instances of an interviewer understanding their crucial role in the creation of testimony. Rather than using the interview as a means to an end, as a way of gathering raw data to be interpreted later by the interviewer, "knowing with" emphasizes a collaborative process, in which much of the interpretation is arrived at together, by both interviewer and subject, *within* the conversation.[39] As Henry Greenspan and Sydney Bolkolsky have written, "The issue here is not being 'open' (a concept that has caused a good deal of mischief) but rather being *in*: *in* the process, *in* the rhythm, *in* the co-laboring. . . . Collaborations of this sort are not simply knowing from people (the 'interviewees') but rather knowing with them."[40]

Institutions

Archival testimony projects deliberately create and collect recordings for posterity. Studying the institutions, their processes and motivations, therefore, is key to understanding and interpreting the meaning of a specific testimony. Freund writes that institutions create the conditions for trustworthiness and believability that undergird oral testimony: "Institutions serve to vouch for claims, giving those selected as representatives standing, authority, and, ultimately, make them trustworthy to institutional audience."[41] Yet, problems arise when we situate testimony in the complex and often contested world of human rights and competing truths. The breakup of Yugoslavia, the genocide in Rwanda, the Israel–Palestine conflict, and the testimonies of the Stolen Generations' Indigenous and native peoples have all produced significant amounts of testimony that, deliberately or not, contradict other institutional truths and testimonies. The agendas, mandates, and priorities of the institutions that oversee testimony projects have profound impacts on the recordings they create. The support these institutions provide is intimately connected to larger, more collective truths that the institution supports (i.e., the remembrance of the Holocaust, acknowledging human rights abuses against Indigenous communities, etc.).[42] These institutions, both large and small, determine who qualifies as a witness and determine the framing of the witness testimony, both in its creation and its dissemination, therefore influencing its reception as authentic and trustworthy.[43]

Neither can these institutions be separated from the cultural contexts from which they collect. Notions of bearing witness are not static across cultures but are in fact inseparably contingent on cultural and historically situated factors. In contrasting testimonies gathered in Yugoslavia with those gathered in the United States, Holocaust scholar Jovan Byford shows that the ways in which testimony is gathered, interpreted and used have significant contextual differences across cultures who have very different notions of the purpose and meaning of "bearing witness." For example, Byford shows that testimonies from Serbian Holocaust survivors in the 1990s fit uncomfortably into the American institutional collections to which they belong, as "the Serbian accounts were embedded in a culture of remembrance" that was very different from that of the Americans. Furthermore, the institutional use for the testimony can evolve in that culture and the "expectations of what counts as a relevant memory" may change as well. Inevitably, testimony reflects the "complex interplay between the local memory culture, established traditions of bearing witness, and the demands of the specific historical and political moment in which they were recorded."[44] Although scholars have acknowledged the importance of understanding the various dimensions that affect the value of testimony as evidence, Kurasawa notes that the sociocultural practices related to bearing witness remain undertheorized.[45]

Truth and Authenticity

One of the most interesting facets of oral testimony is its relationship to an event as it "actually" happened. Oral testimonies are inherently and necessarily subjective, always representing a one-sided story, from memory, sometimes long after the event. Memory is fickle, and people's stories are influenced by others around them, by popular culture, and by their lives before and after the event. In a telling example, Jeffrey Shandler writes that, since the release of *Schindler's List* in 1995, the film has been referenced in hundreds of videotaped survivor testimonies, acting as a "highly variable catalyst, interacting with wartime memories, other mediations of the Holocaust, and the context of the interview itself."[46] These references reveal how testimony is extensively mediated by other narratives and serves as a reflection on the relationship between recalled experience and its mediation. As mentioned above, traditional historical and archival treatments of documents may face challenges in ascribing trustworthiness or reliability to such documents, so obviously and profoundly affected by outside elements.[47]

Whether one should subject oral testimony to the demands and procedures of verifiable proof is debatable. Some scholars argue that historical truth is a necessarily separate realm from the "truth" of survivor's accounts. As one such scholar, James Young, writes, "Rather than coming to Holocaust narrative for indisputably 'factual' testimony . . . the critical reader might now turn to the manner in which these 'facts' have been understood and reconstructed in narrative."[48] Testimony, it is argued, reflects meaning and truth in "what the informant believes is indeed a fact (that is, the fact as he or she believes it) just as much as what 'really happened.'"[49] Another scholar, Lawrence Langer, argues that historical discrepancies in testimony are "trivial in comparison" to the much more meaningful examination of the person who produced them.[50] However, there are many others who see potentially profound meaning in the gaps between "historical" and "subjective" truth.[51] In studying the factual errors in a Holocaust survivor's testimony, Mark Roseman writes that what is truly revealing about these discrepancies "is often not the contrasts between the *written* and the *spoken* but rather that between perceptions and memories 'fixed' or recorded at different points of distance from the events which they describe, that is, in reports and letters *then*, in interviews and observations *now*."[52] Highlighting the ways in which testimony departs from other written records does not diminish evidentiary value of the oral accounts but instead opens up the possibility for reading testimony as the interplay between the event and the ways in which they are recounted. As Marianne Hirsch and Leo Spitzer write, "In taking into account an affective dimension and the meaning of an event for the teller herself, historians are expanding the notion of truth and are coming to a deeper, more encompassing understanding of what we might now think of as an embodied form of 'truthfulness.'"[53]

Video Testimony

Video testimony brings with it its own sets of meanings, so much so that is often referred to as what Aleida Assmann calls an entirely separate "genre of testimony."[54] While being created and consumed in nonwritten form, the video element of testimony is "substantive evidence. . . . The spoken word is embedded in a setting, a situation, a context. People speak with body language, expression, and tone."[55] Video testimony presents discrete modes of discourse that prescribe different ways in which one can express concepts and information.[56] We see and hear the interviewee, conveying information not just through words but through gestures, facial expressions, inflections, and more. Audio-visual testimony allows for open-ended passages, pauses, silence, uncompleted sentences, and innuendo, all of which contribute and alter meaning in ways that could not be expressed in written testimony.[57] Testimony involves deeply embodied memory,[58] and advocates for video testimony suggest that through the video medium, this embodiment can be witnessed, possibly even offering access to what Langer calls "unmediated truth" about the Holocaust.[59] Through video, silence and the sheer inability to express the trauma of the past become visible and known to the viewer. However, according to Hirsch and Spitzer, foregrounding extratextual elements, such as embodiment, affect, and silence, can risk "occluding the wealth of knowledge and information transmitted"[60] by witnesses of trauma and suffering. Either way, as Shoshana Felman and Dori Laub write, the experience of giving testimony "is not simply the information, the establishment of the facts, but the experience itself of living *through* testimony."[61]

Videotaped testimony also allows for the ability to show objects and to capture the ways in which people use these objects. Furthermore, as Shandler writes, the video represents and shows the interviewee's body, which can deepen their testimony: "The survivor, in the role of curator, provides information that identifies and contextualizes objects and can arrange items to impart added meaning through their juxtapositions."[62] In the mediating atmosphere of the video, everyday objects take on new meanings and contexts that wholly belong to the interviewee and their history and are still recognizable to the viewer. Personal photographs, tattoos, disfigurements, and religious iconography are all present in various Holocaust interviews, testifying to both the event in question, when the object achieved its special meaning, as well as the period endured after the Holocaust. These material objects have been kept for posterity by the survivor and then selected for display in the video, constituting a personal archive of meaning that can also speak to wider societal and collective meanings. In this way, "these objects evince survivors' sense of history, whether personal or on a grand scale, and its materialization."[63]

Audio-visual testimony can also have a unique effect on its viewers. Geoffrey Hartman writes that video testimony positions the viewer as a part of a "provisional community," where the viewer no longer turns away from historical and personal trauma but more intimately recognizes it around them.[64] Hirsch and Spitzer refer to this as "secondary witnessing," in which the listener takes on the responsibility of witnessing and remembering into the future,[65] while Alison Landsberg calls this "prosthetic memory," in which "a person does not simply apprehend a historical narrative but takes on a more personal, deeply felt memory of a past event through which he or she did not live."[66] Few deny that video testimony can elicit strong and long-lasting empathetic responses from those who view it. In creating authentic testimonies, institutions contribute to the formation of what Sara Jones calls "mediated remembering communities," which rely on video testimony to join "primary" and "secondary" witnesses into the a "community of remembrance . . . [to ensure that] commemoration of the victims of violent pasts are firmly embedded in contemporary memory cultures."[67]

Living Archives on Eugenics in Western Canada

The Living Archives on Eugenics in Western Canada project established an online digital archive in 2010.[68] The project team attempts to create and make accessible resources on the history of eugenics, to engage communities of eugenics survivors, and to raise awareness about the link between past and present policies dealing with people who are differently abled. The most powerful and important resources created by the project are the testimonies of sterilization survivors who give firsthand accounts of their experiences. The project sought to empower survivors to tell their own stories rather than have others speak for them. Furthermore, the project aimed to foreground the connection between the experiences of eugenics survivors to the barriers that parents with intellectual challenges face today. According to Robert A. Wilson, the testimonies given by the survivors of Western Canada's eugenics program provide important insights into complex lives, "both of what life was like in the past . . . and of what life is like having survived a traumatic past."[69]

These stories are also historical documents, created to address the dearth of records related to Western Canada's eugenic past. Only in the last few decades have members of the scholarly community begun to study and assess the history and impact of eugenics in Canada.[70] These firsthand accounts highlight the traumatic impact of previous laws and practices that inculcate biases against individuals with perceived intellectual limitations. They tell how the containment in residential facilities and forced sterilization caused great pain and feelings of inadequacy that persist into the present. The videos also show how eugenic thinking continues today. These testimonies manage to both deepen a shallow historical record and raise questions around societal perceptions of who deserves to parent children. The project empowers individuals whom society deemed unworthy by helping them disseminate their stories. According to K. D. Childress, the project also aims to help change attitudes of "able-bodied people toward the disabled . . . through listening to the stories of disabled people and their families."[71]

The testimonies of the Living Archives project lay bare many of the ways in which the relationships and contextualities surrounding testimony play a role in meaning. From its beginning, the project resolved to work "with individuals who have a high level of comfort with their story and who have both antecedent and developing trustful relationships with other team advocates."[72] As such, a person and community partner conducted all interviews. Most important, the men and women who told their stories were encouraged to revisit and edit their testimonies, often collectively, to create a finished video. The end result was an archive of previously unrecorded information gathered through a process by which the survivor and interviewer, as individuals and as a community, created knowledge together.

As previously noted, a community organization with strong links to the interviewees and in partnership with academics helped create the testimonies, lending authority and bringing weight to the stories that survivors told. The institutional support behind the project not only allows for a mainstream acceptance of the experiences of those wrongfully sterilized but also disseminates the testimony through the Eugenics Archives website, a major documentary, and several scholarly publications. The website uses the personal testimony not only to connect with the community but, like many other archival testimony projects, to connect events and trauma of the past with injustices still present.

Finally, the testimonies show the ways in which testimonies are mediated through video. One testimony shows a sterilization survivor sharing images from a photo album with photos of himself before and after his operation. He appears in a few photos that also show the institutions in which he was forcibly housed. He takes care to point out the ways in which the institution forced him to stay, noting the high fence around the grounds, and the consequences of being caught escaping. The video ends with images of him and another survivor, watching their testimony and discussing the ways in which it represents their past and the way in which it might be edited.[73] All of the Eugenics Archives videos conclude with the survivors discussing the ways in which the published video can best reflect their stories, what the survivors want to tell to those who will listen. In this way, the videos can increase awareness surrounding Canada's history of eugenics without limiting the fullness of a survivor's life story. As Nicola Fairbrother, a member of the project, noted, the survivors know their stories, and they just needed a mechanism to disseminate them. One should not question the accuracy of the testimonies; instead, we should ask how best to mobilize these personal stories to change people's understanding and biases of people differently abled.

Conclusion

In this essay we have explored the ways in which personal testimony is contingent on historical, cultural, and societal factors as well as elements specific to its medium of creation. In an archival sense, the evidence presented by testimony is neither innate to the testimony nor wholly apart from it but depends on the relationships, contingencies, and mediations connected to the testimonies. Recent reconsiderations of the record–evidence relationship have allowed us to posit a wider and more encompassing understanding of archival evidence, opening space to infer evidence from traditionally overlooked elements. Under Meehan's conceptualization as evidence, the testimonies of the sterilization survivors do not have inherent evidential value but are always "refer[ring] to events (or facts) outside itself," pointing toward evidence through inference and interpretation. Through the process of inference and interpretation, we can posit that these records can be seen as evidence of facts, as evidence of their creation, and as evidence of wider social and cultural contexts. The Living Archives on Eugenics in Western Canada project makes a compelling case study for Meehan's conception of evidence.

As evidence of fact, these records point to events and histories previously uncaptured, or unpreserved, in the historical record. Where the institutional records of these sterilization survivors' lives fail to capture their full history, their oral testimonies provide an excellent resource to further the historical record on this shameful period in Canadian history. We also see how these videotaped testimonies offer evidence of survivors' deeply embodied memories, not only through their own narratives told many times before but seen in their faces and bodies, in their silences, and through the objects kept as representative of their trauma.

The contextualities surrounding the creation of these testimonies also provides space to infer how the product of these testimonies point to a specific interview process, one that presents beneficial evidence of the participatory model used. The context also lays bare the ways in which testimony is invariably mediated by outside narratives and past relationships. Instead of having to infer the ways in which these testimonies are affected by outside elements, we can actually see the process by which the survivors rely on the influence of others to help shape and inform their own stories. Furthermore, the institutions involved—from the small community organization that facilitated the interviews, to the university that worked to create the archive, to the federal funding structure that allowed the project to take off— all speak to the "institutional embeddedness" of the testimonies, by which the survivors' claims are believable, trustworthy, and authentic.

Finally, as evidence of wider societal contexts, these records point to the paradigm by which testimonies exist today. The creation, preservation, and dissemination of these testimonies point to their contemporary epoch of creation, one that has begun to value participatory archiving and a broadening notion of what, and who, deserves to be in the archives.[74] Each testimony collected in this project serves as excellent evidence of this current archival paradigm. As well, it is not without neglect and ignorance that it has taken till now for these records to be created. These records are evidence that much more work needs to be done.

In today's ubiquitous, transnational, and media-saturated witnessing environment, research in archival theory is needed more than ever to understand the rapidly changing technological and societal landscape in which it functions. This essay has provided a backdrop by which oral testimony can be seen as archival evidence and shown how this expanded understanding of evidence might be applied to a novel, new archival project. However, this essay deals almost exclusively with oral testimony that has emerged as part of an institutionally backed project, such as the USC Shoah Foundation or Living Archives on Eugenics in Western Canada. What archival evidence might we infer in the creation and use of testimony, not through archives but through the mass media? What evidence can testimony provide when it is created in the instant instance of trauma, not years or decades later? To better reflect the many varieties and facets of contemporary testimony, more research into the evidentiary significance of witnessing is called for and will hopefully spur on a deeper understanding of testimony and the contexts through which it is created and put to use.

Notes

[1] See Hilary Jenkinson's article, "Reflections of an Archivist," in *A Modern Archives Reader: Basic Readings on Archival Theory and Practice*, ed. Maygene F. Daniels and Timothy Walch (Washington, DC: National Archives and Records Service, 1984), for a thorough background on the foundations of early-twentieth-century archival theory.

[2] Joan M. Schwartz and Terry Cook, "Archives, Records, and Power: The Making of Modern Memory," *Archival Science* 2, no. 1–2 (March 2002): 7.

[3] For more, see Schwartz and Cook, "Archives, Records, and Power," 1–19; Verne Harris, "The Archival Sliver: Power, Memory, and Archives in South Africa," *Archival Science* 2, no. 1–2 (March 2002): 63–86; Joan M. Schwartz, "'We Make Our Tools and Our Tools Make Us': Lessons from Photographs for the Practice, Politics, and Poetics of Diplomatics," *Archivaria* 40 (Fall 1995): 40–76; Brien Brothman, "Afterglow: Conceptions of Record and Evidence in Archival Discourse," *Archival Science* 2, no. 3 (September 2002): 311–342; Tom Nesmith, "Still Fuzzy, But More Accurate: Some Thoughts on the 'Ghosts' of Archival Theory," *Archivaria* 47 (Spring 1999): 136–150; and Mark A. Greene, "The Power of Meaning: The Archival Mission in the Postmodern Age," *American Archivist* 65 (Spring/Summer 2002): 42–55.

[4] See Heather MacNeil, "Trusting Records in a Postmodern World," *Archivaria* 51 Spring 2001): 36–47; Jennifer Meehan, "Towards an Archival Concept of Evidence," *Archivaria* 61 (Spring 2006): 127–146; and Brothman, "Afterglow," 311–342.

[5] MacNeil, "Trusting Records," 42.

[6] MacNeil, "Trusting Records," 45.

[7] Meehan, "Towards an Archival Concept," 139.

[8] Meehan, "Towards an Archival Concept," 140.

[9] Meehan, "Towards an Archival Concept," 144.

[10] "Testimony," *Oxford English Dictionary* [electronic resource], https://www-oed
-com.myaccess.library.utoronto.ca/view/Entry/199748?rskey=HzYbh1
&result=1#eid.

[11] Camilla Loew, *The Memory of Pain: Women's Testimonies of the Holocaust* (Amsterdam:
Rodopi, 2001), 12.

[12] Jacques Derrida, "'A Self-Unsealing Poetic Text': Poetics and Politics of Witnessing,"
in *Revenge of the Aesthetic: The Place of Literature in Theory Today*, ed. Michael
P. Clark, trans. Rachel Bowlby (Berkeley: University of California Press, 2000),
180–207 (emphasis in original).

[13] The sources used in this paper will refer to testimony in exclusively nonlegal terms.
For a discussion of the evolving use of legal *testimony* in a specifically Canadian
context, see Mary Ann Pylypchuk, "The Value of Aboriginal Records as Legal
Evidence in Canada: An Examination of Sources," *Archivaria* 32 (Summer 1991):
51–77.

[14] See Jean Dryden, "Oral History and the Archives: The Case Against," *Canadian
Oral History Association* 5 (1981): 34–37, for a succinct argument of the problem
of oral history in traditional archive and archivist activities. For an excellent
foundational background of the argument, see Jean-Pierre Wallot and Normand
Fortier, "Archival Science and Oral Sources," in *The Oral History Reader*, ed. Robert
Perks and Alistair Thomson, 2nd ed. (New York: Routledge, 1998), 365–378.

[15] Tony Kushner, "Holocaust Testimony, Ethics, and the Problem of Representation,"
Poetics Today 27, no. 2 (Summer 2006): 275–283.

[16] Michal Givoni, *The Care of the Witness: A Contemporary History of Testimony in
Crises* (New York: Cambridge University Press, 2016), 25.

[17] Testimonies used here will, for the most part, be seen through the experience
and study of Holocaust survivors. There are currently more than one hundred
institutions devoted to Holocaust remembrance worldwide, and Holocaust studies
make up a significant amount of what has been written on the subject of testimony
and its creation, use, dissemination, and theoretical underpinnings. There are
obviously many invaluable contributions, theoretical and practical, drawn from
other disciplines and epistemologies and in response to many different forms
of trauma and life experiences. Holocaust studies have depended on survivor
testimony for quite a few decades now and have produced a vast amount of
literature seen through this lens.

[18] Kushner, "Holocaust Testimony," 275.

[19] Aleida Assmann, "History, Memory, and the Genre of Testimony," *Poetics Today*
27, no. 2 (Summer 2006): 263.

[20] Annette Wieviorka, *The Era of the Witness* (Ithaca: Cornell University Press, 2006),
56–95.

[21] Hannah Arendt, *Eichmann in Jerusalem: A Report on the Banality of Evil* (1963;
New York: Penguin Books, 1994), 229.

[22] Wieviorka, *Era of the Witness*, 88.

23 Geoffrey Hartman, "The Humanities of Testimony: An Introduction," *Poetics Today* 27, no. 2 (Summer 2006): 254.

24 Wieviorka, *Era of the Witness*, 143.

25 Geoffrey H. Hartman, "Learning from Survivors: The Yale Testimony Project," *Holocaust and Genocide Studies* 9, no. 2 (Fall 1995): 197.

26 Hartman, "Learning from Survivors," 200 (emphasis added).

27 Wieviorka, *Era of the Witness*, 97.

28 Andrew Flinn, Mary Stevens, and Elizabeth Shepherd, "Whose Memories, Whose Archives? Independent Community Archives, Autonomy and the Mainstream," *Archival Science* 9, no. 1 (June 2009): 71–86.

29 Wieviorka, *Era of the Witness*, 24.

30 Fuyuki Kurasawa, "A Message in a Bottle: Bearing Witness as a Mode of Ethico-Political Practice," *Theory, Culture & Society* 26, no. 1 (2009): 93.

31 Kurasawa, "Message in a Bottle," 93.

32 Holocaust scholars Tony Kushner and Henry Greenspan are two of the largest opponents of tying Holocaust testimony to any sort of use value. For them, merely listening to the survivors should be reason enough. See Kushner, "Holocaust Testimony," 275–283, and Henry Greenspan, *On Listening to Holocaust Survivors: Beyond Testimony* (St. Paul, MN: Paragon House, 2010), 217–238.

33 Kushner, "Holocaust Testimony" 289–290.

34 Kushner, "Holocaust Testimony" 282.

35 Alexander Freund, "'Confessing Animals': Toward a Longue Durée History of the Oral History Interview," *Oral History Review* 41, no. 1 (January 2014): 23.

36 Excellent examples of this include Marjorie DeVault and Glenda Gross, "Feminist Qualitative Interviewing: Experience, Talk, and Knowledge," in *Handbook of Feminist Research: Theory and Praxis*, 2nd ed. (Thousand Oaks, CA: Sage Publications, 2007), 173–198; Rosario Undurraga, "Interviewing Women in Latin America: Some Reflections on Feminist Research Practice," *Equality, Diversity and Inclusion: An International Journal* 31, no. 5/6 (2012): 418–434; Frederick Anyan, "The Influence of Power Shifts in Data Collection and Analysis Stages: A Focus on Qualitative Research Interview," *The Qualitative Report* (2013): 1–9.

37 Kathryn Anderson and Dana Jack, "Learning to Listen: Interview Techniques and Analyses," in *The Oral History Reader*, ed. Robert Perks and Alistair Thomson, 2nd ed. (New York: Routledge, 2006), 130–42.

38 Greenspan and Sidney Bolkosky, "When Is an Interview an Interview? Notes from Listening to Holocaust Survivors," *Poetics Today* 27, no. 2 (Summer 2006): 437–440.

39 Greenspan, *On Listening to Holocaust Survivors*, 217–238.

40 Greenspan and Bolkosky, "When Is an Interview an Interview?," 432.

41 Aaron Beim and Gary Alan Fine, "Trust in Testimony: The Institutional Embeddedness of Holocaust Survivor Narratives," *European Journal of Sociology* 48, no. 1 (2007): 72.

42 Beim and Fine, "Trust in Testimony," 61.

43 Tamar Ashuri and Amit Pinchevski, "Witnessing as a Field," in *Media Witnessing: Testimony in the Age of Mass Communication* (New York: Palgrave Macmillan, 2009), 133–157.

44 Jovan Byford, "Remembering Jasenovac: Survivor Testimonies and the Cultural Dimension of Bearing Witness," *Holocaust and Genocide Studies* 28, no. 1 (Spring 2014): 58–84.

45 Kurasawa, "Message in a Bottle," 94.

46 Jeffrey Shandler, *Holocaust Memory in the Digital Age* (Stanford, CA: Stanford University Press, 2017), 64.

47 Kushner, "Holocaust Testimony," 275.

48 James Young, *Writing and Rewriting the Holocaust: Narrative and the Consequences of Interpretation* (Bloomington: Indiana University Press, 1988), 10.

49 Paul Thompson, *The Voice of the Past: Oral History*, 3rd ed. (New York: Oxford University Press, 2000), 174.

50 Lawrence Langer, *Holocaust Testimonies: The Ruins of Memory* (New Haven: Yale University Press, 1991), xv.

51 Shoshana Felman and Dori Laub, *Testimony: Crises of Witnessing in Literature, Psychoanalysis, and History* (New York: Routledge, 1992), 59–63; Mark Roseman, "Surviving Memory: Truth and Inaccuracy in Holocaust Testimony," in Perks and Thomson, *Oral History Reader*, 2nd ed., 230–243.

52 Roseman, "Surviving Memory," 232 (emphasis in original).

53 Marianne Hirsch and Leo Spitzer, "The Witness in the Archive: Holocaust Studies/ Memory Studies," *Memory Studies* 2, no. 2 (2009): 162.

54 Assmann, "History, Memory," 264.

55 Dan Sipe, "The Future of Oral History and Moving Images," in Perks and Thomson, *Oral History Reader*, 2nd ed., 282.

56 Dan Sipe, "The Future of Oral History," 408–409.

57 Assmann, "History, Memory," 265.

58 Hirsch and Spitzer, "Witness in the Archive," 158.

59 Langer, *Holocaust Testimonies*, 39–76.

60 Hirsch and Spitzer, "Witness in the Archive," 152.

61 Felman and Laub, *Crises of Witnessing*, 85 (emphasis in original).

62 Shandler, *Holocaust Memory*, 153.

63 Shandler, *Holocaust Memory*, 154.

64 Geoffrey Hartman, "Memory.Com: Tele-Suffering and Testimony in the Dot Com Era," *Raritan* 19, no. 3 (Winter 2000): 10.

65 Hirsch and Spitzer, "Witness in the Archive," 163.

66 Alison Landsberg, *Prosthetic Memory: The Transformation of American Remembrance in the Age of Mass Culture* (New York: Columbia University Press, 2004), 2.

67 Sara Jones, "Mediated Immediacy: Constructing Authentic Testimony in Audio-Visual Media," *Rethinking History* 21, no. 2 (2017): 148.

68 The website and its many resources are found at http://eugenicsarchive.ca.

69 Robert A. Wilson, "The Role of Oral History in Surviving a Eugenic Past," in *Beyond Testimony and Trauma: Oral History in the Aftermath of Mass Violence*, ed. Steven High (Vancouver: UBC Press, 2015), 130.

70 Colette Leung, "Profile: The Living Archives Project: Canadian Disability and Eugenics," *Canadian Journal of Disability Studies* 1, no. 1 (2012): 145.

71 K. D. Childress, "Genetics, Disability, and Ethics: Could Applied Technologies Lead to A New Eugenics?," *Journal of Women & Religion* 20 (2002): 159.

72 Wilson, "Role of Oral History," 131.

73 University of Alberta Living Archives Project, "Glenn Sinclair," YouTube, November 2015, video, 9:02, https://www.youtube.com/watch?v=SPMruq7rA70, captured at https://perma.cc/JD94-QJC9.

74 See Terry Cook, "Evidence, Memory, Identity, and Community: Four Shifting Archival Paradigms," *Archival Science* 13 (2013): 95–120, specifically, "Community."

3

"Carry It Forward"
Community-Based Conceptualizations of Accountability

Michelle Caswell, Joyce Gabiola,
Gracen Brilmyer, and Jimmy Zavala

Introduction

Writing in the 2006 volume *Ethics, Accountability, and Recordkeeping in a Dangerous World*, Richard J. Cox stresses the importance of the *ethical* aspects of accountability, integral to, but distinct from, its legal aspects: "I use the term 'accountability' to refer to processes relating individuals and organizations to a higher authority, the assessment of compliance and related activities and functions, and reporting on the effectiveness of performing certain tasks and responsibilities. Accountability brings together, under one umbrella, notions of responsibility, liability, laws and regulations, and transparency of activities."[1] In this essay, we build on Cox's notion of ethical responsibility to reinterpret accountability through the lens of community-based archives. We agree, as Cox has argued, that what distinguishes records from other forms of information is precisely their evidential quality; records are evidence of action and, as such, can, if properly activated, serve as *instruments of* accountability.[2] However, inspired by Cox's emphasis on *ethical* responsibility, we push beyond standard archival studies' constructions of accountability that rely on legal or academic formations and instead focus on records and archives as instruments through which communities are simultaneously responsible to past and future generations.

Many archival thinkers have constructed accountability as the ultimate raison d'être for archives, such that archives are well known as "arsenals of accountability" in the literature.[3] Writing in 2004, James O'Toole even elevated archivists' conceptions of their own ability and responsibility to hold governments and organizations accountable to a "moral theology."[4] Although corporate accountability is often acknowledged, the focus within archival studies has been on government accountability, such that, as Livia Iacovino posits, "In countries that have a democratically elected government, [accountability] . . . is synonymous with open access to government records."[5] Adding to dominant legal conceptions of accountability, John M. Dirks presents a more expansive notion of "historical accountability," which he defines as "how records help to hold yesterday's organizations and institutions accountable for their actions today, both in moral and (sometimes) legal terms."[6] It is clear through the literature that accountability involves the twin functions of legal and ethical responsibilities to the larger society. However, as Iacovino notes, the postmodern turn in archival studies has added a new dimension for exploring accountability, one that "recognizes how meanings and purposes of records should shift to incorporate the experience of the marginalized to counter the archive as constructed by the powerful."[7] Although we prefer the more nuanced and accurate umbrella term "critical archival studies" to the dated (and indeed often misused) "postmodernism," we are inspired by this emphasis on the experiences of those who are marginalized as we reconceptualize accountability to include community-based formations beyond legal and academic notions.[8]

Drawing on data we culled from focus groups with fifty-four users of five different community archives sites in Southern California, this essay explores how members of marginalized communities—and here we are referring specifically to communities of color and LGBTQ communities—imagine archives as aggregations of evidence that disrupt cyclical violence and hold individuals, institutions, and communities accountable to future generations. Across communities and identities, users of community archives repeatedly expressed fear of history repeating itself and articulated conceptions of archives as crucial sites to connect past injustice with contemporary activism and future possibilities. Accountability is thus reframed as an ethical commitment to care across generations.[9] This essay reimagines dominant conceptions of evidence and accountability to accommodate community-based notions of those concepts that are not dependent on the legal or academic conceptions from which archival studies traditionally draws. It argues that members of communities marginalized by race, gender, and sexual orientation interpret the archival function of accountability in terms of intergenerational responsibility to document past cycles of oppression and interrupt them for future generations. More specifically, the interviews we conducted with people of color and LGBTQ communities who use community archives revealed the ways in which marginalized people see history repeating itself and the hopes they have that archival labor—including their own volunteer labor—will intervene in that repetition as a form of accountability to future generations of community members.

Methods

From November 2016 to May 2017, we conducted ten focus groups with a total of fifty-four community members at five different community archives sites in Southern California. Our intention was to uncover the affective impact of community archives on their users so that we could both better understand such organizations as cultural phenomena and create a toolkit that would enable community archives to easily assess and leverage their own impact.

Although we originally intended to study the users of community archives, it quickly became clear that the distinction between user, board member, volunteer, and donor of materials is exceptionally blurry in community archives—such that it is more accurate to say that we studied the communities coalescing around and represented by community archives. We defined community-based archives as grassroots efforts by marginalized communities to document their own histories; while such organizations take a variety of forms and may collaborate to varying degrees with mainstream university or government repositories, a defining characteristic of community archives is that community members themselves maintain some degree of autonomy over the collections in terms of physical custody, appraisal, description, and/or access practices.[10]

The participating sites were the Southeast Asia Archive at the University of California, Irvine, which represents Vietnamese, Laotian, and Cambodian American refugee and immigrant communities; the Little Tokyo Historical Society, which represents descendants of Japanese Americans who were forcibly removed from downtown Los Angeles during World War II; Lambda Archives in San Diego, which is an LGBT archives; La Historia Society, which represents what until recently was a Chicanx/Latinx farm-working community in the city of El Monte, east of Los Angeles; and the Studio for Southern California History, which is a public history organization that collects oral histories and creates other documentary history projects from the bottom up. We chose the sites because they reflect the diversity of community archives in Southern California; they represent a range of marginalized identities (LGBTQ, Latinx, and Asian American); occupy a range of spaces (pop-up events at scattered locations, storefronts in strip malls, and university libraries); and are governed by a variety of structures, from total autonomy as stand-alone nonprofit organizations to integration within large public universities. Although this wide variety of identities, locations, and organization types makes it difficult to compare across cases without collapsing important differences between communities and archives, common themes occurred across sites that we think may resonate with many community archives in the American context.

We employed a semi-structured protocol to conduct the focus groups. Focus group sessions ranged from 60 to 120 minutes. We recorded the focus groups and then transcribed and coded for themes. Rather than attempt to create generalizations of community archives through a representative sample, this research aims to provide details on a phenomenon about which little is known. This essay attributes quotations from interview subjects by name, with their consent, as a way of assuring that intellectual credit is given to those interviewed and, by extension, the community archives themselves. We have deliberately maintained the length of the included quotations from our focus groups so that the voices of the participants remain within context and are understood as intended.

We, the members of the research team and the authors of this essay, think it is necessary to acknowledge our own positionalities, given the interpretivist paradigm in which this research was conducted. This is done to ensure transparency of possible factors that may affect researcher/participant relations and inherent power structures of the focus group format. We occupy multiple and diverse identities; in some cases we were insiders to the communities we studied and in other cases we were outsiders. Michelle Caswell identifies as a white, straight, cisgender woman who grew up in a working-class home and is in the first generation of her family to graduate from high school. Joyce Gabiola identifies as a queer Filipinx American from a middle-class background. Gracen Brilmyer identifies as a white, disabled, gender nonconforming queer person from a middle-class background. Jimmy Zavala identifies as a Chicano with a working-class background and is a first-generation college student. We openly discussed and reflected on these differences and commonalities and believe this multiplicity ultimately strengthened the research, allowing us to collectively see more than each individual team member could alone.

Accountability to the Past

Across sites, participants described working in archives both as volunteers and as users as a way to honor and be responsible to previous generations of community members. In this regard, through archival work, they hold themselves accountable to the generations that came before them.

Dolores Haro, the past board president of La Historia Society, addressed her motivations for being involved in the organization, recounting the hard labor, school segregation, and poor living conditions that her parents' and grandparents' generation survived. Describing the feelings she gets when she sees her ancestors and other community elders in the collection of historic photographs on display at La Historia, she said, "every single picture is a tremendous, beautiful story. So I feel when I walk in . . . I don't even have the word for it, it's . . . not just historical, but it's just so important to continue their legacy."[11] Lucy Vera Pedragon, a former board member of La Historia, agreed, describing her experiences of looking at the organization's collection of photographs documenting the *barrios*, or camps, her farm-working ancestors lived in: "How do I feel? Well, they suffered. They worked hard to make a living and feed their children. And this . . . was a segregated community where we had invisible barriers, and yet, their children became successful, and I think we owe them to keep the history alive. I think that's why we're all here as well, to keep the history alive about a certain time in this community."[12] Teresa Gutierrez, a college student whose grandfather founded the organization, concurred, saying that when she comes to La Historia Society, she feels, "Proud. Proud of the legacy we get to carry and the history that we get to share because I know, and that was [something] my grandpa . . . said, this history was not being represented in other museums, so now we get to represent it and share it with everybody."[13] At La Historia, it was clear that users of and volunteers for the organization do so, in part, out of a sense of ethical responsibility to past generations.

Despite the differences in historical, political, and cultural contexts, the theme of honoring the legacies of previous generations was also prevalent at the Little Tokyo Historical Society, which, in part, documents the forced evacuation of Japanese Americans from the neighborhood during World War II. As volunteer archivist Marcus Mizushima said,

> I just know there's a concern each generation has, I think there's an importance for them to know what happened here before them, because I wouldn't be here if my grandparents didn't make the sacrifice to come to this country and all the things that they went through. . . . Each generation, if there is not an effort to share that, they just lose it. . . . I think that is a big part of what historical societies are helping to do, to help that preservation for people to understand. . . . Each generation, they are here because of what the generation before had done and sacrificed.[14]

In this conceptualization, contemporary community members have an ethical responsibility to understand and share stories from the past.

Invoking nonbiological conceptions of ancestry and lineage, at Lambda Archives, Frank Nobiletti described his work teaching younger generations of LGBTQ people the history of their community in San Diego using materials in the archives, particularly in the aftermath of the AIDS crisis of the 1980s and early 1990s. He said, "There came a generation that didn't grow up with the older people and they were like, 'Oh my god, I had no idea that happened,' and then,

'They did *that* for us? They were thinking of us then?'"[15] Imparting the knowledge of how LGBTQ community members historically fought against oppressive systems is a form of holding younger generations accountable to past generations. Such accountability is particularly important given the generational gap caused by the devastation of AIDS.

Across all of our research sites, the possibility of archives being activated for legal accountability was never mentioned. Instead, accountability was framed as a relationship of care and responsibility to previous generations of community members.

History Repeating Itself

Across sites, we found a prevailing sense that community members see history repeating itself. Again and again, participants described how the historic trauma their communities had suffered not only was never addressed or redressed but that the same oppressive tactics community elders had experienced decades ago were being used in the current moment and that white supremacy and hetero-patriarchy were manifesting in the same ways as they had in the past. And yet, across communities and identities, users of community archives also articulated conceptions of archives as spaces to connect past injustice with contemporary activism and future possibilities, to disrupt cycles of oppression, and to hold each other accountable for imparting knowledge of and strategies for resistance to future generations.

For example, At Lambda Archives, Frank Stefano, a community elder and board member, spoke about how many younger LGBTQ people, who came of age during the Obama administration, might not yet see the political significance of their identity. They might think, "So what, you're gay? Who cares?"[16] However, in Frank's eyes, their identity would take on new meaning as their rights were "retrenched" under the then-new Trump administration. Drawing a chilling parallel, Paul Detwiler, a filmmaker in his forties, responded to Frank, "I thought all the queers in the Weimar Republic probably thought things were fine. . . . They were like 'this is great, we're having a great time, we can do whatever [we want], and we're free and then it's like, kaboom."[17] Edith Benkov, a professor teaching a LGBTQ history class, responded:

> You know, I always teach [the history of the Weimar Republic] and I was teaching that the night of the election . . . and I was like, well guys, this is really interesting but I'm really not talking about [Donald Trump, I'm talking about Hitler]. It was very freaky. It was very, very freaky. But I think when we came back the next week . . . and all these folks came back and said this sounds like last week's lecture and I said yeah, you know these things swing back and forth so you have to kind of keep in mind that [society] may have seemed really wonderful but just like the good old Weimar Republic . . . [things changed].[18]

A sense of terror and dread, the realization of how bad things may get given how awful histories repeat themselves, permeated the room.

Yet, users of Lambda Archives also spoke of archives as sites of political action, where they as individuals and their communities as a whole are responsible for breaking cycles of oppression through resistance. For Angela Risi, a recent college graduate, archival materials can inspire new activism and teach key political strategies from the past:

> We have the collection of associated student council meeting minutes, and so I went into those that week and I found the meeting minutes of when the Gay Liberation Front was proposed to be passed as a recognized student organization and it was approved. That was a really neat thing to find. That was one thing I was really impressed by, especially with activism happening today. I think that people think that activists who came before our time were this entity that had power and control and were official, but the records show it's just a handful of people to get together and scribble some things down on a notepad and that it evolves into something you could never have foreseen. . . . I don't know if [activists] are currently using [the archives] but I think certainly one way that they could use it is just as pure motivation to believe in the work that they're doing and see it is important, and . . . also to learn how activism has and hasn't been successful in this specific context of the city of San Diego, what tactics have worked, what haven't, or is there maybe a historic theme of police using certain strategies to try and regulate a movement such as permits or raids.[19]

Angela also drew trans-generational connections between anti-gay legislation from the past and President Trump's current Muslim ban:

I can't help but see the parallels between laws that Trump is putting into place—for example, the ban on people from the seven majority Muslim countries—and how the administration is saying this isn't a Muslim ban but it effectively works as a Muslim ban, and how laws from the 50s and 60s were often explicitly anti-gay, but even if they weren't, they were crafted in a way to target the gay community. It's sneaky and manipulative and it's been happening for a long time.[20]

Risi, like many other focus group participants, suggested that communities turn to archives to learn about and from past activist strategies. Benkov concurred that Lambda can be of much use to activists, because "the more you know about the past, you'll see things that are happening again, but we will know how to counteract things better if we see what was done before, especially in our own community.[21]

At La Historia Society, volunteer archivist Rosa Peña also tied her archival work to contemporary politics:

You don't realize how it repeats itself if you don't learn the history. . . . If you don't know, even in like the 1940s, Americans that were of Mexican descent were sent back to Mexico. Like, it could happen again this time because it's like, somebody that's searching for a Mexican is not going to see a Mexican American . . . just like they did back then, they're just going to round them up, just like they did with the Japanese. . . .[22]

Jazmin de la Cruz, a young college student and volunteer, echoed Rosa's sense of the cyclical nature of time but also added that archival work can help stop cycles of oppression: "Like Rosa said, history repeats itself [but] it can be stopped if you know the history."[23] Focus group participants at La Historia Society appeared to be in agreement that preserving and educating young people about the community's history is a way to resist and intervene on cycles of racism and state violence.

At Little Tokyo Historical Society, Shelly Niimi talked about the importance of community elders who had survived incarceration as children speaking out about their experiences in light of ongoing Islamophobia:

> Part of [the story of internment has been] covered up because of
> the cultural thing to not talk about negative things, but it was a bad
> experience that we don't want to happen to other people. [We don't
> want] that same mistake happening to Muslims after 9/11. . . . I feel
> like it's really sort of honorable that [the elders] are talking about
> [internment] so much now because that's helping Muslim people,
> to fight that Muslim ban, so it's like even more of an honorable
> thing to do even though it's culturally uncomfortable.[24]

Again, community members connected past and contemporary
oppression as a form of interruption in the historical cycle and a way
to leverage records to build a more just future.

As our research demonstrated, members of marginalized
communities themselves articulated the repetition of history and the
cyclical nature of oppression, making connections between oppression
that their own community has experienced or is experiencing and that
of other communities. Yet they also saw remembering and preserving
and storytelling as a way to break that cycle, to be responsible *to* the
past and *for* the future.

Accountability to the Future

Across sites, participants talked about their responsibility to younger
and future generations of community members and discussed archival
work as a way to hold themselves—and each other—accountable
to younger and future generations. This conveyed to us a sense of
accountability to the future that extends dominant interpretations of
accountability.

Participants actively imagined future generations of community
members coalescing around the archives. At Little Tokyo Historical
Society, Michael Okamura spoke about building a sense of community
among Japanese Americans centered around the neighborhood's
history:

> We should have a voice, and yes, we're proud of who we are, we've
> been here a long time and we've contributed to this society for many
> generations, and we're so proud of this community here physically that
> we will fight for it and not get drowned out by all these other people or
> groups that have different interests and want to dictate what they want
> to do for this neighborhood too. So that's why instilling in the younger

generation, growing that pipeline of leadership, which the community is doing now, to get them involved rather rapidly, because I'm getting a little bit older and it needs to be passed on to . . . younger people. . . . And then those stories will be gone, so how to have that connection still while we can retrieve those stories? The archives will help out a lot too, but if we can have those personal ties to the archives, better yet, and then, carry it forward.[25]

The theme of "carrying it forward" resonated across sites. At La Historia Society, Teresa Gutierrez spoke about forming the organization after realizing that Mexican American stories were left out of the official El Monte history museum: "We couldn't connect to the history. . . . Our history wasn't very apparent there, so we have this [organization] to connect with and to build not just this past history, but future history."[26] Similarly, community elder Val Rodriguez explained, "you don't see this [Mexican American history] in the books, you can't find this in books, [you won't learn it] unless you meet somebody . . . and learn from them, now it's up to me to share to younger people, "hey this is it, [if] you lose it, you lose it." He later said, "I want to make sure I give life to my younger generation so they can continue," adding, "We the people have our responsibility to keep our community alive."[27]

At the University of California, Irvine's Southeast Asia Archive, Kevin Duc Pham, a Vietnamese American undergraduate student, spoke about using a collection of records created by Vietnamese refugees:

It makes me very emotional. I've teared up a couple of times just seeing what these people went through, what they've had to experience, just knowing how I'm still affected by it, how lots of members of my community are still affected by it. Seeing how all these people were put into these refugee camps, these re-education camps, all the ways that they suffered, all the ways that they've tried so hard to come out and reach America and how, even though they have started a new life here, a lot of them are still affected by what had happened before. I see a lot in my own family, how they're experiencing things like PTSD because . . . they're victims of war and they went through all these horrible, traumatic experiences and I'm still affected by it, and a lot of other people I know are still affected by it too. So [using the archives] definitely helps re-coincide our present with our past, that we're able to move forward towards the future.[28]

As Pham eloquently put it, working in and with archives anchors a sense of ethical responsibility across generations, leveraging the past as a way to hold ourselves accountable to the future.

Conclusion

Our research at community archives in Southern California shows how members of marginalized communities conceptualize accountability, moving away from legal adjudication toward a broader sense of community-based responsibility. Indeed, for communities for whom legal justice remains elusive, accountability is rooted in ethical relationships with each other rather than with the (failed) state.[29] We thus conceptualize accountability in a community archives setting as a relationship to the past and the future—specifically, as an obligation to preserve evidence *in the now* that both honors past generations of elders and imagines possibilities for future generations. In our reframing, records are still evidence of activity but primarily serve internal community-based needs rather than the external demands of academic epistemologies or the legal system.

Ignited by Richard Cox's insistence that we interpret accountability beyond a legal purview, this essay has explored the ways in which communities that coalesce around community archives view archival work as an instrument through which they are responsible to past and future generations. It is no coincidence that, for many of the communities we studied, legal accountability is a political impossibility, has failed entirely, or has only partially or symbolically repaired past and ongoing injustice. For communities still marginalized by white supremacy and hetero-patriarchy, legal accountability is but one avenue of redress; *ethical* accountability, as evidenced by a sense of responsibility to past and future generations of community members, is another. It is this ethical dimension of accountability that was reflected in our focus group data. Community-based forms of responsibility may take the form of paying respect, listening, sharing stories, educating, making connections, learning strategies, speaking out, intervening, and imagining more just futures. In practicing these techniques, members of marginalized communities forge mutual responsibilities, envisioning and enacting a community-based conception of accountability.

Notes

[1] Richard J. Cox, *Ethics, Accountability, and Recordkeeping in a Dangerous World* (London: Facet, 2006), xxx.

[2] For more on evidence, see Richard J. Cox, *No Innocent Deposits* (Lanham, MD: Scarecrow Press, 2004), 165–200.

[3] Terry Eastwood, "Reflections on the Development of Archives in Canada and Australia," in *Archival Documents: Providing Accountability Through Recordkeeping*, ed. Sue McKemmish and Frank Upwards (Melbourne: Ancora Press, 1993), 36; Livia Iacovino, "Archives as Arsenals of Accountability," in *Currents of Archival Thinking*, ed. Terry Eastwood and Heather MacNeil (Santa Barbara, CA: ABC-CLIO, 2010), 181–212.

[4] James O'Toole, "Archives and Historical Accountability: Toward a Moral Theology of Archives," *Archivaria* 58 (Fall 2004): 3–19.

[5] Iacovino, "Archives as Arsenals," 181.

[6] John M. Dirks, "Accountability, History, and Archives: Conflicting Priorities or Synthesized Strands?," *Archivaria* 57 (2004): 30.

[7] Iacovino, "Archives as Arsenals," 188.

[8] For a definition of critical archival studies, see Michelle Caswell, Ricardo Punzalan, and T-Kay Sangwand, "Critical Archival Studies: An Introduction," *Journal of Critical Library and Information Studies* 1, no. 2 (2017), https://doi.org/10.24242/jclis.v1i2.50.

[9] For further details on care ethics in archives, see Michelle Caswell and Marika Cifor, "From Human Rights to Feminist Ethics: Radical Empathy in Archives," *Archivaria* 81 (Spring 2016): 23–43.

[10] Andrew Flinn, Mary Stevens, and Elizabeth Shepherd, "Whose Memories, Whose Archives? Independent Community Archives, Autonomy, and the Mainstream," *Archival Science* 9 (2009): 75.

[11] Dolores Haro, Focus Group at La Historia Society, El Monte, CA, February 18, 2017.

[12] Lucy Vera Pedragon, Focus Group at La Historia Society, El Monte, CA, February 18, 2017.

[13] Teresa Gutierrez, Focus Group at La Historia Society, El Monte, CA, February 18, 2017.

[14] Marcus Mizushima, Focus Group at Uyehara Travel, Los Angeles, CA, March 4, 2017.

[15] Frank Nobiletti, Focus Group at Lambda Archives, San Diego, CA, February 5, 2017.

[16] Frank Stefano, Focus Group at Lambda Archives, San Diego, CA, February 6, 2017.

17 Paul Detwiler, Focus Group at Lambda Archives, San Diego, CA, February 6, 2017.

18 Edith Benkov, Focus Group at Lambda Archives, San Diego, CA, February 6, 2017.

19 Angela Risi, Focus Group at Lambda Archives, San Diego, CA, February 6, 2017.

20 Risi, Focus Group.

21 Benkov, Focus Group.

22 Rosa Peña, Focus Group at La Historia Society, El Monte, CA, February 18, 2017.

23 Jazmin de la Cruz, Focus Group at La Historia Society, El Monte, CA, February 18, 2017.

24 Shelly Niimi, Focus Group at Uyehara Travel, Los Angeles, CA, March 3, 2017.

25 Michael Okamura, Focus Group at Uyehara Travel, Los Angeles, CA, January 7, 2017.

26 Gutierrez, Focus Group.

27 Val Rodriguez, Focus Group at La Historia Society, El Monte, CA, March 18, 2017.

28 Kevin Duc Pham, Focus Group at Southeast Asia Archive, University of California, Irvine, Irvine, CA, February 3, 2017.

29 We are not claiming that legal accountability for injustice is not important but rather that many see it as an unrealistic and even unattainable luxury.

4

Of Truth, Evidence, and Trust

Records and Archives in the Era of Misinformation and Disinformation

Luciana Duranti

What is truth? Most definitions refer to a verifiable and indisputable fact, that is, an event or human conduct that actually happened. How do we know that a fact actually happened? We rely on evidence. For centuries, records and archives have formed the evidentiary infrastructure through which beliefs and values have been upheld and understood. In his definition of archival documents, or records, Sir Hilary Jenkinson established their two qualities of impartiality and authenticity, stating, "Provided, then, that the student understands [the records'] administrative significance, they cannot tell him anything but the truth."[1] Of course, what Jenkinson was talking about is documentary truth, as historical truth cannot be directly accessed. Yet, documentary evidence has been recognized by most legal systems and scientific researchers as a highly reliable conduit to the truth, because, placed in its contexts (be they administrative/juridical, provenancial, procedural, documentary, or technological), it shows the relationship between a fact to be proven and the fact that proves it.[2] Lately, though, the public appears to disregard this fact infrastructure in favor not only of information coming from more easily accessible sources, such as social media, but also of its own feelings and opinions.

The term *post-truth* was coined in 1992 to refer to "circumstances in which objective facts are less influential in shaping public opinion than appeals to emotion and personal belief."[3] The term came in common use in 2016 due to a rise of anti-intellectualism that began to undermine faith in the professional integrity of all knowledge fields and in the value and authority of records and archives as sources. A related phenomenon, called either "alternative facts" or "disinformation," arose at the same time; these terms refer to the deliberate propagation of information that is incorrect by design and used by those who wish to disseminate confusion and deceit through alternative versions of the facts. Furthermore, the growth of technical infrastructures that are increasingly complex, often invisible, and hidden, is fostering the spreading of "misinformation," that is, information that is erroneous by mistake or because of incompleteness or decontextualization. In the past, these phenomena were dealt with through the mediation exercised by records managers and archivists, but today these professionals find themselves at a loss to capture much, if any, contextual data about the information found in these infrastructures and, often, even to understand their scope and scale or who controls them. This problem is due not only to the constant connectivity that characterizes our time and lets disinformation and misinformation circulate at rates unimaginable only a few decades ago but also to the pervasiveness of distribution channels that tend to sidetrack traditional institutions in favor of social environments where reputation as a trusted source no longer carries any weight.

In the past, records and archives professionals have provided a reasonable guarantee of the accuracy, reliability, and authenticity of the documentary evidence for which they are responsible. However, the phenomena described above have been so highly politicized that reliance on records and archives as primary sources of evidence seems hopelessly mired in partisanship,[4] while it becomes increasingly unclear who is responsible for the truthfulness of information circulated through the news or social media, and we know that at least one form of social media is filtered in order to reinforce members' beliefs and those of their friends and family.[5] Contributing to this situation, the creation and maintenance of records is falling victim to politicians and administrators who fear being held accountable for their actions, a behavior that reached a turning point in Canada in

2015–2016, when the Information Commissioner of Canada and the Information and Privacy Commissioner for British Columbia called for a legislated "duty to document."[6]

Finally, there is the purposeful will of third parties to document facts and actions as they happen by saving related videos and news but without access to the original sources, as in the case of the Internet Archive's Trump Archive. The introduction to the Archive states that "while largely curated by hand, the collections demonstrate how Artificial Intelligence algorithms could be used to create such resources, for example with voice and/or facial recognition. These evolving non-commercial, searchable collections are designed to preserve the historical record for posterity."[7] Clearly, the terms *evidence* and *truth* cannot be associated with such an endeavor. A more thoughtful undertaking is Wikipedia's plan for a crowd-funded news website offering stories by journalists and volunteers working together to counter the spread of fake news. Charlie Beckett, media professor at the London School of Economics, welcomed Wikitribune as an attempt to tackle a lack of public trust in mainstream media but questioned whether this is a remedy against inaccuracy: "There's nothing magical about being a citizen. As a citizen, you have your own bias and prejudice and experience as well."[8] This is true, unless the citizens use records and archives as primary sources of evidence for the specific facts presented on such a medium. Some groups and individuals feel a sense of injustice and are attempting to unearth the truth through the use of hacktivism,[9] while others are using encryption and decentralized information-processing technologies, such as blockchain, to protect the "truth" as well as their privacy.[10] In the past few years, many different knowledge fields have addressed this truth issue.

Library and information science scholars, noting that misinformation and disinformation, and the need to combat them, are nothing new, cite as an evaluation method Socrates' "test of three": is the information true, is the intent to share it good, and is the fact of knowing it useful to the recipient of the information?[11] Calls to "certify" information acknowledge the challenge of doing so, citing the volume of information; the democratization of information creation, which makes it difficult to know what source is authoritative; and the potential for falsity and pretense. Most of the literature emphasizes the important role of critical thinking and media/information literacy in fighting misinformation and argues that librarians and other information professionals have the key responsibility of serving as impartial mediators: educating the public on how to think critically about information presented to them and to understand the inherent and explicit biases of those who create and disseminate information, and promoting the importance to democracy of facts and evidence.[12] In collection management literature, a major talking point has been whether to "collect" misinformation and disinformation and how to contextually present it to users.[13] The literature acknowledges that any collection is "filtered" but argues that the ethics and professional skills of information professionals mitigate the risk of extreme bias.[14]

A key theme emerging from this literature is the changing way in which society assigns value to information: no longer is this determined by the authoritativeness or reliability of the source or the aggregation in which the information resides but rather by the breadth of its circulation. A recent Pew Research Center survey observed that Americans are losing faith in institutions, such as government, archives, libraries, museums, and the traditional media,[15] and perceived trust is identified as a key factor when assessing user perceptions toward information. Information ethicist Luciano Floridi states that "the cost of misinformation may be hard to reverse, especially when confidence and trust are undermined" and calls for the creation of an "ethical infosphere" to reestablish "credibility, transparency and accountability."[16]

Legal scholarship focuses on the erosion of the persuasive value of evidence and on the view of facts as threats,[17] but most authors do not go beyond acknowledging that the law is simply inadequate to the task of keeping the disinformation of the current moment in check. Members of the legal profession have expressed the belief that standards are the most effective way of dealing with the determination of what is evidence in the digital environment. In Canada, Section 6 of the *Uniform Electronic Evidence Act* provides that, "for the purpose of determining under any rule of law whether an electronic record is admissible," a judge may consider whether or not the disputed electronic record was created or stored in compliance with appropriate standards of recordkeeping.[18] According to the fundamental distinctions between rules of law and questions of fact, and between material facts and preliminary facts, Section 6 classifies standards as questions of preliminary fact: they do not have the status of laws or of material facts but are admissible as preliminary facts to be considered by judges in determining the admissibility of disputed electronic records. Thus, the recently published Canadian standard CGSB 72:34-2017, *Electronic Records as Documentary Evidence*,[19] explicitly addresses social media and cloud computing and issues a serious warning about the trustworthiness of these records creation/recordkeeping environments but offers no solutions to redress the problem.

In the social sciences, on the contrary, there is an abundance of literature on misinformation, concentrated mostly within psychology, political science, and social science and focused largely on the question of correcting misperceptions, with the proliferation of false facts about politics, climate change, and the safety of childhood vaccinations as the examples most frequently examined. The work of Brendan Nyhan and Jason Reifler on correcting political misperceptions is cited repeatedly in both the political science and psychology literature, as well as outside of it, perhaps because of the surprising nature of their finding that corrections often fail to reduce misperceptions and may actually increase the persistence of a misperception through the repetition of it.[20] However, there is no discussion in this literature about ways of facilitating access to reliable sources.

The literature of computational science flags very significant issues with how algorithms work and their interactions with fake news. After the October 1, 2017, mass shooting in Las Vegas—and notwithstanding pressure from FactCheck.org, PolitiFact, Snopes, The Weekly Standard, ABC News, and the Associated Press—Google allowed a 4chan thread to trend in its Top News section, and Facebook had a top-trending article from the Gateway Pundit: both sources are notorious for spreading false news and toxic rumors, but the popularity-first focus of social media algorithms pushed these items to the top.[21] The entire December 2017 issue of the *Journal of Applied Research in Memory and Cognition* is about post-truth, disinformation, and misinformation; one of the articles proposes "technocognition," an interdisciplinary approach joining technology and philosophy as the solution.[22] However, so far philosophy has only contributed insights into the production, dissemination, and reception of disinformation: epistemology, skepticism, ethics, agnotology (i.e., the study of willful acts aimed to spread confusion and deceit),[23] and philosophy of information. A recent article takes up post-truth politics and education by re-asserting the primacy of objective truth and independent facts, the decline of which is attributed to the work of constructivist, postmodernist, and postcolonial theorists.[24] Maren Behrensen engages with post-truth politics by examining "why people cling so closely to poor information in the first place" and identifying a totalizing mistrust against entire institutions as the culprit, because it lets opportunistic agents of manipulation fill the resulting vacuum.[25]

Although very interesting, the above literature does not shed much light on what records and archives professionals can do to address the "truth issue" in such a way that the public will turn to the primary sources of evidence and instruments for accountability—records and archives—to discover facts and to make decisions on the basis of reliable information. Economics scholars state that humans use heuristics to make decisions, often "satisficing"—that is, accepting any available option as good enough rather than selecting the optimal outcome. "Nudges," small stimuli used to influence individuals or organizations, can lead people to make better decisions, though many consider them manipulative and paternalistic, as they can be deployed for nonaltruistic reasons, and fake news (particularly when targeted to gain endorsements within social networks) might be considered a "nudge" to undermine democracy in its own right.[26] However, medical literature suggests that people may not respond to "the best evidence," whether due to developments in human psychology (e.g., the influence of technology on the way we think and process information), changes in the external environment (e.g., the demise of the traditional media), or other factors. Psychology scholars in particular think that, by trying to correct erroneous beliefs caused by misinformation or disinformation, we may actually reinforce those beliefs. More successful corrections might be to repeat the true information often; ignore the false information, and don't repeat it; make true information as accessible as possible; and prepare information recipients to expect misinformation. Efforts to correct misinformation must be mindful of how people assess and accept the "truth" of evidence. The source of the correction also matters, as we are more accepting of evidence that is contrary to our beliefs when the source of that correction has a vested interest in that correction being untrue.[27]

Given all of the above, what can records and archives professionals do? The obvious answer is to reestablish the lost trust in the fact infrastructure provided by archives. What does trust involve? Some view it as a four-level progression: from *individual*, as a personality trait, to *interpersonal*, as a tie directed from one person to another (son to father), to *relational*, as a property of a mutual relationship (people doing business), and then to *societal*, as a feature of a community as a whole.[28] InterPARES Trust (ITrust), an international multidisciplinary research project focused on the trustworthiness of records in the cloud environment,[29] defines *trust* as "confidence of one party in another, based on an alignment of value systems with respect to specific actions or benefits, and involving a relationship of voluntary vulnerability, dependence, and reliance, based on risk assessment."[30] Substantially, trust involves acting without the knowledge needed to act by substituting the information that one does not have with other information, such as the testimony of witnesses, oral tradition, records, or archival institutions. A 2015 study by Devan Ray Donaldson and Paul Conway shows that the public in general trusts information when it is in the custody of archival institutions.[31] However, such information is not easily accessible to the general public. Thus, ITrust developed ways of making records and archives accessible to the general public by entrusting it to a cloud environment that is secure, available,[32] reliable,[33] and cross-jurisdictional.

The key to a trustworthy cloud environment is the contract made between the cloud service provider (CSP) and the owner of the records or their designated preserver (e.g., an archival institution). ITrust researchers produced checklists for contracts that address "data ownership; availability, retrieval, and use; data retention and disposition; data storage and preservation; security; data location and data transfer; and end of service/contract termination."[34] On the basis of the contract requirements, digital preservation standards, other ITrust studies on open government, privacy, public trust, security classification, and economic models, the research team proceeded to develop a model of Preservation as a Service for Trust (PaaST).[35] The model defines a comprehensive set of functional and data requirements that support preservation of digital information regardless of the technologies used or who uses them. The requirements are intended to enable authentic digital preservation in the cloud, but they are valid in other scenarios as well, including in-house preservation and situations in which digital preservation includes both in-house and contracted services. In addition, PaaST requirements are applicable to cases that include heterogeneity in the types of information objects being preserved; variety in applicable directives, such as laws, regulations, standards, policies, business rules, and contractual agreements—including varying conditions of ownership, access, use, and exploitation; variation in institutional arrangements and relationships between or among the parties involved; and a wide spectrum of circumstances from best practices to worst cases. The PaaST requirements supplement the Open Archival Information System (OAIS) Reference Model[36] in that they are intended to be directly implementable in software. However, PaaST does not specify what technology should be used; rather, it defines what the technology must be able to do.[37]

As the focus of PaaST is preservation, any system developed that respects its requirements would allow for an inference of authenticity for the records managed by the system from the moment they are entrusted to it. Thus, there is no guarantee that the records ingested in any kind of service respecting PaaST requirements were authentic before transfer. For this reason, ITrust investigated the possibility of technological authentication for records generated with and without a digital signature by studying ways of connecting records contained in blockchains to a records management system via a blockchain aggregator and, in turn, connecting the recordkeeping system to a preservation system based on PaaST requirements. A team of researchers designed a TrustChain system that relies on the involvement of a group of trusted archival institutions and the records creators from whom they receive records transfers. The TrustChain is designed to provide confirmation of integrity, time of creation/existence, sequence of records, nonrepudiation, continuing validity of e-signatures after the expiration of the related certificates, and an unbroken chain of evidence from creation to archival preservation.[38]

The models developed by ITrust are very promising and it is very likely that they will be implemented, either in part or in their entirety. With implementation, the material created, managed, and preserved respecting PaaST and TrustChain requirements will be trustworthy as a source of evidence, as documentary truth. Will it be trusted, though? More important, will this infrastructure for trust imply that—to paraphrase a line in a popular film—"if [we] build it, [they] will come"?[39] Not likely. It is not sufficient—though it is essential—to move forward and deal with constant technological change, to conduct interdisciplinary, international research in collaboration with the industry and across sectors to generate public interest in it. Neither is it sufficient—though it is a necessary prerequisite—to develop and implement strong recordkeeping and records preservation systems supported by advanced authentication technology, in collaboration with information technology experts, to attract the public to it as its primary source of information. To counteract misinformation and disinformation and once again make records and archives the centerpiece of what the public will regard as the best evidence of facts and actions and the most effective instrument of accountability, records and archives professionals must do much more. They need to develop tools to "nudge" people toward their infrastructure for documentary truth (recordkeeping and preservation systems), even if it means slicing and dicing the related information for targeted audiences, just like Facebook does. They have to create different blueprints for characterizing their infrastructure to potential users, just like Google does. Finally, they need to design and implement capabilities enabling people to easily trace, access, and assess records in context, click after click, fast and easily, just like Wikipedia does. Most important, they need to do all of the above ethically, on the basis of a true understanding of the facts and of a willingness to let those facts speak for themselves.[40]

Ethical considerations concerning presentation of records and archives through traditional channels of communication do not translate seamlessly to online communities, however. Records and archival professionals traditionally have been guided by codes of ethics and aspirational sets of principles for ethical behavior, but those codes and principles are not easy to enforce. In 2006, Richard Cox stated that the problem was in the field of ethics itself.[41] There are too many ethical theories, he said, and they are often in conflict with each other, overlapping, and unable to prove that a certain behavior is unethical regardless of the perspective or implications.[42] One might add that these theories, which tend to be based on consequences, duties, rights, or virtues,[43] are more relevant to communication between individuals than to the creation, use, keeping, and maintenance of information. What is relevant to professionals in the digital online environment is rather "responsibility," which can be enforced through legislation and regulations.[44] A "duty to document" one's action, ensconced in legislation, might be able to do just that, requiring administrators of all kinds, including records managers and archivists, to record all of their actions and decisions, especially when it comes to providing access to the information they hold in trust. Only then will the public rediscover that records and archives are the necessary instruments for unveiling and denouncing misinformation and disinformation and get to the truth.

Notes

[1] Hilary Jenkinson, *A Manual of Archive Administration*, 2nd ed. (1937; repr., London: Percy Lund, Humphries & Co., 1965), 12.

[2] Luciana Duranti, "The Archival Bond," *Archives and Museum Informatics* 11 (1997), 214. See also Jason R. Baron, "Documentary Evidence," in *The Encyclopedia of Archival Science*, ed. Luciana Duranti and Pat Franks (Lanham, MD: Rowman & Littlefield, 2015).

[3] "Word of the Year 2016 Is . . . ," Oxford Dictionaries, 2016, https://en .oxforddictionaries.com/word-of-the-year/word-of-the-year-2016.

[4] George Depres, "Fact Denial and the Record Under Threat," *Brandeis Records Manager*, December 21, 2016, https://gdrecordsmanager.blog/2016/12/21/fact -denial-and-the-record-under-threat, captured at https://perma.cc/6WLB-DPPY.

[5] Shannon Greenwood, Andrew Perrin, and Maeve Duggan, "Social Media Update 2016," Pew Research Center, Internet & Technology, November 11, 2016, http://www.pewinternet.org/2016/11/11/social-media-update-2016, captured at https://perma.cc/72TE-LA7Y; Frederic Filloux, "Facebook's Walled Wonderland Is Inherently Incompatible With News," in *Monday Note* (blog), December 4, 2016, https://mondaynote.com/facebooks-walled-wonderland-is-inherently -incompatible-with-news-media-b145e2d0078c.

[6] Office of the Information Commissioner of Canada, "Backgrounder on a Duty to Document," news release, October 27, 2016, https://www.oipc.bc.ca /media/16822/2016-01-25-backgrounder_duty-to-document_en.pdf; Elizabeth

Denham, *Submission to the Special Committee to Review the Freedom of Information and Protection of Privacy Act* (Victoria, British Columbia: Office of the Information and Privacy Commissioner for British Columbia, November 18, 2015), https://www.oipc.bc.ca/special-reports/1884, captured at https://perma.cc/295T-RC5D; Elizabeth Denham, *Access Denied: Record Retention and Disposal Practices of the Government of British Columbia,* Investigative Report F15-03 (Victoria, British Columbia: Office of the Information and Privacy Commissioner, October 22, 2015). See also Elizabeth Denham, "The Extent of Our Care: Archives, Memory and Information Rights," Information Commissioner's Office, January 25, 2017, https://ico.org.uk/about-the-ico/news-and-events/news-and-blogs/2017/01/the-extent-of-our-care-archives-memory-and-information-rights/, captured at https://perma.cc/Y95Y-K3QA.

[7]   Trump Archive, https://archive.org/details/trumparchive&tab=about; see also Kalev Leetaru, "What Data-Mining TV's Political Coverage Tells Us," *Real Clear Politics,* August 10, 2017, https://www.realclearpolitics.com/articles/2017/08/10/what_data-mining_tvs_political_coverage_tells_us.html, captured at https://perma.cc/5GML-QDH6.

[8]   Charlie Beckett, "Wikitribune: Can Crowd-sourced Journalism Solve the Crisis of Trust in News?," *Polis: journalism and society at the LSE* (blog), London School of Economics and Political Science, April 28, 2017, https://blogs.lse.ac.uk/polis/2017/04/25/wikitribune-can-crowd-sourced-journalism-fight-fake-news/, captured at https://perma.cc/UT2B-TKFA.

[9]   Christie Thompson, "Hacktivism: Civil Disobedience or Cyber Crime?," *ProPublica,* January 18, 2013, https://www.propublica.org/article/hacktivism-civil-disobedience-or-cyber-crime, captured at https://perma.cc/33GE-UE6X.

[10] Sarah Underwood, "Blockchain Beyond Bitcoin," *Communications of the ACM* 59, 11 (2016): 5–17. See also Syrian Archive, https://syrianarchive.org, and Blockchain@UBC, https://blockchainubc.ca/.

[11] Nick Poole, "Evidence and Trust in a Post Truth World," *CILIP,* September 12, 2017, https://archive.cilip.org.uk/news/evidence-trust-post-truth-world, captured at https://perma.cc/M5MT-AGXF.

[12] Claire Laybats and Luke Tredinnick, "Post Truth, Information, and Emotion," *Business Information Review* 33, no. 4 (2016): 204–206; Kayleigh Bohémier, Melanie Maksin, and Gwyneth Crowley, "Wayfinding the Web: Applying Critical Information Literacy to a Google Instruction Session," *Online Searcher* 41, no. 4 (July/August 2017), http://www.infotoday.com/OnlineSearcher/Articles/Features/Wayfinding-the-Web-Applying-Critical-Information-Literacy-to-a-Google-Instruction-Session-119313.shtml, captured at https://perma.cc/PTM8-2F2G.

[13] Rick Anderson, "Fake News and Alternative Facts: Five Challenges for Academic Libraries," *Insights: The UKSG Journal* 30, no. 2 (2017): 4–9.

[14] Laybats and Tredinnick, "Post Truth."

[15] John B. Horrigan, "How People Approach Facts and Information," Pew Research Center, Internet & Technology, September 11, 2017, http://www.pewinternet.org/2017/09/11/how-people-approach-facts-and-information/, captured at https://perma.cc/T62Y-4U2C.

[16] Luciano Floridi, "Fake News and a 400-Year-Old Problem: We Need to Resolve the 'Post-Truth' Crisis," *Guardian,* November 29, 2016, https://www.theguardian.com /technology/2016/nov/29/fake-news-echo-chamber-ethics-infosphere-internet -digital, captured at https://perma.cc/3VKB-9J2J.

[17] S. I. Strong, "Alternative Facts and the Post-Truth Society: Meeting the Challenge Essay," *University of Pennsylvania Law Review Online* 165 (2017): 137–146.

[18] Uniform Law Conference of Canada, Uniform Electronic Evidence Act, September 1998, https://www.ulcc.ca/en/older-uniform-acts/electronic-evidence /1924-electronic-evidence-act.

[19] *Electronic Records as Documentary Evidence,* CAN/CGSB 72:34-2017 (Gatineau, Canada: Canadian General Standards Board, 2017).

[20] Brendan Nyhan and Jason Reifler, "When Corrections Fail: The Persistence of Political Misperceptions," *Political Behavior* 32, no. 2 (2010): 303–330.

[21] See Charlie Warzel, "The Big Tech Platforms Still Suck During Breaking News," BuzzFeed News, October 2, 2017, https://www.buzzfeed.com/charliewarzel/the -big-tech-platforms-are-still-botching-breaking-news, captured at https://perma.cc /9EAW-RJR8.

[22] Stephan Lewandowsky, Ullrich K. H. Ecker, and John Cook, "Beyond Misinformation: Understanding and Coping with the 'Post-Truth' Era," *Journal of Applied Research in Memory and Cognition,* 6, no. 4 (2017): 353–369.

[23] Georgina Kenyon, "The Man Who Studies the Spread of Ignorance," BBC, January 6, 2016, http://www.bbc.com/future/story/20160105-the-man-who-studies-the -spread-of-ignorance, captured at https://perma.cc/XTC9-R49S.

[24] Kai Horsthemke, "'#FactsMustFall'? Education in a Post-Truth, Post-Truthful World," *Ethics and Education* 12, no. 3 (2017): 273–288.

[25] Maren Behrensen, *The State and the Self: Identity and Identities* (New York: Rowman & Littlefield, 2017).

[26] Julia M. Puaschunder, "Nudgital: Critique of Behavioral Political Economy," *Archives of Business Research* 5, no. 9 (2017): 54–76.

[27] Neil Levy, "Nudges in a Post-Truth World," *Journal of Medical Ethics* 43, no. 8 (2017): 495–500; Norbert Schwarz, Eryn Newman, and William Leach, "Making the Truth Stick & the Myths Fade: Lessons from Cognitive Psychology," *Behavioral Science & Policy* 2, no. 1 (2016): 85–95.

[28] Kari Kelton, Kenneth R. Fleishmann, and William A. Wallace, "Trust in Digital Information," *Journal of the American Society for Information Science and Technology* 59, no. 3 (2008): 364.

[29] See http://www.interparestrust.org.

[30] InterPARES Trust Terminology Project, http://arstweb.clayton.edu/interlex/en /term.php?term=trust, captured at https://perma.cc/ACR2-VCCL.

[31] Devan Ray Donaldson and Paul Conway, "User Conceptions of Trustworthiness for Digital Archival Documents," *Journal of the Association for Information Science and Technology,* January 30, 2015, https://doi.org/10.1002/asi.23330.

[32] "Cloud availability" refers to availability of the infrastructure, hardware, and software—that is, to the amount of time that a system is expected to be in service, expressed statistically or as a percentage. Availability facilitates the retrieval and readability of the records, because technical difficulties might slow the process.

[33] Cloud reliability is the characteristic of behaving consistently with expectations in terms of consistency of access—that is, copies of the records that are distributed across several data centers to ensure that redundancy remains consistent while users access the same data at the same time. It is the copies of records that remain consistent as they are distributed across several data centers to ensure redundancy.

[34] Jessica Bushey, Marie Demoulin, and Robert McLelland, "Cloud Service Contracts: An Issue of Trust," *Canadian Journal of Information and Library Science* 39, no. 2 (June 2015): 128–153.

[35] Luciana Duranti, Adam Jansen, Giovanni Michetti, Courtney Mumma, Daryll Prescott, Corinne Rogers, and Kenneth Thibodeau, "Preservation as a Service for Trust (PaaST)," in *Security in the Private Cloud,* ed. John Vacca (Boca Raton: CRC Press, 2017), 47–72.

[36] *Space Data and Information Transfer Systems—Open Archival Information System—Reference Model,* No. ISO 14721:2012 (Geneva, Switzerland: International Organization for Standardization, 2012).

[37] Kenneth Thibodeau, Daryll Prescott, Richard Pearce-Moses, Adam Jansen, Katherine Timms, Giovanni Michetti, Luciana Duranti, Corinne Rogers, Larry Johnson, John R. Butler, Courtney Mumma, Vicki Lemieux, Sarah Romkey, Babak Hamidzadeh, Lois Evans, Joseph Tennis, Shyla Seller, Kristina McGuirk, Chloe Powell, Cathryn Crocker, and Kelly Rovegno, *Preservation as a Service for Trust: Functional and Data Requirements for Digital Preservation,* InterPARES Trust Report (unpublished), January 2018.

[38] Most research documents are not published yet, but some reports are posted on the ITrust website. See, for example, Mats Stengård, Hans Almgren, and Hrvoje Stancic, *Model for Preservation of Trustworthiness of the Digitally Signed, Timestamped and/or Sealed Digital Records (TRUSTER Preservation Model) (EU31)—Case Study 3,* https://interparestrust.org/assets/public/dissemination/EU31_20170511_TRUSTER_CaseStudy3_v1-4.pdf, captured at https://perma.cc/CZ33-4CNG. See also Victoria L. Lemieux and Manu Sporny, "Preserving the Archival Bond in Distributed Ledgers: A Data Model and Syntax," in *Proceedings of the 26th International Conference on World Wide Web Companion* (Perth, Australia, April 3–7, 2017): 1437–1443; and the ITrust spinoff, Blockchain at UBC, https://blockchainubc.ca.

[39] Phil Alden Robinson, *Field of Dreams* (screenplay), 1989.

[40] Elena Danielson, *The Ethical Archivist* (Chicago: Society of American Archivists, 2010), 18.

[41] His statement was part of a presentation at the Society of American Archivists' annual meeting and later published in an article, "Digesting the Raisins of Wrath: Business, Ethics, and the Archival Profession," *American Archivist* 71 (Spring/Summer 2008): 203–209.

42 Cox, "Digesting," 205.

43 Don Fallis, "Information Ethics for Twenty-first Century Library Professionals," *Library Hi Tech* 25, no. 1 (March 13, 2007): 23–36.

44 Corinne Rogers and Luciana Duranti, "Ethics in the Cloud," *Journal of Contemporary Archival Studies* 4, no. 2 (2017): 4, http://elischolar.library.yale.edu /jcas/vol4/iss2/2.

5

Commentary
Accountability and Evidence

Heather Soyka

When Richard Cox published *Ethics, Accountability, and Recordkeeping in a Dangerous World* in 2006, it was in reaction to the events of September 11, 2001, and other contemporary events, using corporate and government scandals to examine the role of recordkeeping and archivists in a post-truth climate. Within that volume, he defined the term *accountability* to refer to processes relating individuals and organizations to a higher authority, to the assessment of compliance and related activities and functions, and to the formation of reporting on the effectiveness of performing certain tasks and responsibilities. Accountability brings together, under one umbrella, notions of responsibility, liability, laws, regulations, and transparency of activities.[1] In terms of archives, records, and information, accountability assumes that issues—such as explaining the importance of records, working against unwarranted secrecy, the importance of corporate and societal memory, and trust—are necessary between government and its citizens.[2] These themes are of central relevance to the discourse around records and their creation, access, and use. The research that Cox generated in this area continues to engage and provide space for provocative, complex conversations about power, accountability, and evidence.

The four essays in this section are all concerned with expanding applications of accountability and evidence within archival theory and practice. David Wallace focuses on power, narratives, and the limitations of records as evidence and as objects of accountability; Wendy Duff and Jefferson Sporn examine the idea of oral testimony as an expansion of collaborative archival evidence; Michelle Caswell, Joyce Gabiola, Gracen Brilmyer, and Jimmy Zavala explore conceptualizations of accountability as a community-based obligation for preservation; and, finally, Luciana Duranti identifies a need for rebuilding trust in institutions with documentary infrastructure. All four essays demonstrate the importance of acknowledging the different ways that notions of transparency, collaboration, responsibility, trust, and power related to archives and records have been described, used, and understood under the concept of accountability.

These essays make explicit contributions to the discussion of accountability and evidence, which is one of the four overall themes that form *Defining a Discipline*. Across the four essays, several common threads emerge that reflect ongoing conversations and indicate future directions for research in the archival profession.

The first thread centers the needs of communities and individuals around evidence and accountability to past and future generations. Caswell, Gabiola, Brilmyer, and Zavala's analysis of their ongoing community archives research study demonstrates a reconceptualization of accountability, casting it as a community-based responsibility that honors previous generations and suggests possibilities for future generations of a community. Rather than relying on the authority of official systems and institutions, this research imagines and promotes recordkeeping frameworks that are reflections of community motivations, voices, and realities and not subsumed by external systems and hierarchies. This added dimension of ethical accountability, described as a sense of obligation to past and future generations of the community, may provide an alternative pathway for the documentation and explication of past events. Duff and Sporn contend that the evidentiary value of oral testimonies acquired by archives is related to connecting testimonies with people, using archives as sites of ethical responsibility for people who have been marginalized or historically excluded. Using the collaborative concept of "knowing with" to emphasize a collaborative process of shared interpretation and co-labor, Duff and Sporn argue that oral testimony is a means of transmission to future generations and that video testimony positions the viewer as a member of a "provisional community" where the listener takes the responsibility for witnessing and remembering into the future. Collaborating with communities is not merely collecting from communities but sitting in community with members as a central part of the process.

The second common thread brings together considerations around institutions and authority. Wallace's examination of the politics and documentary process around American war crimes in Vietnam outlines the limitations of using records as tools of accountability, describes their contextual messiness, and underscores problems of institutional legitimacy, knowledge generation, agency, and narrative construction. Comprising many parts, what Wallace terms a "multifaceted documentary archipelago" of institutions and authorities plays a role in the complicated and shifting understandings of the conflict. Because the official record maintained by the government does not exist in isolation, the unsanctioned and unofficial may come together to form a more nuanced, complicated understanding that should provoke thoughtful interrogation of national memory and who/what purpose it serves.

Whereas Wallace focuses on powerful actors and the question of whether official institutions are suitable arbiters of social memory, Duranti makes the case that in an era of misinformation, it is important to nudge people toward the infrastructures for authoritative documentary truth. Describing current iTrust research, Duranti argues that regaining public trust in archives and other government institutions will rely on making complex infrastructures more transparent and visible; nurturing confidence in standards, institutions, and authentic transfer; and designing tools and systems that allow people to trace, access, and assess records in context.

Understanding the limitations of institutional authority for evidence and accountability is important to reading how communities are fostering and conceptualizing their own recordkeeping practices and values for memory and accountability. Removing governmental or institutional actors from the central recordkeeping role allows communities to envision different structures that meet their unique needs. In their research study, Caswell, Gabiola, Brilmyer, and Zavala showed that the expanded concept of ethical accountability is rooted in relationships between members of the community instead of relationships between individuals and the state or individuals and institutions. The sense of responsibility for documentation is to honor past generations and provide support for future generations by telling the stories of the community. Duff and Sporn also have examined the role of institutions, their processes, and the motivations for collecting oral testimonies as part of their research. Noting that the institution cannot be divorced from its contexts, they show that, through the process of selection, archivists and curators determine authenticity, trustworthiness, and who is eligible to qualify as a witness. When, as in the case study from the Living Archives on Eugenics cited by Duff and Sporn, institutional records fail to capture the full picture, oral history testimonies allow evidence and an additional vector for understanding this part of Canadian history. Oral testimony is a means of transmitting evidence about more than just the event but of life lived before and after.

A third thread, and one of the core challenges of recordkeeping, is the notion of trust. How do communities build and understand trust? How can communities develop mechanisms for trust that serve as alternatives to or alongside of institutional frameworks for recordkeeping? In regards to responsibilities to past and future members of the community, is trust activated by demonstrating fidelity to the past that can be carried into the future? Caswell, Gabiola, Brilmyer, and Zavala show that communities have a need for trust that is based in accountability. By developing alternative frameworks for recordkeeping, community members are able to establish and reflect on evidence outside of official systems that honors their experiences and brings them to a shared set of truths that make sense *for* the community, even if it is different than institutional or organizational records created *about* the community and its members. Similarly, Duff and Sporn outline possibilities for community members working together with researchers and institutions to refocus on both narrator and questioner as co-producers of knowledge in order to build shared trust in both process and outcome.

Along similar lines, how do institutions build trust with communities that they purport to serve? Duranti describes "post-truth" misinformation and disinformation practices that have developed with the express purpose of confusing the public and undermining faith in the value and authority of records. Duranti describes trust as a four-level progression from individuals to interpersonal, relational, and societal relationships[3] and suggests that reestablishing trust in what Duranti terms "fact infrastructure" is the key way that archivists can contribute to solving this problem. By following the PaaST system requirements for building trusted recordkeeping systems, Duranti posits that institutions could provide confirmation of authenticity, integrity, and continued validity for records managed within trusted systems and that archives professionals need to nudge people toward using that infrastructure.

Historically as well as in the present, many communities and individuals have had reasonable cause to distrust governments and institutions and the records generated by official processes. Wallace's concept of the "documentary archipelago" as a multifaceted dance between official and unofficial records illustrates some of the problematic, embedded realities and processes that shape and form records. But it also suggests different ways that people have built individual trusted relationships and alliances around the unofficial, unsanctioned, and complex record in order to better understand events and situations. Still, Wallace's essay shows that the difficult work of interrogating and unpacking the complex layers of powerful actors, silences, deliberate falsification, and more must be thoughtfully undertaken by archivists.

Together, these essays provide evidence of a sustained and expanding dialogue around notions of accountability and the roles of records and archivists. Ongoing and future considerations for the archival profession may be found in these common threads; there continues to be a clear need for more work that is centered on the needs of communities for accountability; for work that continues to examine and interrogate concerns around the positioning of power and institutional authority; and for work that delves deeply into complex notions of trust, authority, and truth. Applicable broadly to researchers, practitioners, educators, and students, the four essays in this section serve as a reminder for archivists and memory workers to continue to explore accountability, both in broad terms and in ways that resist, complicate, and confound simple answers.

Notes

1 Richard J. Cox, *Ethics, Accountability, and Recordkeeping in a Dangerous World* (London: Facet, 2006), xxx.

2 Richard J. Cox and David A. Wallace, eds., *Archives and the Public Good: Accountability and Records in Modern Society* (Westport, CT: Quorum Books, 2002).

3 InterPARES Trust (ITrust), https://interparestrust.org.

THEME TWO
Ethics and Education

Richard J. Cox, *Desert Bloom*, Oil on Canvas, 2014.

6

Records as Evidence, Text, and Narrative
Framing the Ethical Dimensions of Integrity

Heather MacNeil

Introduction

In the concluding chapter of *Ethics, Accountability, and Recordkeeping in a Dangerous World*, Richard Cox suggests that "archivists sometimes face a daunting challenge in building support for their mission" because the meaning of archives is so multilayered. He describes his own habit of reading voraciously across disciplines as an ongoing effort to discover new insights into that meaning, and he urges archivists to join in that effort by "open[ing] up a dialogue with other disciplines in order to reach the greatest possible comprehension of what archives might represent."[1] This essay is a modest response to that urging. Drawing on perspectives from within and without the archival discipline, it aims to uncover a few of the layers of meaning associated with the notion of integrity as an ethical principle and obligation for archivists.

In the *Oxford English Dictionary*, the term *integrity* has two distinct yet overlapping meanings. Its root meaning, deriving from the Latin *integritās*, refers to a state of "wholeness, completeness, or entirety" or an "unimpaired or uncorrupted condition" and is used in a general sense to characterize the quality of a thing. The term also has a specifically moral dimension, referring to an individual's "unimpaired moral state" or "soundness of moral principle."[2] Both senses of the term *integrity* are apparent in the International Council of Archives' (ICA) Code of Ethics. The first principle of the ICA's Code invokes integrity explicitly when it states that "archivists should protect the integrity of archival material and thus guarantee that it continues to be reliable evidence of the past"; the accompanying commentary to that principle invokes it implicitly when it asserts that "the objectivity and impartiality of archivists is the measure of their professionalism."[3] In the principle, integrity corresponds to the complete and unimpaired state of archives (as a corpus of documentation) and is viewed as a precondition for protecting their value as reliable evidence.[4] In the commentary, which lays out the ethical obligations entailed in protecting that value, integrity may be understood as an unstated but implicit virtue-term that encapsulates the qualities of impartiality and objectivity required of archivists to properly fulfill their obligation to identify and preserve archives and make them available for use.

This essay explores some themes and variations on these two dimensions of integrity and is framed around three metaphors: records as *evidence*, archival fonds as *texts*, and records as *narratives*. Metaphors are potentially powerful framing devices because they trigger what L. David Ritchie calls "conceptual structures" that enable us to look at the world in novel ways.[5] The metaphor of records as evidence, referenced in the ICA Code of Ethics, is rooted in law and history and has long functioned as a kind of foundational metaphor for the archival mission. It foregrounds the critical importance of records in rendering an account of the past and in holding records creators to account for their actions in the present and the ethical obligation of archivists to ensure that the account rendered through records is and remains, to the extent possible, complete and uncorrupted. The metaphor of archival fonds as texts draws on insights from contemporary textual scholarship; it focuses attention on the constructed nature of an archival fonds and the complex web of agents and forces that impinge on and shape its meaning in and through time and highlights archivists' ethical obligation to render a complete and transparent account of their own actions with respect to the records in their care.

The metaphor of records as narratives, for its part, is rooted in humanities and social science scholarship and revolves around the positioning of narrative and narrativity over the last few decades as "concepts of social epistemology and social ontology" that are closely linked to the formation of individual and social identity.[6] Unlike the metaphors of records as evidence and archival fonds as texts, which speak to different understandings of the nature of records, the metaphor of records as narratives speaks to the impact of records—both positive and negative—on individuals and communities seeking access to them as part of the process of identity formation. This essay will focus on a particular subset of that metaphor—that is, care records as narratives—that has emerged in the wake of contemporary inquiries into historical institutional childhood abuse. This specific metaphor draws on insights from social and psychological research into the experience of "care leavers," individuals who have spent substantial portions of their childhood in institutional care and who are seeking access to their care records in an effort to understand and recover from a traumatic past. It links integrity, as a condition of wholeness, to the notion of an integrated self and underscores the ethical obligation of archivists to support and advocate on behalf of individuals and communities who are trying to reconcile their present with their past as a means of achieving that wholeness.

Records as Evidence

Nancy Partner writes that evidence is "a metaphor based on visual perception," deriving from the Latin word *ēvidentia*, meaning "that which is manifest or in plain sight."[7] In its metaphorical sense, historical evidence is that which "brings the vanished past into sight."[8] The observational principles on which archivists ground their belief in records as "reliable evidence of the past" thus reflect a conception of records as witnesses to past events and a corresponding view of the world as one that is capable of being so witnessed.

The observational principles underpinning the metaphor of records as evidence are rooted in the philosophy of rationalist empiricism that emerged during the seventeenth century and reoriented knowledge in the direction of empirical inquiry to establish matters of fact. According to that philosophy, the truth of any proposition could be established by reasoning from the relevant evidence, with reason operating within a framework of inferences, generalizations, and probabilities. Rationalist empiricism exercised a significant influence on the emerging fields of law and history because it was assumed that records constituted a form of testimony and thus fell under the general theory of evidence and knowledge. By the end of the nineteenth century, the twin notions of records as evidence and of evidence as inference had found their way into the rationalist tradition of evidence scholarship and the scientific tradition of historical scholarship.[9] Because records were presumed to reflect events in the real world, their reliability was linked to their proximity to the events they purported to record and the credibility of the persons who observed and recorded those events. In both traditions, the methods for assessing records as reliable evidence of the past were directed toward peeling away the distorting layers of time, bias, and interpretation to bring the past "into plain sight."

When European archival theory started to take shape in the late nineteenth and early twentieth centuries, it absorbed these methods and reinterpreted them for the aggregations of documents now in the custody of archival institutions. According to that theory, archives were less susceptible to the distorting influences of time, bias, and interpretation than other kinds of historical sources because they were made or received by an entity in the course of carrying out its activities and in accordance with its own needs rather than the interests of posterity. In Sir Hilary Jenkinson's words, archives were simply "there, a physical part of the facts which . . . happened to survive"[10] and, as such, they constituted "a measure of knowledge which [did] not exist in quite the same form anywhere else."[11] They carried, in consequence, a particular weight as primary evidence for suppositions made or conclusions drawn about those activities.

For the first generation of archival theorists, then, protecting the integrity of archival records as reliable evidence meant protecting their value as impartial witnesses to past events. Accordingly, the principles governing the arrangement of archives were based on the assumption that keeping together "the whole" of the records of a given records creator (an archival fonds) and maintaining them in their original order (the order given to them by that creator) was the best means to preserve the truth-value that attached to records through the circumstances of their creation, maintenance, and custody; in cases in which original order had been damaged or "corrupted,"[12] the archivists' duty was to undo the damage and restore that order.[13] In asserting these principles as the only sound basis for arrangement, archival theorists were asserting the archivist's ethical obligation to protect the integrity of that evidence and to avoid contaminating it in the methods employed to manage archival fonds. The impartiality and objectivity of the archivist, alluded to in the ICA Code of Ethics, is tied to that obligation. Michelle Light and Tom Hyry suggest that, "at their heart, respect for original order and provenance . . . strive to reduce the archivist's meddling impact and influence on the records, so that the context of the records' creation and use is preserved and the authenticity of the records' evidence is maintained."[14]

For much of the twentieth century, the metaphor of records as evidence was linked to the metaphor of archives as laboratories of history, positioning archival institutions as the primary site for the production of historical knowledge and as the place where the most impartial sources of history could be found. In contemporary archival discourse, the metaphor of records as evidence is frequently conjoined with the metaphor of archives as arsenals of administrative, democratic, and historical accountability to highlight the critical role played by records in ensuring that records creators are held to account for their actions in the present as well as the future and to underscore the ethical obligation of archivists to facilitate and promote the creation and maintenance of records that are complete and uncorrupted. Within this accountability frame, the emphasis that contemporary records management standards such as ISO 15489-1:2016(E) place on the creation and capture of records as "evidence of business activity" attests to a continuing concern with ensuring that records can serve as reliable witnesses to the events they document. In the ISO standard, such concern manifests itself in the metadata specifications, which aim to situate records in time and place and in relation to actions and agents from the moment of their creation, and in the procedural controls for monitoring and evaluating records systems, which aim to protect the records in those systems from corruption or tampering within and across time and space.[15]

Within the accountability frame, the metaphor of records as evidence remains compelling, particularly when considered in relation to scandals that have resulted from failures of public and private agencies to provide an adequate account of their actions through their records and in light of the demonstratively negative impact poor recordkeeping practices have had on the ability of official inquiries investigating historical abuse to fulfill their remit. The metaphor links integrity to the capacity of records to bear witness to past events in which society has a vital interest and to the ethical obligation of archivists to protect, nurture, and advocate for that capacity on society's behalf.

Within the laboratories of history frame, however, the metaphor of records as "reliable evidence of the past" has lost some of its cachet, especially when viewed in light of the contemporary archival turn in history. As Ann Laura Stoler explains, "Whether documents are trustworthy, authentic and reliable remain pressing questions, but a turn to the social and political conditions that produced these documents, . . . has altered [our] sense of what trust and reliability might signal and politically entail."[16] Kathryn Burns's study of notarial archives in sixteenth-century colonial Peru speaks to that shift in perspective. Quoting William Hanks, Burns points out that for historians working with colonial records, "'one of the central empirical and methodological problems . . . is *the sheer partiality of what was written*'—its striking incompleteness, as well as the 'power asymmetries' inherent in it."[17] In her study, she describes the recordmaking practices of early modern notaries as acts of "legal ventriloquy" in which notaries created for their clients a first-person subject, an official "I" on whose behalf they ostensibly acted.[18] The templates used by notaries to communicate their client's wishes, however, were designed to register agreement, "not ambivalence or disagreement," and, as she puts it, created "the legal fiction of an 'I' with clear, decisive agency where perhaps none existed."[19] The point of the documents was not to reveal but to "prevail."[20] Burns compares these recordmaking practices to a game of chess—"full of gambits, scripted moves, and countermoves"—and suggests that chessboard may be a more apposite metaphor for the notarial archive than the traditional metaphor of archive as mirror.[21]

Burns's study illustrates one of the ways in which archival turn scholars have troubled the metaphor of records as evidence by positioning historical sources as constituent agents in reconstructing a particular conception of the past rather than as the unselfconscious remains of that past. The implications of such repositioning extend beyond the making of records to the keeping of them; for if recordmaking practices are "full of gambits, scripted moves, and countermoves," so, too, are the archival practices associated with the management of historical records. That being the case, archivists and archival institutions may also be considered constituent agents in reconstructing a particular conception of the past. The metaphor of archival fonds as texts offers a useful frame within which to explore the ramifications of this repositioning for archival understanding of integrity as an ethical value.

Archival Fonds as Texts

We can trace a conceptual trajectory of the term *text* from its early affiliation with philological scholarship focusing on texts as literary objects; to its uptake by postmodern theory and criticism, which extended its reach to include any form of representation and turned text into what Neil Fraistat and Elizabeth Bermann Loizeaux call "a function of signifying practices"; to its current incarnation as a pivot point for a host of disciplinary fields concerned with the production, consumption, reception, editing, and sociology of texts, broadly defined.[22] As David Greetham describes it, "this shift from modernist text to postmodernist text" corresponds roughly to the shift in meaning "between the two main strands of the etymological *text*: from the *textus* to the *textile*."[23] *Textus* is linked, historically, to "the validity and definitiveness of the biblical text" and is affiliated with the notion of text as authority, revealed truth, and originality. *Textile*, deriving from the Latin *texĕre*, is affiliated with the notion of text as a weaving, a tapestry, a network, a web;[24] in this latter strand, what constitutes a text, according to D. F. McKenzie, "is not the presence of linguistic elements but the act of construction."[25]

Within the Anglo-American tradition of textual criticism, the shift in meaning from revealed to constructed text corresponds to two distinct approaches to the preparation of critical editions—that is, the authorial approach and the sociological approach.[26] In the authorial approach, the task of the textual critic is to reconstitute, from among the many "corrupt" variants of a literary text that have existed over time, the authentic or "ideal" text, namely, the one that best embodies the final intentions of the author. Once the text has been revealed through that act of editorial reconstitution, it is then contextualized through the preparation of a critical apparatus that contains notes and commentary on the text, the history of its variants, an essay outlining the editorial principles followed, and so forth.

Textual critics who adopt a sociological approach call into question the centrality of final authorial intentions in the preparation of critical editions. They take the view that the production of a literary text is not the individual endeavor of an author but a collaborative enterprise between and among the author, editors, publishers, and readers; variant versions of a text are not "corruptions" to be eliminated but, rather, legitimate textual formations worth studying in their own right; and the primary task of the textual critic is not to reconstitute authorial intentions through the establishment of a single definitive text but, rather, to expose the complex and open-ended histories of textual change and variance through the presentation of multiple texts. As Renaissance textual scholar Leah Marcus cautions,

> No single version of a literary work can offer us the fond dream of unmediated access to an author or to his or her era; the more aware we are of the processes of mediation to which a given edition has been subject, the less likely we are to be caught up in a constricting hermeneutic knot by which the shaping hand of the editor is mistaken for the intent of the author, or for some lost, "perfect" version of the author's creation.[27]

Marcus proposes the term "new philology" to describe the shift in editorial attention from idealized to historicized literary texts. The "dominant textual paradigm" of this new philology is a "network," within which "the text loses its privileged separateness and is conceptualized as part of a much wider vectoring of forces and objects"[28]—including the shaping hand of editors themselves.

We can trace a similar trajectory from revealed to constructed text through the archival literature reexamining the principles that underpin the arrangement of a fonds and its parts. In that literature, the valorization of a unitary original order—that is, one bounded by the lifespan of the creator—and the idealized model of the fonds as a totality of records that revolves around a single creator have been disputed on the grounds that each has acted, in its own way, to obscure the complex history of a fonds and its parts, thereby effacing much of its meaning. There is a growing recognition that the material and intellectual orders of records within a fonds are not stabilized at any single point in time; they are continually being shaped and reshaped as those records are resituated in different environments and territorialized by different authorities. Like variant versions of literary texts, these different orders are viewed increasingly by archivists not as a contamination to be eradicated but simply part of the history and evolving meaning of those records and, therefore, should be made visible through the critical apparatus of description. The recognition that multiple agents and authorities participate in the creation and ongoing history of a fonds and its parts has also thrown into question the current boundaries of the fonds that effectively subordinate these many agents and authorities to a single primary creator and shrink the totality of records to the physical aggregations of records that have survived and are held in a given archival institution.

Viewed through the lens of the sociological approach to textual criticism, the metaphor of the archival fonds as texts focuses archival attention on the inevitably constructed nature of a fonds and its parts as well as the process of that construction—that is, the ways in which a web of records and their relationships are formed and reformed over time and the wider vectoring of agents and circumstances that have shaped their history. Most important for present purposes, the metaphor draws the agency of archivists into that history—that is, the role they play in shaping the contours and meaning of archival aggregations through their practices of appraisal, arrangement, description, and preservation. In so doing, it uncouples integrity, as a quality of character, from impartiality and objectivity and expands the notion of accountability to encompass the ethical obligation of archivists to hold themselves to account for the actions and decisions they have taken with respect to the records in their care and, as much as possible, to make those actions and decisions known to users. In this context, integrity finds its location in the completeness of the account rendered and in the qualities of critical self-reflection and transparency that inform it.

The metaphor of archival fonds as texts supports and reinforces the insights of archival turn and textual scholarship concerning the constructed nature of the historical record and the multiple agencies at play in that construction. It acts as a necessary corrective to the metaphor of records as evidence by drawing attention to the incompleteness and partiality of that evidence. It does not, however, cancel out the ethical obligation that is linked to the evidence metaphor within the accountability frame—that is, to work toward strengthening the capacity of records to hold records creators to account for their actions. It simply extends that obligation by situating archivists within the accountability frame, holding themselves to account for their actions through their own documentation practices and making those actions visible to users.

The metaphors of records as evidence and archival fonds as texts speak to different understandings of the nature of records and their capacity to reveal the past. The metaphor of care records as narratives speaks instead to the impact of records—both positive and negative— on individuals and communities whose need for records to reveal the past is an urgent and deeply felt one. The metaphor communicates the emotional significance that care leavers attach to the records documenting their time in care—that is, their belief that these records will provide the foundation on which they might begin to build a coherent narrative of their lives and, in so doing, come to terms with a traumatic past. It also highlights the ethical obligation of archivists to assist care leavers in navigating the disjunction between the different understandings of records as reliable evidence of the past and as a partial—that is, incomplete and biased—construction of that past.

Care Records as Narratives

Since the 1980s, official inquiries into historical institutional child abuse have been established in at least twenty jurisdictions across Europe, Canada, New Zealand, Australia, and the United States, and the number of inquiries has been steadily rising since the mid-2010s.[29] Care-related records have featured prominently in such inquiries. For the authorities investigating historical abuse, such records are critical sources for gaining insight into the systemic factors that contributed to it. For care leavers, they are critical sources for learning about and recovering from their life in institutional care. The metaphor of care records as narratives speaks to the role that records are perceived to play in the latter process. As Margaret Somers observes,

It is through narratives that we come to know, understand, and make sense of the social world, and . . . through narratives . . . that we constitute our social identities. . . . all of us come to *be* who we *are* (however ephemeral, multiple, and changing) by being located or locating ourselves (usually unconsciously) in social narratives *rarely of our own making.*[30]

There is a substantial body of research, primarily in the fields of social work, sociology, and psychology, that explores the connection between narrative, records, and the social identity of care leavers. As Christine Horrocks and Jim Goddard explain,

Leaving care research has shown that reaching into the past can be important in the construction of a "coherent narrative of their [care leavers'] lives that can connect past and present." . . . [In that research] identity is seen as a "dynamic project" that is ongoing, developing— being revised throughout the life course. These revisions are not only influenced by personal events/biographies, but they are also situated and influenced by wider societal understandings; the self is an ever- developing story that can be added to, amended, and transformed. Accessing child care files, with their mixture of new and forgotten personal information, can be a hugely significant event in the self- identity storytelling project of these adults. Moreover, . . . they mark the interaction of different sources of identity, our self-reflection and the interpretations of professionals involved in our childhoods.[31]

That research has also shown that children who have grown up in care share a number of distinct characteristics associated with their social identity. The first is the experience of separation and loss that results from their being removed from their birth families; that separation and loss is exacerbated by the secrecy associated with being a child in substitute care. Gill Pugh observes that, for much of the twentieth century, the pendulum of prevailing wisdom swung back and forth between a belief in severing all links between children taken into care and their birth parents—the so-called fresh start approach—and a belief in preserving biological links and continuity.[32] Until the latter part of the twentieth century, the former approach—which was based on the assumption that a child could not form meaningful attachments in their new life if they still had attachments to their former life—was dominant and carried with it "a desire to suppress not only contact with, but knowledge of people and information from the past ('secrecy')."[33] That approach may explain, in part, why many care leavers lack basic information about their background, including their parentage, medical history, the existence of siblings or other relatives, the reasons they entered care, and even their age.

The social identity of care leavers is also shaped by the experience of "genealogical bewilderment"; this is a knock-on effect of secrecy and "describes the state of confusion and uncertainty said to be experienced by the child (or adult) 'who either has no knowledge of his natural parents or only uncertain knowledge of them.'"[34] That state of bewilderment intensifies the care leavers' need to know about their past; a need fueled by their belief that filling in the gaps will somehow heal them or at least help them come to terms with that past.

Finally, children who have grown up in institutional care share the experience of stigma that attaches itself to them simply because they are different. As Pugh observes, "the 'differences' of those growing up in care are frequently all too visible. Children may attract attention . . . from the necessity for statutory visits from social workers, from difficulties in accounting for the absence of parents or siblings, transport in vehicles with distinctive identifying logos, and so on."[35] This stigma is gradually internalized as the children come to understand that their own life story

> is at odds with cultural ideas/stories of what is normal. While a considerable number of other people one knows might share a life story that tells of being "looked after" by a local authority, this is by no means storied as "normal." Such life stories, which do not adhere to normalcy, become stories of disruption. They are defined by their difference, leaving the person feeling at odds with others. It is therefore no surprise that issues of stigmatization and self-esteem loom large in the leaving care literature.[36]

Given these painful childhood experiences of separation and loss, secrecy, genealogical bewilderment, and stigma, it is also no surprise that care-leaver narratives are sometimes described as "narratives of lost origins" in which care leavers try to make sense of a past and present self in the absence of what Suellen Murray et al. call "reliable markers about what happened, and why";[37] and no wonder that care

leavers look to their records as a kind of historical repository of their
lives,[38] a foundation on which to recover their lost origins and begin
the process of constructing a more integrated narrative of the self.

Care leavers form one part of a growing community of archival
users seeking access to records as a way of coming to terms with a
traumatic past and as a first step in achieving justice for the historical
wrongs committed against them. When they enter the archives, these
users carry with them a profound legacy of pain, shame, confusion,
and anger, along with a tangled mix of needs, expectations, hopes,
and fears. As Gudmund Valderhaug describes it:

> Individuals who approach the archives to find documentation of
> injustice committed against themselves are very often strangers to the
> archives. . . . They approach us with their demands for justice, with their
> angst and their hopes, with their wants and desires; they are coming to
> change their lives. The archives are strange to them; they know little
> about what may be found there, but they know that the archives are part
> of the same public system that some years ago neglected or mistreated
> them. And they may even be strangers *in* the archives, because their
> lives are poorly documented—and sometimes totally absent—in the
> records.[39]

Valderhaug's last point underlines a depressingly common finding
of official inquiries into historical institutional child abuse—that
the records documenting the lives of children in care are filled with
gaps and omissions and that the most significant omissions are the
voices of the children themselves. It also echoes the observation of
Michael Jones and Cate O'Neill that "the fragmented, disordered
documentary traces of children's experiences in institutional care in
some ways mirror the situations of the families that these children
come from, and many children's journey through the system."[40]

What ethical obligations do archivists have toward these so-called
strangers in our archives? The research on care leavers suggests that
the first obligation is to actively support their efforts to identify and
locate their care records from a stance of engagement and empathy
rather than one of impartiality and objectivity.[41] It may not be within
the power of archivists to alleviate the pain of care leavers when they
discover, as they so often do, that their voices are largely absent in their
own care records. But it is within archivists' power to create access tools

for care leavers that offer easily navigable pathways to a range of care-related records, along with contextual information to enable them to decipher and interpret those records; to prepare supplementary textual and visual resources relating to the histories of care institutions that, in the absence of their own care records, may enable them to reconstruct at least some parts of their life in care; and to incorporate annotation tools that will allow care leavers to add their voices, however belatedly, to those records and resources.[42] It is also within the power of archivists to advocate for the creation of care-related records that provide a more complete account of the experiences of children in institutional care and that place them at the center rather than the margins of those experiences; and to work toward ensuring that those records are properly identified, managed, described, and made accessible in the recordkeeping and documentation systems of both records creators and records preservers.[43]

The metaphor of care records as narratives thus invites archivists to think about integrity as a quality of wholeness and completeness of a person, a coherent and integrated self. Viewed from that perspective, the archivist's ethical obligation is to support the efforts of care leavers to create an integrated narrative of their lives—notwithstanding the fragmented and partial evidence on which that narrative will be built—and to actively work, on behalf of care leavers and society as a whole, toward strengthening the capacity of care-related records to serve as reliable evidence of the past. By highlighting the enormous emotional significance that care leavers attach to these records, the metaphor also invites archivists to link archival integrity to a willingness to engage with and, to the extent possible, empathize with the particular needs of individuals and communities who are seeking access to records as part of the process of coming to terms with a traumatic past.

Conclusion

The overarching aim of this essay has been to contribute to Richard Cox's effort to broaden and deepen our understanding of the archival mission by drawing on different disciplinary perspectives to help illuminate the various meanings associated with integrity as an ethical principle and obligation for archivists. The metaphors that have been explored in this essay are complementary conceptual frames for thinking through those meanings. While each metaphor triggers different interpretations of integrity as both a desirable condition of wholeness and a desirable quality of character, all three are bound together by an ethic of accountability, broadly interpreted. The metaphor of records as evidence highlights the role archivists play in preserving and protecting records in the service of historical, administrative, and democratic accountability and the qualities of impartiality and objectivity traditionally associated with accomplishing that role. The metaphor of archival fonds as texts shifts attention to the obligation of archivists to hold themselves to account for their actions and foregrounds the qualities of critical self-reflection and transparency needed to fulfill that obligation, while the metaphor of care records as narratives speaks to the obligation of archivists to take into particular account the access needs of individuals and communities whose lives are documented—for better or for worse— in records and the qualities of engagement and empathy essential to meet those needs in a meaningful way.

Each metaphor also functions as a kind of corrective to the other ones. The metaphor of archival fonds as texts acts as a corrective to the metaphor of records as evidence by drawing attention to the incompleteness and partiality of that evidence. The metaphor of records as narratives, for its part, acts as a corrective to the metaphor of archival fonds as texts because, while it acknowledges the limitations of the evidence metaphor, it also underscores the necessity for archivists to maintain their faith in the capacity of records to serve as reliable evidence of the past and to actively work toward protecting and promoting that capacity.

Notes

1 Richard J. Cox, *Ethics, Accountability, and Recordkeeping in a Dangerous World* (London: Facet, 2006), 233–234, 254.

2 "Integrity," *Oxford English Dictionary* (Oxford: Oxford University Press, 2017), https://www.oed.com/view/Entry/97366?redirectedFrom=integrity#eid.

3 International Council on Archives, *Code of Ethics*, September 6, 1996, http://www .ica.org/sites/default/files/ICA_1996-09-06_code%20of%20ethics_EN.pdf, captured at https://perma.cc/QPC5-5R92.

4 This interpretation of *integrity* is consistent with the one found in the 1988 edition of the *ICA Dictionary of Archival Terminology*. There, *archival integrity* is defined as

"a basic standard derived from the principle of *provenance* and the *registry principle* which requires that an *archive/record group* shall be preserved in its entirety without division, mutilation, *alienation*, unauthorised destruction or addition, except by *accrual* or *replevin*, in order to ensure its full evidential and informational value." Peter Walne, ed., *Dictionary of Archival Terminology/Dictionnair de terminologie archivistique*, 2nd ed. (Munich: K. G. Saur, 1988).

5 L. David Ritchie, *Metaphor* (New York: Cambridge University Press, 2013), 202.

6 Margaret Somers, "The Narrative Constitution of Identity: A Relational and Network Approach," *Theory and Society* 23 (1994): 606.

7 Nancy Partner, "Making Up Lost Time: Writing on the Writing of History," *Speculum* 61 (January 1986): 105.

8 Partner, "Making Up Lost Time," 105.

9 For a detailed discussion of the evolution of legal and historical methods for assessing the trustworthiness of records as evidence, see Heather MacNeil, *Trusting Records: Legal, Historical, and Diplomatic Perspectives* (Dordrecht: Kluwer, 2000), 1–31.

10 Hilary Jenkinson, "Reflections of an Archivist," in *A Modern Archives Reader: Basic Readings on Archival Theory and Practice*, ed. Maygene F. Daniels and Timothy Walch (Washington, DC: National Archives and Records Service, 1984), 18.

11 Jenkinson, "Reflections," 15.

12 Hilary Jenkinson, *A Manual of Archive Administration* (Oxford: Clarendon Press, 1922), 32.

13 S. Muller, J. A. Feith, and R. Fruin, "The Arrangement of Archival Documents," *Manual for the Arrangement and Description of Archives*, 2nd ed., trans. Arthur H Leavitt (Chicago: Society of American Archivists, 2003), sec. 16, 59.

14 Michelle Light and Tom Hyry, "Annotation and Colophon: New Directions for the Finding Aid," *American Archivist* 65 (Fall/Winter 2002): 219–220.

15 *Information and Documentation: Records Management: Part 1: Concepts and Principles*, 2nd ed., ISO 15489-1:2016(E) (Geneva, Switzerland: International Organization for Standardization, 2016).

16 Ann Laura Stoler, "Colonial Archives and the Arts of Governance: On the Content in the Form," in *Refiguring the Archive*, ed. Carolyn Hamilton et al. (Dordrecht: Kluwer Academic Publishers, 2002), 85.

17 Kathryn Burns, *Into the Archive: Writing and Power in Colonial Peru* (Durham, NC: Duke University Press, 2010), 127, quoting William F. Hanks, *Intertexts: Writings on Language, Utterance, and Context* (Lanham, MD: Rowman & Littlefield, 2000), 12 (emphasis by Burns).

18 Burns, *Into the Archive,* 125–126.

19 Burns, *Into the Archive,* 127.

20 Burns, *Into the Archive,* 124.

21 Burns, *Into the Archive,* 124.

22 Neil Fraistat and Elizabeth Bermann Loizeaux, "Introduction: Textual Studies in the Late Age of Print," in *Reimagining Textuality: Textual Studies in the Late Age of Print* (Madison: University of Wisconsin Press, 2002), 5.

23 David Greetham, "The Philosophical Discourse of [Textuality]?," in *The Pleasures of Contamination: Evidence, Text, and Voice in Textual Studies* (Bloomington: Indiana University Press, 2010), 278 (emphasis added).

24 David Greetham, "What Is Textual Scholarship?," in *A Companion to the History of the Book*, ed. Simon Eliot and Jonathan Rose (West Sussex: Wiley-Blackwell, 2009): 24.

25 D. F. McKenzie, *Bibliography and the Sociology of Texts* (Cambridge: Cambridge University Press, 1999), 43.

26 For a detailed discussion of these approaches and their analogies to archival arrangement and description, see Heather MacNeil, "Deciphering and Interpreting an Archival Fonds and Its Parts: A Comparative Analysis of Textual Criticism and the Theory of Archival Arrangement," in *Research in the Archival Multiverse*, ed. Anne J. Gilliland, Sue McKemmish, and Andrew Lau (Melbourne: Monash University Press, 2016), 161–197.

27 Leah S. Marcus, *Unediting the Renaissance: Shakespeare, Marlowe, Milton* (New York: Routledge, 1996), 3.

28 Marcus, *Unediting the Renaissance, 22–23.*

29 A research project housed at La Trobe University in Melbourne, Australia, is currently mapping the rise of inquiries into historical institutional child abuse over time and across national contexts. See Katie Wright, Shurlee Swain, and Johanna Sköld, "The Age of Inquiry: A Global Mapping of Institutional Abuse Inquiries," La Trobe University, 2017, https://doi.org/10.4225/22/591e1e3a36139. For analyses of specific inquiries into historical abuse of children in care, see Johanna Sköld and Shurlee Swain, eds., *Apologies and the Legacy of Abuse of Children in "Care": International Perspectives* (Basingstoke: Palgrave MacMillan, 2015).

30 Margaret Somers, "The Narrative Constitution of Identity: A Relational and Network Approach," *Theory and Society* 23 (1994): 606 (emphasis in original).

31 Christine Horrocks and Jim Goddard, "Adults Who Grew Up in Care: Constructing the Self and Accessing Care Files," *Child & Family Social Work* 11 (2006): 265.

32 Gill Pugh, *Unlocking the Past: The Impact of Access to Barnardo's Childcare Records* (Aldershot, UK: Ashgate Publishing, 1999), 7.

33 Pugh, *Unlocking the Past,* 7.

34 Pugh, *Unlocking the Past,* 35.

35 Pugh, *Unlocking the Past,* 34.

36 Horrocks and Goddard, "Adults Who Grew Up in Care," 266.

37 Suellen Murray, John Murphy, Elizabeth Branigan, and Jenny Malone, *After the Orphanage: Life Beyond the Children's Home* (Sydney: UNSW Press, 2009), 53.

[38] Shurlee Swain and Nell Musgrove, "We Are the Stories We Tell About Ourselves: Child Welfare Records and the Construction of Identity Among Australians Who, as Children, Experienced Out-of-Home 'Care,'" *Archives and Manuscripts* 40 (2012): 6.

[39] Gudmund Valderhaug, "Memory, Justice and the Public Record," *Archival Science* 11 (2011): 21 (emphasis in original).

[40] Michael Jones and Cate O'Neill, "Identity, Records and Archival Evidence: Exploring the Needs of Forgotten Australians and Former Child Migrants," *Archives and Records* 35 (2014): 113.

[41] For a discussion of how empathy might inform archival theory and practice more generally, see Michelle Caswell and Marika Cifor, "From Human Rights to Feminist Ethics: Radical Empathy in the Archives," *Archivaria* 81 (Spring 2016): 23–43.

[42] The *Find & Connect* online resource, which contains history and information about Australian children's residential homes and institutions, provides an example of what such a resource might look like. See https://www.findandconnect.gov.au.

[43] The need for more comprehensive and inclusive care records is discussed in Heather MacNeil, Wendy Duff, Alicia Dotiwalla, and Karolina Zuchniak, "'If There Are No Records, There Is No Narrative': The Social Justice Impact of Records of Scottish Care-Leavers," *Archival Science* 18 (2018): 1–28, esp. 21–24. For more on the need for archivists to advocate for the creation of a more comprehensive and inclusive record in the context of individuals and communities who are trying to come to terms with a different kind of traumatic past, such as the Yugoslav wars of the 1990s, see Anne Gilliland, "Moving Past: Probing the Agency and Affect of Recordkeeping in Individual and Community Lives in Post-conflict Croatia," *Archival Science* 14 (2014): 249–274.

7

NARA and the Private Email Account

The Agency's Response to the Clinton Email Case

Eleanor Mattern

Introduction

On March 2, 2015, Michael Schmidt of the *New York Times* broke a story headlined "Hillary Clinton Used Personal Email at State Dept., Possibly Breaking Rules," in which he reported that the former secretary of state used a nongovernmental email account during her tenure.[1] What followed was intense media coverage and further revelations about a privately managed server. Criticism dogged Secretary Clinton for the entire 2016 presidential election, and the FBI launched an investigation into Clinton's handling of classified information that ultimately cleared her of wrongdoing.

There were few, if any, days between the publication of Schmidt's report and the presidential election on November 8, 2016, on which the media did not cover the case or Clinton's dissenters did not use it as a vehicle for critiquing her ethics and, even, her abidance of the law. While there are a host of perspectives on the factors that led to her loss, Clinton has attributed it to the matter involving her emails.[2] Because records were at the forefront of the public dialogue during this election, it is worthwhile to probe the response from the National Archives and Records Administration (NARA) and lessons learned concerning records management. In this essay, I consider the relevant records management regulatory ecosystem and the actions and response of NARA before, during, and after this case.

The Case

The FBI's July 2016 report on its investigation of Clinton's emails provides a detailed account of the servers that Clinton, her husband Bill, and their staffs utilized for email hosting since 2008. Although I will not focus on what ultimately drove the FBI's inquiry—the handling of classified information—the report provides a useful overview of the administration of and changes made to the email systems used by the Clintons. In all, Clinton's team managed or contracted the management of three server systems in the period between 2008 and 2015, two based in the Clintons' Chappaqua, New York, residence and a third at a data center in New Jersey.[3] In January 2009, Clinton asked her aides to create the private email domain clintonemail.com, which was hosted on the private server. During her service as secretary of state from January 21, 2009, to February 1, 2013, Clinton used a total of eleven BlackBerry devices associated with a personal email account.[4]

The FBI report provides insight into Clinton's motivations for using a personal email address and a personal BlackBerry for both private and work email. It credits the following explanation to Clinton's deputy chief of staff Huma Abedin: "State advised personal e-mail accounts could not be linked to State mobile devices and, as a result, Clinton decided to use a personal device in order to avoid carrying multiple devices."[5] Former FBI director James Comey also cited convenience as the apparent driver for Clinton's approach to email management for her personal and business communication.[6] Clinton has affirmed this characterization, citing her discomfort with technology and the hassle of toting two devices as the primary drivers for her reliance on one device synced with her personal account.[7]

A frequent defense from Clinton's camp has been that she was not unique in her use of a personal email account for State Department business.[8] A 2016 report by the State Department's Office of Inspector General (OIG) corroborates that Colin Powell indeed used a personal email account for public business; Madeleine Albright did not use email and Condoleezza Rice used an agency address alone.[9] During the height of the controversy, the Clinton team was also quick to point to its efforts in 2014 to turn over records to the State Department in compliance with the Federal Records Act and records management guidance published in the aftermath of her term.

In November 2014, Patrick F. Kennedy, undersecretary of state for management and senior agency official for records management, wrote to the representatives of the most recent secretaries of state and informed them that NARA's guidance regarding email records had been updated. He asked that the former secretaries produce copies of any State Department records created using personal accounts.[10] In December 2014, Clinton's former chief of staff responded to Kennedy's request and provided an assurance that Clinton's team would later often use: because the former secretary directed email to government addresses, her records would be captured within the government recordkeeping systems.[11] Clinton would later maintain,

> As for recordkeeping, because the overwhelming number of people with whom I was exchanging work-related emails were government personnel on their ".gov" email addresses, I had every reason to think the messages I sent should have been captured by the government's servers, archived, and made available for Freedom of Information Act (FOIA) requests.[12]

Still, Kennedy's request prompted action on the part of Clinton's team, who turned over hard copies of around 30,000 emails that they determined to be public, totaling roughly 55,000 pages.[13] At the urging of NARA, the State Department later requested and secured the emails and associated metadata in digital format from Clinton's attorney.[14]

In this essay, I examine or cite only a small portion of the enormous number of press articles on the Clinton email scandal. Law and policy provide the most substantial background for the discussion that follows. In terms of scholarly publications, research revealed that academics have not yet substantively tackled this case. The few that have written about it have done so from a legal standpoint.[15] This essay is an information professional's effort to understand the records management issues at play and the role that NARA played in this story.

Relevant Legislation and Guidance

Schmidt's *New York Times* headline posited that Clinton may have broken regulations by using a personal email account. As a consequence and escalation of this assertion, Michael Flynn, former advisor to Donald Trump, led Republican National Convention attendees in a chant to "lock her up."[16] The Republican chairman of the Senate Judiciary Committee, Senator Chuck Grassley, questioned the legality of using a private email server.[17] Although the FBI focused on whether classified information was compromised, here I consider the law and policy that set requirements and procedure for the management of federal email records and the involvement of NARA in this regulatory ecosystem.

Understanding NARA's place in this case involves understanding policy. The following sources contribute to this landscape: the Federal Records Act, the Code of Federal Regulations, Executive Memoranda, NARA Bulletins, and State Department Records Management Guidance. As demonstrated below, an examination of this ecosystem reveals that law, regulations, and guidelines regarding email management have changed much during this decade alone and in the years during and since Clinton's tenure as secretary of state.

The Federal Records Act

In 2014, the Federal Records Act updated its definition of federal records to include "recorded information . . . created, manipulated, communicated, or stored in digital or electronic form."[18] Before this expansion, the definition still encompassed digital communication, with *records* including "machine-readable materials, or other documentary materials, regardless of physical form or characteristics."[19] Under the Federal Records Act, the Archivist of the United States has the final determination on whether a document meets the definition of a "record."[20] The head of each federal agency is responsible for ensuring that employees are creating and preserving documentation that sufficiently captures the "organization, functions, policies, decisions, procedures, and essential transactions of the agency" and for enacting safeguards that prevent the removal or loss of records.[21] The Archivist is charged with empowering the agency to do so, by providing "guidance and assistance to Federal agencies with respect to ensuring adequate and proper documentation of the policies and transactions of the Federal Government and ensuring proper records disposition."[22]

In November 2014, a year and a half after Clinton completed her tenure as secretary of state, there was a notable addition made to the law that clarified the responsibilities of government employees who use personal messaging accounts. The section states that employees of an executive agency may not use non-official accounts unless they copy their messages to their government address or forward a copy of each to their official account within twenty days.[23]

The *Code of Federal Regulations* (CFR)

The *Code of Federal Regulations* (CFR) provides standards and procedures to guide compliance with federal statutes.[24] These regulations include NARA's responsibilities to set guidance for agencies on the creation, management, and disposition of federal records.[25] Agencies, in turn, are required to implement a records program that complies with NARA's requirements and to report any unlawful "removal, defacing, alteration, or destruction of Federal records" to NARA.[26] The CFR sets a procedure for NARA to follow upon receiving such an alert; NARA followed this procedure in the case involving Clinton's emails.[27]

NARA made an addition to the CFR in 2009 that is particularly relevant to this case; it stated that agencies that allow employees to use personal email accounts "must ensure that Federal records sent or received on such systems are preserved in the appropriate agency recordkeeping system."[28] This section is revealing in two ways. First, it suggests that, at the time of the addition of this section, agencies were able to make a determination as to whether an employee could use a nongovernmental system. Second, it places the onus on the agency to ensure that, if employees use such systems, the records are preserved within the governmental recordkeeping system.

Executive Memorandum and NARA Bulletins

Pertinent to contemporary activities related to email retention and management is President Barack Obama's Memorandum on Managing Government Records, issued on November 28, 2011. In this document, the president called on heads of executive departments and agencies to improve records management policies and practices and to submit a plan to the Archivist of the United States and the director of the Office of Management and Budget (OMB) on how they would do so, particularly with regard to digital records.[29] In response, in 2012, NARA and the OMB issued the *Managing Government Records Directive* (M-12-18), which set goals for state agencies and an accompanying schedule to strengthen digital records management.[30]

NARA also published two bulletins that provided guidance for sound management of federal records: *Bulletin 2013-02* in August 2013 and *Bulletin 2013-03* in September 2013. The dates are notable; email management guidance from NARA was growing and strengthening in the months after Clinton completed her service. *Bulletin 2013-02* established the "Capstone" approach to email disposition and calls for agencies to designate senior officials whose emails would be transferred to NARA in total.[31] In September 2015, there were around 200 individuals in the State Department who were identified as "Capstone" officials and, as agency head, the secretary of state would certainly be among them.[32] In *Bulletin 2013-03*, NARA provides a clear statement on the use of personal email accounts for federal business: an employee should only do so if the situation requires. Archivist of the United States David S. Ferriero cited this bulletin in 2013 during the House of Representatives Committee on Oversight and Government Reform. He explained that if an email is sent or received using a personal account, it would have to "be moved to the official recordkeeping system of the agency as soon as practicable, and then managed according to the Federal Records Act."[33]

State Department Guidance and Records Retention Schedules

Since 1995, the State Department's *Foreign Affairs Manual* (FAM) has set agency-level guidelines for email management that reiterates that email messages received or created as part of public business meet the definition of "record" under the Federal Records Act.[34] However, explicit discussion of the use of personal addresses in the FAM was put in place after Clinton's tenure and the 2014 amendment to the Federal Records Act.

Today, the State Department's manual for its employees discourages the use of a personal email account for government business
except in outlying circumstances such as system outages.[35] The
influence of the Clinton case can be observed in updated guidance.
The FAM renders "convenience" as an illegitimate rationale for use of
a personal email account and discourages the practice except in cases
that are unavoidable. The State Department also put measures in
place that employees must follow if such unavoidable situations arise,
including a requirement that the sender copy their own government
account on the message.

NARA Activities in Response to the Email Controversy

As the above section suggests, NARA has a large role in setting
standards and regulations for email management. Its activities in this
regulatory space intensified in the years during and after Clinton's
term as secretary of state. This section considers NARA's direct
engagement with this particular case, drawing heavily from records
that the agency has made available on its website.[36] Figure 1 illustrates
some of NARA's key actions and the records-related developments in
the case.

Just days before he broke his story, Michael Schmidt of the *New
York Times* contacted NARA General Counsel Gary M. Stern and
requested time to talk off the record. "I'm working on a story about
government employees who use their personal email addresses to
conduct government business," Schmidt told Stern.[37] On learning
that Schmidt was investigating Clinton's use of a personal email
address, Stern told the reporter that

> NARA does look into allegations of this type, with our interest
> being to ensure that the agency recovers any alienated records. . . .
> This case, if true, would present a concern, although it may be
> the case that the State Department has already taken appropriate
> action to recover the records.[38]

This initial communication was followed by action within NARA
that can be categorized along five areas: communication and
engagement with the State Department; communication with the

Judiciary Committee; contributions to the State Department's Office of Inspector General's investigation; public statements; and the publication of *Criteria for Managing Email Records* in spring 2016.[39]

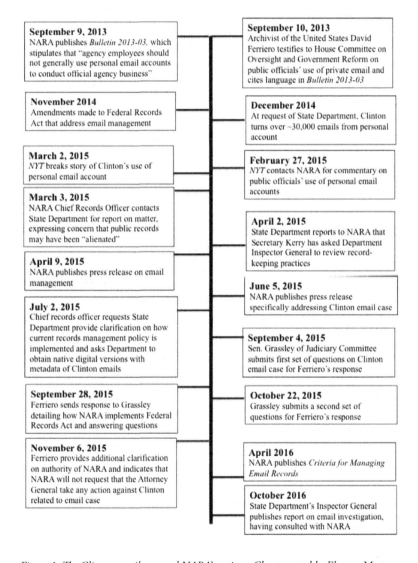

September 9, 2013
NARA publishes *Bulletin 2013-03*, which stipulates that "agency employees should not generally use personal email accounts to conduct official agency business"

September 10, 2013
Archivist of the United States David Ferriero testifies to House Committee on Oversight and Government Reform on public officials' use of private email and cites language in *Bulletin 2013-03*

November 2014
Amendments made to Federal Records Act that address email management

December 2014
At request of State Department, Clinton turns over ~30,000 emails from personal account

March 2, 2015
NYT breaks story of Clinton's use of personal email account

February 27, 2015
NYT contacts NARA for commentary on public officials' use of personal email accounts

March 3, 2015
NARA Chief Records Officer contacts State Department for report on matter, expressing concern that public records may have been "alienated"

April 2, 2015
State Department reports to NARA that Secretary Kerry has asked Department Inspector General to review record-keeping practices

April 9, 2015
NARA publishes press release on email management

June 5, 2015
NARA publishes press release specifically addressing Clinton email case

July 2, 2015
Chief records officer requests State Department provide clarification on how current records management policy is implemented and asks Department to obtain native digital versions with metadata of Clinton emails

September 4, 2015
Sen. Grassley of Judiciary Committee submits first set of questions on Clinton email case for Ferriero's response

September 28, 2015
Ferriero sends response to Grassley detailing how NARA implements Federal Records Act and answering questions

October 22, 2015
Grassley submits a second set of questions for Ferriero's response

November 6, 2015
Ferriero provides additional clarification on authority of NARA and indicates that NARA will not request that the Attorney General take any action against Clinton related to email case

April 2016
NARA publishes *Criteria for Managing Email Records*

October 2016
State Department's Inspector General publishes report on email investigation, having consulted with NARA

Figure 1. The Clinton email case and NARA's actions. Chart created by Eleanor Mattern.

Communication and Engagement with the State Department

NARA was most involved in the Clinton email case through its interactions with the State Department, with Chief Records Officer Paul M. Wester Jr. leading NARA's communications. Concern that records were outside of government custody drove NARA's immediate action. The day after the *New York Times* report ran, Wester acted in accordance with the CFR by contacting Margaret P. Grafeld, deputy assistant secretary for Global Information Services at the State Department, to inquire whether records had escaped public custody and to request a report on measures to retrieve and safeguard agency records. Wester also asked that the State Department submit to NARA its broad internal guidance for employees on email management and, more specifically, its internal guidance for employee management of records created through personal email accounts.[40] Grafeld's response followed on April 2, 2015, with two notable pieces of information. First, Grafeld relayed that the State Department had contacted the offices of the most recent secretaries of state and had obtained 55,000 pages of email records from Clinton. Second, Grafeld conveyed that Secretary of State John Kerry called for the Department's Inspector General to review recordkeeping practices in the agency and make recommendations for improvement in consultation with NARA.[41]

NARA continued its engagement with the State Department following this communication. The agency, through Wester, demonstrated an interest in ensuring that safeguards and systems were in place to avoid another incident like the Clinton case. Wester asked for updates and for confirmation that the State Department had "discussed the responsibilities for managing Federal records in government and personal email accounts with your agency head [Kerry]" and were ensuring "that Federal records created or received in a personal email account used by your agency head are captured in an agency recordkeeping system."[42] The State Department contact responded that both were done.

NARA also advocated for preservation of Clinton's emails in their native digital form. The records suggest that their influence was impactful here. In December 2014, the Clinton team transferred printed copies of the emails to the State Department. In follow-up correspondence with Clinton's attorney, the State Department cited

NARA's recommendation that the emails and associated metadata should be transferred in digital format.[43]

Communication with the Judiciary Committee

Although NARA sought information from the State Department, at least one unit within the government requested answers from NARA. On September 4, 2015, Senate Judiciary Committee Chairman Chuck Grassley wrote to Archivist of the United States David Ferriero. In his letter, Grassley cited NARA's responsibility to oversee proper records management and to put measures in place to prevent unauthorized removal. Grassley questioned whether NARA:

- Was aware of Clinton's use of a nongovernmental email account for business purposes
- Had expressly permitted this use
- Had conducted an inspection of the State Department's records management program during Ferriero's tenure
- Had initiated a formal investigation following the discovery of Clinton's practices[44]

Ferriero's response was detailed and accompanied by documentary evidence. He explained that NARA had learned of Clinton's use of a personal email account from the *New York Times* reporter and not before and that it was deferring to the State Department's investigation on the matter.[45] Although Grassley pushed back with a second letter, it was evident that Ferriero viewed the matter as sufficiently handled by the State Department and was of the opinion that NARA's efforts would be best directed to measures that would help mitigate the likelihood of a similar situation occurring.[46]

In his communications to Grassley, Ferriero reported that no formal inspection of the State Department had been conducted since he had taken office in 2009. His response points to the resource-related challenges of conducting formal, intensive inspections of agency records management programs. NARA has increasingly relied on self-reporting and self-assessments, which NARA uses to identify specific elements of a program to inspect and, if necessary, improve.[47] As Ferriero explained to Grassley,

> The criteria for selecting agencies for an inspection or records management program review include . . . the results of an agency's annual

records management self-assessment, the significance of certain records
and the related business processes, the risk of improper management
of records, and the presence of important issues that are relevant to the
management of federal records in general. Until March 2013, the State
Department records management had not, based on NARA's analysis
and these criteria, exhibited risk sufficient to warrant an inspection.[48]

This was, arguably, NARA's most surprising revelation during the case.

Contributions and Response to State Department's Office of Inspector General's Investigation

On March 23, 2015, then secretary of state John Kerry called for
the Office of Inspector General (OIG) to conduct a review of his
agency's recordkeeping and preservation practices and to put forward
a series of recommendations for improvements.[49] The OIG's report,
published in May 2016, identified a series of weaknesses in records
management within the agency, including "a limited ability to
retrieve email records, inaccessibility of electronic files, failure to
comply with requirements for departing employees, and a general
lack of oversight."[50] The Federal Records Act, regulations, and NARA
guidance feature heavily in this report, which states:

> Sending emails from a personal account to other employees at their
> Department accounts is not an appropriate method of preserving any
> such emails that would constitute a Federal record. . . . At a minimum,
> Secretary Clinton should have surrendered all emails dealing with
> Department business before leaving government service and, because
> she did not do so, she did not comply with the Department's policies
> that were implemented in accordance with the Federal Records Act.[51]

It is evident that the OIG had an open line of communication with
NARA during the review. NARA offered its feedback on the OIG's
final summation and, in doing so, made one of its most significant
contributions to the case. The OIG stated that "NARA agrees with
the foregoing assessment but told OIG that Secretary Clinton's
production of 55,000 pages of emails mitigated her failure to properly
preserve emails that qualified as Federal records during her tenure and
to surrender such records upon her departure."[52] With this, NARA
expressed the position that the outcome was sufficient.

Public Statements

NARA's official commentary on the Clinton email controversy was measured, infrequent, and high-level. In the wake of Schmidt's story, Wester sent a message to NARA colleagues, stating,

> We will likely see a lot of press about this issue in the coming days. We will probably not have much more to say about the matter itself immediately, beyond reiterating all of our well-established guidance related to email management and generally letting everyone know we are working on the issue with State.[53]

A day after the article's publication, NARA officials circulated talking points internally, which cited relevant policy, stressed the State Department's responsibility to ensure that similar events do not occur, and emphasized NARA's commitment to assisting agencies as they develop procedures for email management.[54]

The talking points confirm that NARA officials were not interested in passing judgment on Clinton's email practices and instead wanted to focus on facts—namely, what NARA officials did in the wake of the discovery and what relevant guidance exists. In a follow-up to his article, Schmidt and a co-author cited a NARA spokesperson who pointed to the 2009 addition to the CFR dealing with the management of records sent or received through nongovernmental accounts. In offering this commentary, the spokesperson was in keeping with Wester's indication that comments should be limited and focused on the talking points.[55] NARA General Counsel Gary M. Stern was similarly direct in another *New York Times* article. He pointed to requirements to retain and preserve public records under the Federal Records Act but acknowledged the demands that the volume of email presents. He said, "It doesn't matter on what medium or in what form it occurs . . . [but] there's such a challenge with email, because everyone gets a couple of hundred a day and nobody has the time to go through and say, 'Is this a record, or is it not?'"[56]

There was indeed little in the way of NARA commentary in the press coverage that followed Schmidt's story. Instead, NARA engaged with the public most directly through press statements posted to its website. NARA released three statements: in April, June, and December of 2015.[57] The April 2015 release was NARA's attempt to publicly communicate relevant policy and guidelines regarding email management. NARA officials used the June press statement to directly address the Clinton email case and counter uncited media reports that "have given the false impression that the National Archives and Records Administration . . . did not discharge our duties appropriately."[58] They further highlighted their actions with the State Department and emphasized the responsibility of agencies in implementing an effective records management program.[59] NARA made a clear statement to the public with its June press release: there was no misstep on its part and, instead, the records management shortcomings were at an individual level. This is the closest that NARA officials have come to criticizing Clinton's decision-making and practices.

It was a former NARA employee who was most vocal in the press. Jason Baron, NARA's director of litigation for thirteen years, went on the record for Schmidt's original article to offer some provocative remarks. Unlike current NARA officials who were reserved in their criticism of Clinton's use of a personal email account, Baron was reproachful:

> It is very difficult to conceive of a scenario—short of nuclear winter—where an agency would be justified in allowing its cabinet-level head officer to solely use a private email communications channel for the conduct of government business. . . . I can recall no instance in my time at the National Archives when a high-ranking official at an executive branch agency solely used a personal email account for the transaction of government business.[60]

Baron expressed discomfort with the Clinton team defense that emails would have been captured in the government systems because Clinton was sending to government accounts.[61] He raised the possibility that, if business emails were sent to nongovernment accounts, they would not have been preserved, and he questioned the Clinton team's process for identifying which records were public.[62]

Publication of *Criteria for Managing Email Records*

In April 2016, NARA published the *Criteria for Managing Email Records in Compliance with the Managing Government Records Directive (M-12-18)*, a positive step toward improving the public sector's understanding of email management requirements. This document outlines "success criteria" for agencies' email management programs and expressly states that a policy on "how to appropriately handle email messages . . . created on nonofficial or personal electronic messaging accounts" is part of a successful program.[63] This document compiles email management requirements, offering a useful spreadsheet that maps these requirements to associated law, regulation, or NARA guidance.[64]

In addition, in 2016, NARA made modifications to the process guiding agencies' self-reports on email management, using the published success criteria to frame a new "maturity model" survey and scoring system. The maturity model "provides five scenarios with progressively improving descriptions for each of the four domains—policies, systems, access, and disposition. Agencies chose which scenario best describes their current state of email management."[65] In turn, NARA uses the scores to identify agencies that are at high risk for inadequate treatment of email. NARA is now publishing the data that the agencies have provided in response to the maturity model assessment, along with an analysis in "Federal Email Management Annual Reports."[66] This is a good step toward transparency and provides accountability for agencies' email management policies and practices.

These "Federal Email Management Annual Reports" also include validation methods that NARA is now employing to check for misrepresentation or misreporting by agencies. For example, in the FY2017 report, NARA cites among its validation methods requesting "copy of approved policies from a random sample" of agencies that indicate they have policies on the use of personal email accounts. NARA provides the results of the validation, and, in FY2017 there was a definite disconnect between reported data and reality; only 54 percent of the policies submitted by the sample respondents included policy on the use of personal email accounts.[67] What is unknown from this report are the subsequent steps that NARA and the agencies take in response to inaccurate data or the reason for inaccurate self-reporting. Even without this knowledge, these validation methods, if they are new practice since the Clinton case, are a movement toward ensuring that the picture NARA has of agencies' records management practices is aligned with reality.

Discussion

The archival community and public can gain some insight into NARA's regulations, priorities, practices, and workflows through this case. The agency demonstrated an openness to engage with the media, as exhibited by Stern's acceptance of Schmidt's request for comments on email regulations. However, NARA officials consistently retained a neutral tone, hesitating to either offer criticism or to condone Clinton's reliance on personal email. The agency's approach was to concentrate on internal action, rather than on directing blame. NARA was, first, focused on working with the State Department to ensure that appropriate measures were taken to recover records and, second, to develop stronger guidance related to email management. NARA officials displayed an interest in allowing the State Department to direct the response and, by doing so, suggested that the onus was largely on an agency to oversee a working records management program. Since the events of this case, there is evidence that NARA is taking a more proactive approach to mitigating problematic email management programs within agencies; this is to the benefit of both agencies and the public at large.

Delving into federal records rules reveals that there is a complex network of statutes, federal regulations, agency requirements, and guidelines. It is a diffuse network, with these different regulatory components living in different sections of the law, in different manuals and bulletins, on different portals and websites. An obvious lesson from this case is that policies and guidelines around email management have been consistently evolving in the last ten years. Although, as cited earlier, a 2009 update to the CFR did address the use of personal email accounts by calling on agencies to "ensure that Federal records sent or received on such systems are preserved in the appropriate agency recordkeeping system," it appears that the State Department had not caught up to this update. For its part, NARA, the regulatory body behind this update, remained unaware that Clinton's emails were not being preserved in agency recordkeeping systems during her tenure. In the case of email management in the public sphere, good practices have not arrived as immediately as the guidelines that have been put in place.

The density of the regulatory fabric raises the importance of facilitating understanding among public employees. In its training role, NARA should work closely with agencies to ensure that requirements and responsibilities for public employees are coherent and understood and to evaluate this training for efficacy. With this case so plainly demonstrating that public sector employees have misconceptions around records management, NARA has an ethical responsibility, along with a mandate, to improve understanding. The 2016 publication of *Criteria for Managing Email Records*, complete with its distilled compilation of pertinent rules, is one example of NARA addressing this responsibility. Working with the agencies to develop mechanisms for evaluating employees' understandings of the regulations and to assess the efficacy of training would be a positive next step to mitigating email mismanagement and the use of personal accounts.

From a records management perspective, the most troubling revelation in this case was the failure of NARA's approach to monitor agencies' compliance with regulations and records management practices. It is indeed unsettling that it was the press, rather than the State Department's self-assessment, that brought the use of Clinton's personal email account to NARA's attention. The late discovery of Clinton's use of a personal email account, along with other records management issues that the State Department's OIG unearthed, revealed a deficient process.

NARA has made strides to modify the agency self-reporting process, but, in the aftermath of this case, NARA has an obligation to regularly monitor, evaluate, and revise the process and the new maturity model. In addition, NARA should revisit the decision-making framework it uses to determine whether to complete a formal inspection and explore how internal resources may support a timeline of scheduled inspections of all agencies as a complement to self-reports. NARA's strategic plan for 2018–2022 indicates that the latter is happening. The plan includes a strategic goal that reads: "by FY 2019, NARA will conduct inspections of records management practices at 10 percent of Federal agencies per year." With this goal, NARA recognizes its responsibility to ensure understanding and compliance among agencies and to "provide its stakeholders with reasonable and independent assurance that those agencies are complying with relevant laws and regulations."[68]

Where there is a public-sector process that is known to be deficient, the responsible agency has a duty and an ethical commitment to the public to remedy the failings. In the years before the Clinton email case, NARA could have been more proactive in providing oversight over email management practices by placing less trust in the accuracy of agencies' self-reports. However, there are extremely positive indicators that NARA has prioritized appropriate management of email and regulatory compliance among agencies at this point in time. Future action—for example, monitoring and adjusting the new maturity model approach to agency reporting—is as critical as the immediate steps that NARA took to ensure that Clinton's emails were in public custody.

Conclusion

Although Clinton and her supporters are bound to see few positive outcomes of the media attention and fallout regarding her emails, there is a silver lining: it is unlikely that a public official of Clinton's stature will make the same missteps in the future. NARA's previous position and tack was to trust that agencies were acting as responsibly with regard to records as they reported. This proved an insufficient approach, with this case revealing pain points in the self-reporting approach to records management reviews. In the aftermath of this case, NARA's ethical approach must be a commitment to mitigate recurrences in the future and an improvement of the auditing measures; this is critical for the archival record, for a participatory government, and for government transparency.

There are indicators that NARA is taking that commitment seriously. For the fiscal years of 2016 and 2017, NARA implemented a stronger monitoring approach, requiring agencies to submit an annual report on their email policies and systems. Agencies are now expected to describe their policies concerning the use of personal email accounts in these reports. NARA scores these reports for risk level and program maturity and posts them on its website.[69] This is a more proactive approach than had been in place, but NARA must continue to be vigilant to the accuracy of these self-reported measures.

In his essay-length response to Nicholson Baker's best-selling book *Double Fold*, Richard J. Cox begins with the following reflection:

> Imagine that you woke up one morning to discover that archives, historical manuscripts, rare books, and newspaper collections were the subject of journalists, book reviewers, and radio and talk show hosts around the country. Imagine that the issue of preservation . . . was being contemplated by the news media. Imagine that the purpose of libraries and archives was being considered, anew, by social pundits through every conceivable media outlet.[70]

With the publication of Schmidt's article, archives and records management were again thrust into the public consciousness, with a case that had arguably far greater public impact than the microfilming of historic newspapers that Baker discussed.

This essay serves as an initial effort to probe the Clinton email case in an archival and records management context. As among NARA's many stakeholders, members of the archival community should remain curious about developments regarding email management in the public sector. There is space and opportunity for continued investigation and a need to observe how this case influences email management practices and oversight in federal agencies moving forward.

Notes

[1] Michael Schmidt, "Hillary Clinton Used Personal Email at State Dept., Possibly Breaking Rules," *New York Times*, March 2, 2015, https://www.nytimes.com/2015/03/03/us/politics/hillary-clintons-use-of-private-email-at-state-department-raises-flags.html?_r=0, captured at https://perma.cc/H4ZY-YLDR.

[2] Hillary Rodham Clinton, *What Happened* (New York: Simon and Schuster, 2017), 289, 323.

[3] Federal Bureau of Investigation, "Clinton E-mail Investigation," July 2016, 3, https://vault.fbi.gov/hillary-r.-clinton/Hillary%20R.%20Clinton%20Part%2001%20of%2035/view, captured at https://perma.cc/6Z7B-MMFT.

[4] Federal Bureau of Investigation, "Clinton E-mail Investigation," 2–8.

[5] Federal Bureau of Investigation, "Clinton E-mail Investigation," 8.

[6] *Hearing Before the Committee on Oversight and Government Reform of the House of Representatives*, 114th Congress, July 7, 2016, testimony of James Comey, 20, https://web.archive.org/web/20181225205104/https://oversight.house.gov/wp

-content/uploads/2016/07/7-7-2016-Oversight-of-the-State-Department.pdf; CSPAN, *Hillary Clinton Email Investigation, Part 1* (video), July 7, 2016, https://www.c-span.org/video/?412315-1/fbi-director-james-comey-testifies-hillary clinton email probe, captured at https://perma.cc/B5FF-N4R7.

[7] Clinton, *What Happened*, 292–293.

[8] Clinton, *What Happened*, 296.

[9] Office of Inspector General, United States Department of State, *Office of the Secretary: Evaluation of Email Records Management and Cybersecurity Requirements* (May 2016), 3, https://fas.org/sgp/othergov/state-oig-email.pdf.

[10] Letter from Patrick F. Kennedy to Cheryl Mills, November 12, 2014, https://www.archives.gov/files/press/press-releases/2015/pdf/attachment4-clinton-letter.pdf, captured at https://perma.cc/64GX-R4TQ.

[11] Letter from Cheryl Mills to Patrick F. Kennedy, December 5, 2014, https://www.archives.gov/files/press/press-releases/2015/pdf/attachment8-clinton-reply-letter.pdf, captured at https://perma.cc/DAB2-VC3D.

[12] Clinton, *What Happened*, 296.

[13] Federal Bureau of Investigation, "Clinton E-mail Investigation," 15; Clinton, *What Happened*, 300.

[14] Letter from Patrick G. Kennedy to David E. Kendell, June 15, 2015, attachment B6, 3–4, https://www.archives.gov/files/press/press-releases/2016/pdf/nara-response-to-grassley_attachment-b.pdf, captured at https://perma.cc/QC2Z-U7Z6.

[15] See Shannon Fields, "Intent or Gross Negligence: Hillary Clinton Should Be Charged under 18 U.S.C. Sec. 793 for Mishandling Classified Information," *Regent University Law Review* 30, no. 1 (2017): 149–172; Bill Aleshire, "'Hillary' Emails and the Unenforceable Texas Public Information Act," *Texas Tech Administrative Law Journal* 17, no. 2 (Summer 2016): 175–212.

[16] Ryan Teague Beckwith, "Michael Flynn Led a 'Lock Her Up' Chant at the Republican Convention. Now He's Charged With Lying to the FBI," *Time*, December 1, 2017, http://time.com/5044847/michael-flynn-hillary-clinton-republican-convention-lock-her-up/, captured at https://perma.cc/73KZ-UN38.

[17] "Sen. Chuck Grassley: Hillary Could Be Charged in Email Case," *Newsmax*, March 31, 2015, https://www.newsmax.com/Newsfront/charles-grassley-hillary-clinton-private-email/2015/03/31/id/635635/, captured at https://perma.cc/8KAH-3YNS.

[18] United States Code: Disposal of Records, 44 U.S.C. § 3301, Historical and Revision Notes, Legal Information Institute, https://www.law.cornell.edu/uscode/text/44/3301, captured at https://perma.cc/EM8X-P.

[19] United States Code: Disposal of Records, 44 U.S.C. § 3301, Historical and Revision Notes, Legal Information Institute, https://www.law.cornell.edu/uscode/text/44/3301; NARA, "National Archives Welcomes Presidential and Federal Records Act Amendments of 2014," National Archives and Records Administration, news release, December 1, 2014, https://www.archives.gov/press

/press-releases/2015/nr15-23.html, captured at https://perma.cc/63BP-FJTB.

20 United States Code: Disposal of Records, 44 U.S.C. § 3301, Legal Information Institute, https://www.law.cornell.edu/uscode/text/44/3301, captured at https://perma.cc/B4DK-5KFH.

21 United States Code: Records Management by Federal Agencies, 44 U.S.C. § 3105, Legal Information Institute, https://www.law.cornell.edu/uscode/text/44/3105, captured at https://perma.cc/MH74-AMPU.

22 United States Code: Records Management by the Archivist of the United States, 44 U.S.C. § 2904, National Archives and Records Administration, https://www.archives.gov/about/laws/records-management.html, captured at https://perma.cc/XT4B-JNBT.

23 United States Code: Records Management by the Archivist of the United States, 44 U.S.C. § 2911.

24 "Frequently Asked Questions (FAQs)," National Archives and Records Administration, updated March 18, 2019, https://www.archives.gov/about/regulations/faqs.html, captured at https://perma.cc/4897-9YNY.

25 Code of Federal Regulations: National Archives and Records Administration, 36 CFR § 1220.12a, Legal Information Institute, https://www.law.cornell.edu/cfr/text/36/part-1220.

26 Code of Federal Regulations: National Archives and Records Administration, 36 CFR § 1220.30; 36 CFR 1230.14, Legal Information Institute, https://www.law.cornell.edu/cfr/text/36/part-1230.

27 Code of Federal Regulations: National Archives and Records Administration, 36 CFR § 1230, Legal Information Institute, https://www.law.cornell.edu/cfr/text/36/part-1230.

28 Code of Federal Regulations: National Archives and Records Administration, 36 CFR § 1236.22, Legal Information Institute, https://www.law.cornell.edu/cfr/text/36/part-1230.

29 "Presidential Memorandum—Managing Government Records," The White House, November 28, 2011, https://obamawhitehouse.archives.gov/the-press-office/2011/11/28/presidential-memorandum-managing-government-records, captured at https://perma.cc/D9LJ-GGQA.

30 Jeffrey D. Zients and David S. Ferriero, "Memorandum for the Heads of Executive Departments and Agencies and Independent Agencies" (M-12-18), August 24, 2012, https://www.archives.gov/files/records-mgmt/m-12-18.pdf, captured at https://perma.cc/T374-T8S7.

31 National Archives and Records Administration, "Bulletin 2013-02: Guidance on a New Approach to Managing Email Records," August 29, 2013, https://www.archives.gov/records-mgmt/bulletins/2013/2013-02.html, captured at https://perma.cc/8967-4HK4.

32 Office of Inspector General, *Office of the Secretary*, 8.

33 *Testimony of David S. Ferriero, Archivist of the United States, before the House Committee on Oversight and Government Reform, U.S. House of Representatives on*

Preventing Violations of Federal Transparency Laws, September 10, 2013, https: //docs.house.gov/meetings/GO/GO00/20130910/101277/HHRG-113-GO00 -Wstate-FerrieroD-20130910.pdf, captured at https://perma.cc/N67L-4U34.

[34] United States Department of State, 5 FAM 443.2, https://fam.state.gov/FAM /05FAM/05FAM0440.html, captured at https://perma.cc/G8T2-RSHP.

[35] United States Department of State, 5 FAM 443.7.

[36] NARA posted a collection of records associated with this Clinton email case alongside a press release. See "Statement from the National Archives: Update on NARA's Activities and Communications Related to Email Management at the Department of State," news release, December 7, 2015, https://www.archives .gov/press/press-releases/2016/nr16-29.html, captured at https://perma.cc/U7YD -37VE.

[37] Email from Michael Schmidt to Gary M. Stern, National Archives and Records Administration, February 27, 2015, https://www.archives.gov/files/foia/state -department-emails/pdf/27-nara-email-fwd-nyt-redacted.pdf, captured at https: //perma.cc/CK5X-VLH3.

[38] Email message from Gary M. Stern to David Ferriero and Paul Wester, National Archives and Records Administration, March 1, 2015, https://www.archives.gov /files/foia/state-department-emails/pdf/28-nara-eamil-fwd-re-fwd-nyt-very-close -hold-redacted.pdf, captured at https://perma.cc/4HRD-6AR4.

[39] National Archives and Records Administration was involved in a dismissed lawsuit related to the Clinton email controversy, brought by the Cause of Action Institute against John Kerry and David S. Ferriero. The plaintiff asked the court to order the State Department and NARA to take additional action to recover records on Clinton's server. The judge dismissed it as "moot," because the defendants had been working toward the recovery of the emails at the time of the complaint. See "Judge Dismisses Pair of Lawsuits Arising from Clinton Emails," *AP News*, January 11, 2016, https://apnews.com/b219d2da39454b799b653187d6ab2831/judge-dismisses -pair-lawsuits-arising-clinton-emails, captured at https://perma.cc/W2PZ-BB2T.

[40] 36 CFR 1230; Letter from Paul M. Wester Jr. to Margaret P. Grafeld, March 3, 2015, https://www.archives.gov/files/press/press-releases/2015/pdf/nara-letter-to-state -department-3-3-15.pdf, captured at https://perma.cc/9H9M-UUWJ.

[41] Letter from Margaret P. Grafeld to Paul M. Wester Jr., April 2, 2015, attachment B2, 1–2, https://www.archives.gov/files/press/press-releases/2016/pdf /nara-response-to-grassley_attachment-b.pdf, captured at https://perma.cc/RG32 -CK42.

[42] Letter from Patrick F. Kennedy to Paul M. Wester Jr., June 12, 2015, attachment B3, 1, https://www.archives.gov/files/press/press-releases/2016/pdf/nara-response -to-grassley_attachment-b.pdf, captured at https://perma.cc/6XMN-P6Y9.

[43] Letter from Patrick F. Kennedy to David E. Kendall, May 22, 2015, attachment B6, 3, https://www.archives.gov/files/press/press-releases/2016/pdf/nara-response -to-grassley_attachment-b.pdf, captured at https://perma.cc/HE8V-4LCQ.

44 Letter from Charles E. Grassley to David S. Ferriero, September 4, 2015, https://www.archives.gov/files/press/press-releases/2016/pdf/nara-response-to-grassley_2015-9-28.pdf, captured at https://perma.cc/N4KF-QHZ4.

45 Letter from David S. Ferriero to Charles E. Grassley, September 28, 2015, https://www.archives.gov/files/press/press-releases/2016/pdf/nara-response-to-grassley_2015-9-28.pdf, captured at https://perma.cc/L4CY-2X3C.

46 Letter from Ferriero to Grassley, September 28, 2015, https://www.archives.gov/files/press/press-releases/2016/pdf/nara-response-to-grassley_2015-9-28.pdf, captured at https://perma.cc/P9VZ-J8JQ.

47 Letter from Ferriero to Grassley, September 28, 2015, https://www.archives.gov/files/press/press-releases/2016/pdf/nara-response-to-grassley_2015-9-28.pdf, captured at https://perma.cc/N9M8-5JR8.

48 Letter from Ferriero to Grassley, September 28, 2015, https://www.archives.gov/files/press/press-releases/2016/pdf/nara-response-to-grassley_2015-9-28.pdf, captured at https://perma.cc/MU7F-8ZRP.

49 Letter from John F. Kerry to Steve A. Linick, March 23, 2015, attachment B2, 31–32, https://www.archives.gov/files/press/press-releases/2016/pdf/nara-response-to-grassley_attachment-b.pdf, captured at https://perma.cc/BM7D-WRGY.

50 Office of Inspector General, *Office of the Secretary*, "What OIG Found."

51 Office of Inspector General, *Office of the Secretary*, 23.

52 Office of Inspector General, *Office of the Secretary*, 23.

53 Email from Paul Wester to AC-All@nara.gov, March 3, 2015, https://www.archives.gov/files/foia/state-department-emails/pdf/32-nara-email-nyt-article-on-hillary-clintons-emails.pdf, captured at https://perma.cc/Y8HN-3HEJ.

54 National Archives and Records Administration, "Talking Points: State Department/Hillary Clinton Email," March 3, 2015, https://www.archives.gov/files/foia/state-department-emails/pdf/34-state-talking-points.pdf, captured at https://perma.cc/7Q2M-WCHA.

55 Michael S. Schmidt and Amy Chozick, "Using Private Email, Hillary Clinton Thwarted Record Requests," *New York Times*, March 3, 2015, https://www.nytimes.com/2015/03/04/us/politics/using-private-email-hillary-clinton-thwarted-record-requests.html, captured at https://perma.cc/M2UZ-RTVY.

56 Julie Hirschfeld Davis, "Vague Email Rules Let Federal Agencies Decide When to Hit Save or Delete," *New York Times*, March 13, 2015, https://www.nytimes.com/2015/03/14/us/politics/vague-email-rules-let-federal-agencies-decide-when-to-hit-save-or-delete.html, captured at https://perma.cc/8JQP-8LLG.

57 National Archives and Records Administration, "National Archives Releases State Department Letter re: Email Recordkeeping," April 9, 2015, https://www.archives.gov/press/press-releases/2015/nr15-65.html, captured at https://perma.cc/2FZ8-4CK3; National Archives and Records Administration, "Statement on NARA's Records Management Activities," June 5, 2015, https://www.archives.gov/press/press-releases/2015/nr15-86.html, captured at https://perma.cc/QLC5-RFJK; National Archives and Records Administration, "Statement from the National

Archives: Update on NARA's Activities and Communications Related to Email Management at the Department of State," https://www.archives.gov/press/press releases/2016/nr16-29.html, captured at https://perma.cc/2Z84-24P3.

[58] National Archives and Records Administration, "Statement on NARA's Records Management Activities."

[59] National Archives and Records Administration, "Statement on NARA's Records Management Activities."

[60] Schmidt, "Hillary Clinton Used Personal Email."

[61] Melissa Block, "Clinton's Use of Personal Email Could Hamper Archiving Efforts," *All Things Considered*, NPR, March 4, 2015, https://www.npr .org/2015/03/04/390757750/clintons-use-of-personal-email-could-hamper -archiving-efforts, captured at https://perma.cc/QM54-HLJB.

[62] Alex Altman and Michael Scherer, "The Problem With Hillary Clinton's Email Record Search," *Time*, March 11, 2015, http://time.com/3740357/hillary-clinton -emails-search/, captured at https://perma.cc/KKT2-BWYW.

[63] National Archives and Records Administration, *Criteria for Managing Email Records in Compliance with the Managing Government Records Directive (M-12-18)*, April 6, 2016, 3, https://www.archives.gov/files/records-mgmt/email-management/2016 -email-mgmt-success-criteria.pdf, captured at https://perma.cc/L8EY-U6EK.

[64] National Archives and Records Administration, *Criteria for Managing Email Records*, Appendix B.

[65] National Archives and Records Administration, *Federal Agency Records Management: 2017 Annual Report*, August 2018, 9, https://www.archives.gov/files /records-mgmt/resources/2017-farm-annual-report.pdf, captured at https://perma .cc/RM6Q-78JP.

[66] National Archives and Records Administration, "Federal Email Management Annual Reports," updated on May 31, 2019, https://www.archives.gov/records -mgmt/resources/email-mgmt-reports, captured at https://perma.cc/YLN3 -FMQY.

[67] National Archives and Records Administration, *Federal Agency Records Management: 2017 Annual Report*, Appendix IV, 4, https://www.archives.gov/files/records-mgmt /resources/2017-farm-annual-report.pdf, captured at https://perma.cc/RM6Q -78JP.

[68] National Archives and Records Administration, 2018–2022 Strategic Plan, February 2018, 11, https://www.archives.gov/files/about/plans-reports/strategic -plan/2018/strategic-plan-2018-2022.pdf, captured at https://perma.cc/2ML2 -YYT7.

[69] National Archives and Records Administration, "Federal Email Management."

[70] Richard J. Cox, "Don't Fold Up: Responding to Nicholson Baker's Double Fold," Society of American Archivists, April 18, 2001, https://www2.archivists.org /news/2001/dont-fold-up-responding-to-nicholson-bakers-double-fold-by -richard-j-cox, captured at https://perma.cc/Y698-MCR6.

8

Movement and Transformation
Teaching to the Fourth Dimension

Anne J. Gilliland and Kathy Carbone

Introduction

Movement and transformation are intrinsic to archives because the physicality, interrelationships and valence of records[1] continually change as records move and compound through time and space and are used for different purposes and in different historical and sociopolitical contexts. The archive and its individual contents also change physically and intellectually as a result of handling, interpretation, and "making" and encounters with the archive. In addition, in such encounters, the crossing and re-crossing of contexts, temporalities, subjectivities, and materialities, as well as the unexpected emergence or absence of materials and information, can invoke affective, even transformational responses.[2] Archival education, however, has rarely focused specifically on the ways in which movement and transformation occur with and within archives or on the implications for archival praxis. In the twenty-first century, these aspects can no longer remain implicit. The archival field needs to be able to respond to overt examples of how records and related phenomena move; are understood across different circumstances, considerations, contestations, and creative activities; and are fragmented, compiled, augmented, and transformed as a result of globalization, networking, big data, and digital asset management as well as mass population movements. The archival field further needs to contemplate the affective charges that records conduct, the intensities they build and the impacts they have, and the ways in which records (or the lack thereof) impede or facilitate, constrain or help people move toward—or away from—something.

In the first part of this essay, we briefly review how ideas of movement and transformation have been previously raised, in particular within the framework of the records continuum and its fourth dimension, Pluralize. We then introduce two pairs of archival courses, each taught by one of us, that explicitly addressed different aspects of movement and transformation. Each course focused on how to engage diverse student populations with the archive/archives and especially how records and their human relations move (both literally and affectively) and are transformed (physically and cognitively) over time, space, and standpoint. One pair of courses addressed archival issues associated with global movements of records and of people as a result of conflicts, colonization, exploitation, and other human and natural events, while the other two emphasized the transformation of records through "making." Three courses were offered at the University of California, Los Angeles (UCLA), to cohorts including undergraduate, professional graduate, and doctoral students from archival studies and several other fields, and one course was offered at the California Institute of the Arts (CalArts) to undergraduate and graduate art students. We discuss how the need for these courses emerged organically out of the contexts of both institutions, how we approached these courses pedagogically, and how, in different ways, we addressed and elicited movement and transformation. We conclude with a reflection on what we found to be particular benefits of these kinds of courses for the archival field and for other fields experiencing archival turns.

Movement, Transformation, and the Fourth Dimension of the Records Continuum

Archival thought-leaders in several different countries and archival traditions have argued for almost a century that there are more forms of movement and transformation in records, recordkeeping, and the use of records than only those aspects that are implicit in concepts such as original order, singular provenance, and fixity that consume so much professional attention. These ideas came to a head in a couple of different ways by the end of the twentieth century. Terry Cook, Joan Schwartz, and Eric Ketelaar, among others, took up the ideas of postmodernists that had been circulating within academia since the late 1950s and argued that the same records could be interpreted in many different ways and also that archivists play an active and power-laden role in shaping the record and how it is interpreted through their professional actions. However, it was the exposition of the records continuum model in Australia in the mid-1990s, with its "multi-dimensional and multi-layered views of recordkeeping and archiving in different spacetimes,"[3] that for the first time provided a framework within which complexities, contingencies, and also contestations and paradoxes inherent to records, recordkeeping, and records use might be theoretically contemplated as well as practically addressed. Ideas about movement and transformation across time, space, and context began to be implemented in particular through description and through electronic recordkeeping systems design. For example, building on Peter Scott's ideas about how the physical and intellectual instability of the fonds might be addressed through archival description and, within the framework of the records continuum, Chris Hurley demonstrated how simultaneous multiple and parallel provenances could be at work for the same records.[4] Hurley and other records continuum thinkers were also influenced by archival consultant David Bearman's efforts in the 1980s and early 1990s to delineate electronic records, the dynamics, fuzziness, relational components, and migration requirements of which challenged traditional archival ideas about the nature of the record, pointing instead to records' transactionality and functions.

As these examples would suggest, those articulating "continuum thinking" have wrestled with issues and observations that challenge simplistically articulated precepts related to fixity, singular provenance, and original order that remain widely accepted as sine quibus non in modern professional archival practice. "Continuum thinking" underscores the fundamental point that is so often missed when archival ideas and practices are being taught—that there are dynamics and a depth of complexity, change, and contingency associated with records and archives, and, as a result, there can be no two same archival moments within the continuum. Fundamental to the continuum's time-space conceptualization are the potential for and arguably the inevitability of the movement and transformation of records across its four dimensions (Create, Capture, Organize, and Pluralize) and the facets represented on its axes (Transactionality, Evidentiality, Identity, and Recordkeeping Containers). However, movement and transformation are the very essence of the fourth dimension, Pluralize, which, as Sue McKemmish articulates it, "involves disembedding the record from its original multiple organisational and/or personal contexts and carrying it through spacetime."[5] Pluralization speaks to the societal dissemination, interpretation, and exploitation of records well beyond the confines, oversight, and perhaps even expectations or anticipations of archivists, archives, or the archival profession. It speaks also to the participation of records in the formation of collective memory and identities. In this dimension, records join with what Frank Upward calls other "memory banks across even wider reaches of time or space"[6] and are open to new and potentially multiple uses and meanings and a plethora of new and free-forming relations between people, events, history, memory, objects, temporalities, discourses, and so forth. In the fourth dimension, records are no longer primarily the concern of the recordkeeping fields. The pluralization of the record or, in the spirit of Gilles Deleuze and Felix Guattari, the *deterritorialization* and *reterritorialization*[7] of the record—its movement away from archives and into different spatial and temporal relations and realities—creates new potentials and directs the future movements of bodies, actions, knowledge, and meaning-making processes of many individuals, communities, and disciplines. Although the records continuum explicitly contemplates movement in terms of how recordkeeping phenomena traverse and change across time and space, inevitably this involves "movement" and often "transformation" in the affective sense also.

Terry Cook, whose visits to Australia were influential in the early development of the records continuum model, was already arguing in 1993 about the importance of the societal pluralizing role of archives that is represented by the fourth dimension.[8] In addition to Cook, several other influential archival scholars have called for the Pluralize dimension to receive more consideration.[9] A small number of recent studies by emerging scholars have applied or demonstrated fourth-dimension ideas about how records move and are transformed across time, agents, geographies, and cognitive and affective states to phenomena in online spaces of cultural heritage, such as YouTube;[10] the making and sharing of records within (and beyond) the Los Angeles-based community arts group Machine Project;[11] police surveillance records transformed into poetry objects, spoken-word performances, and sculptures;[12] and mug shots of Tuol Sleng prison victims.[13] The societal, translocal, creative, and affective implications of pluralization have also penetrated into disciplinary discussions in the social sciences, arts, and humanities through the so-called archival turns. One turn, Eric Ketelaar suggests, is away from a view of archives as sources to "archives as epistemological sites and outcomes of cultural practices." He writes that archival turns can take on linguistic, social, performative, and representational forms.[14] Therefore, the need for those entering the archival field to understand such turns and transformations, as well as to bring their own professional perspectives to these wider experiences and discussions, calls for interinstitutional, interdisciplinary, and imaginative innovations in curricula and pedagogy, both inside archival education programs and in other fields.

Designing Archival Curricula to Address Movement and Transformation

We specifically designed the courses we taught at UCLA and CalArts to bridge disciplinary areas (e.g., the arts and humanities as well as different area studies), distances (e.g., across national, regional, community, and ideological borders), and diasporas (of people, of records, and of cultural production). Through the courses, we sought to surface the presence and valence of affective phenomena that have recently been articulated in the field and that have engendered considerable resonance among a wide range of disciplines and user communities[15] and demonstrate how these may occur across the records continuum. Affective phenomena speak not only to how archives and the archival field can capture the imagination of users and the public more broadly but also to the need for the field to actively engage with personal and community imaginaries, storytelling, and acts of creativity that are inspired by contact with or meaningful absence of archival evidence and other traces of the past.

For example, Anne Gilliland and Michelle Caswell have argued that affect plays an important role in forming and transforming individual and collective imaginings about the nature of the archive and its contents, even to the point where the imagined archive may develop its own agency, and Kathy Carbone has argued for understanding records as affectively charged objects able to move people into new ways of doing and being that can reveal the workings and significance of records in people's lives.[16]

Pair 1: Movement of People, Movement of Records

UCLA's master's specialization in archival studies was established in 1995 in the Department of Information Studies (UCLA's iSchool), which prioritizes social justice and human rights concerns as well as engagement with California's diverse communities and their various connections to other parts of the globe. This distinctive critical and ethical orientation has been influential in decisions made about what is taught in archival studies and how it is taught. Courses emphasize the central and proactive roles and ethical responsibilities of archives and archivists with regard to accountability, the construction and contestations of memory and identity in and across different communities and cultures, and inequitable and affective aspects of records and recordkeeping. Increasingly, these courses have attracted doctoral and undergraduate students from other fields who are engaged in "archival turns," in using the archives in their own scholarship, and, perhaps most compellingly, in finding themselves and their communities. For many of these students, engagement in archival courses is a deeply personal and transformative experience. Teaching to the fourth dimension, then, has emerged organically out of this space.

The first pair of courses described below specifically addressed the movement and fragmenting of both records and peoples across and outside national and community domains; how the relationships between the records and those to whom they pertain or who use them move and transform across time, space, generation, and positionality; and what archivists needed to know in order to be better positioned to address such movement and transformation. In 1967, Ernst Posner, the first full-time archival educator in the United States, lamented that archivists still operated within their own archival domains and traditions and were unfamiliar with others.[17] Despite extensive professional and technological developments in the archival field in the intervening years, this remains the case. In 2011, an essay written by archival academics from multiple countries and institutions described the urgency of a pluralized approach to education—and, in particular, teaching to the archival multiverse, a concept considerably broader than what Posner had envisaged.[18] This was further reinforced in an edited volume of essays, *Research in the Archival Multiverse*, published in 2016.[19] Nevertheless, in archival education little emphasis is placed on preparing professionals to address issues that arise when individuals and organizations, their activities, and the records and other documentation and memorialization of those activities move, for all sorts of reasons, beyond and across institutional boundaries, community spaces, and national borders.[20] Although these concerns certainly fall within the scope of traditional archival practice across the first three dimensions of the records continuum, the movements of records, people, and memory across geographies, time and generations, institutional responsibilities, and the formations of personal and collective memory and identity bridge into the fourth dimension.

Migrating Memories: Diaspora, Archives, and Human Rights

In fall 2014, Anne Gilliland and Bosnian-Australian anthropologist Hariz Halilovich addressed several aspects of these concerns when they jointly taught an intensive five-week course, "Migrating Memories: Diaspora, Archives, and Human Rights." The course, which drew master's and doctoral students from anthropology, Chicanx studies, education, English, and history in addition to information studies, explored the (re)construction of migrants' memories and identities as distinct transnational and translocal practices taking place in both private and public domains, in reality and imagination, and in the realms of real and cyber space.[21]

Students were introduced to the significance of memory in establishing diasporas and to various forms and practices, both tangible and intangible, of memory and memory work in migrant and refugee communities: from oral histories and testimonials to performative enactments of memories (e.g., through commemorations, art and music, and virtual villages) to the establishment of more formal memory structures such as archives, libraries, museums, monuments and memorials, and documentary and print production. Students and instructors discussed fourth-dimension aspects of how novels and creative nonfiction as well as documentary and autobiographical films have creatively and affectively engaged records, archives, and memories in (re)presenting personal and community stories of contemporary and historical migration and human rights issues as well as the dynamics of identity formation. While the instructors introduced literature and film in part to illustrate how creative endeavors can serve as alternative forms of archives and expressions of memory, students were able to connect their own experiences to those media as well as to the short ethnographic projects that they chose to carry out for the class. Indeed, their projects were often specifically designed to help them better understand their own community's memory-making processes. The class discussions proved to be very important pedagogically, not only in teasing out relationships between records, memories, identity and healing after trauma and diaspora, and understanding the professional and ethical challenges involved in working with diaspora communities, but also in helping participants to connect their own experiences and feelings, and those of their families, to what they were learning about in class. Thus, this connection increased both their awareness and their empathy, states that the instructors believed to be essential in enhancing professional practice in support of diaspora needs of archives.

Locating and Using Records as Evidence in Human Rights Activities

Records provide essential evidence for many human rights as well as other kinds of government, corporate, and personal activities. Records are needed by international tribunals prosecuting war crimes; watchdog agencies documenting human rights abuses; nongovernmental organizations working with forcibly displaced persons; refugees and others in diaspora seeking asylum, resettlement, or family reunification; and victims, migrants, and family members looking for missing or "disappeared" individuals, pursuing reparations claims, or reclaiming confiscated or looted property. Missing or dispersed records, poorly funded records repositories, inadequate description and lack of digital access, linguistic and script differences, varying legal requirements, and uncooperative authorities all present challenges. Often, those seeking records are attempting to do so from countries other than those where the needed records might be located.

Following up on the ground opened by the previous course, "Locating and Using Records as Evidence in Human Rights Activities," a quarter-long seminar taught by Gilliland, was aimed more directly at master's and doctoral students in archival studies but with a longer-term view to building it out further as a joint clinic engaging both law and archival studies students. Its conception was also influenced by a course offered at the Donald and Vera Blinken Open Society Archives at Central European University in Budapest, "Archives, Evidence and Human Rights," which is mandatory for students in the Human Rights Program of the Legal Studies Department and cross-listed to the History Department. That course seeks to attract students with different backgrounds who are working on topics related to recorded memory, historical analysis and representations of oppressive regimes, and retroactive justice in order to educate them on ways of locating, assessing, collating, and challenging recorded evidence.[22]

The UCLA course used actual transinstitutional and transnational cases to build student understanding about the role of and requirements for consulting and producing records in different contexts and, in particular, the depth of knowledge about the nature of the records and recordkeeping processes and events that are needed. It also sought to confront students with the possibilities of not being able to satisfactorily resolve the cases or locate the evidence that they were seeking. This approach was intended not only to give them a better sense of the difficulties, affect, and imaginings of archival users who might attempt such quests but also to encourage them to identify and propose effective and state-of-the art description, seeking, and interpretive strategies whereby archivists in one country might support individuals in locating, accessing, using, and challenging records as documentary evidence that might exist in various other locations. Speakers from archives in countries around the world where relevant records are located presented virtual lectures on the state of those records (provenance, reliability, completeness, condition, idiosyncrasies, and so forth), how those records are described and organized and possible uses, and other locations where complete or partial copies might be located, as well as legal, political, and procedural considerations. As with the previous course, students pursued projects that often had strong personal resonances, including looking for documentation that might assist in writing a magical realist novel about the 1992 Analco explosions in Guadalajara, helping victims of the 2013 Rana Plaza collapse in Bangladesh in securing compensation, identifying unacknowledged victims and additional evidence of what occurred during the Tlatelolco massacre of students and other civilians in Mexico City in 1968, locating the fate of a family member still unaccounted for after the Holocaust, and putting together cases on behalf of California Native American communities for federal tribal recognition.

Without a doubt, both courses were highly affective and engaging for all of the students. Regardless of their academic backgrounds, students were completely absorbed. Hierarchies and disciplinary divides in the classroom between master's and doctoral students, between fields, and between students and instructors broke down, and the very real roles that records, memory, and identity play in personal and community lives became readily apparent. The importance of archival practices and at the same time their very real limitations were driven home, as were the limitations of simplistic archival conceptualizations. In the second course, students realized—more, perhaps, than in conventional appraisal, description, or reference courses—that they could not do this kind of work without adequate historical understanding and knowledge about recordkeeping systems and practices. The course also palpably demonstrated how there are some questions that the existing records and archival infrastructure are simply unable to answer satisfactorily and the disappointments and frustrations that this outcome can engender. Pedagogically, however, such inability was not a failure if the students then could discern what could be improved and propose ways in which that could be achieved.

Pair 2: Transforming Records
Archives and Art-Making at CalArts

The archive is an opportunity to create and construct.

—Dany Naierman,
"The Anxiety Archive: The Psycho-
Dimension of Dealing with Past," 2016

In 1961, Walt Disney founded CalArts, a "community of the arts"
dedicated to "radical cultural innovation."[23] It was the first degree-
granting institution of higher learning in the United States created
specifically for students of both the visual and the performing arts
and in which all of the arts were—and continue to be—taught
together on one campus and in one building. Comprising the Schools
of Art, Theater, Music, Film/Video, Critical Studies, and Dance,
CalArts offers more than seventy degree-granting programs at the
undergraduate and graduate levels. It is devoted to experimentation,
innovation, project-based learning, critical thinking, and reflecting
on how one's art practice can be a productive force in cultural and
social transformations.

The CalArts Institute Archives serves as the university's collective
memory and holds materials generated by faculty, staff, students,
academic programs, administrative offices, and campus organizations
as well as materials that document the history of the Chouinard Art
Institute and the Los Angeles Conservatory of Music. Situated in the
CalArts Library, the Institute Archives is an underused and somewhat
mysterious place to many on campus—especially the student
population. Out of a desire to create new pathways into the archives
for students, foster archival curiosity and investigation, and stimulate
dialogue between arts disciplines and archival studies (people,
practices, and discourses),[24] Carbone developed and taught "Archives
and Art-Making" in spring 2016 to graduate and undergraduate
students from across CalArts' six schools. The course followed three
interwoven trajectories: exploring archival principles, practices, and
theory; examining the ways in which contemporary performing,
visual, and literary artists approach and create with the archive(s);[25]
and making art inspired by or with records from the Institute Archives.

The class consisted of two separate (but interrelated) modes of engaging archival matters. First, each class started with student-led discussions of the weekly readings, which comprised a mixture of archival studies literature and humanities literature focused on the archival turn in contemporary art practice. Interesting to note is that while all of the students were familiar with the archives-focused humanities literature, none of the students knew about the existence of archival studies literature. All of the readings centered on notions about archives common to both sets of literature, such as memory and counter-memory, identity formations, power dynamics, and omissions and silences in archives as well as the body and performance as archives, archival imaginaries, and artists' archives. In our class discussions and their weekly writing assignments, students inventively and productively intermingled and debated these ideas—especially the workings of memory and power in archives and archival artworks.

Then, during the second part of the class, students researched archival materials for their art projects via finding aids and reference interactions with me (as archivist) and by roaming the stacks of the archive—opening boxes and looking through collections freely on their own. Liberating the space of the archive in this manner gave the students very direct, tactile, and embodied archival experiences and a greater sense of the materiality and scope of the collections (as well as the processing activities that occur in the space). This unfettered access to the archives also encouraged serendipity—chance discoveries in which students made connections between CalArts' past and present-day approaches to art-making and arts pedagogy, student life, and academic programs that could only happen by being physically present in the space of the archive.

Students made a diverse array of artwork for their final projects. For example, one student created a mixed-media installation at a campus swimming pool. The installation featured present-day swimming trunks hung on a fence surrounding the pool as well as a screen set beside the pool onto which the student projected a montage of black-and-white archival photographs of students and faculty using the pool in the 1970s. Accompanying this was an audio recording of the student reading a letter penned by a CalArts community member in the 1970s who was upset about CalArts' Board of Trustees' desire to close the pool because of the nude swimming that was going on at the time. One of the students produced a small (4" x 2") flipbook of black-and-white photographs of former and current music faculty while another made an installation titled, "Living archive/archive of degradation," which comprised small, clear plastic boxes containing soil, seeds, leaves, and fruit that the student found on the grounds of CalArts and hung from the branches of a tree on campus. There was also a spoken-word performance with simultaneously projected visuals of black-and-white photographs from a 1950s masquerade ball at Chouinard Art Institute collaged with text culled from correspondence and memoranda related to the institutional transition from the Chouinard Art Institute to CalArts during the 1960s.

Through their archival art-making, the students in the course *deterritorialized* archives and *reterritorialized* them into campus spaces and contexts where they had never been before, transforming relations between records, people, campus locales, and a university's history. These archival movements also transformed relations between students and the Institute Archives: some ten students who came across one of the artworks on campus—but who had never heard of the Institute Archives—visited the repository. The course also transformed students' perceptions about the nature of records and what happens (and can happen) in archival spaces; that is, students began to see records as tools and materials with which to think and do things, and the archive as an art studio in which to work, broadening their ideas about the types of resources they can deploy in their art practices and the kinds of spaces in which they can create.

Archives and Art-Making at CalArts

> **I went into the archive and came out a completely different way.**
>
> —Herbert U. Serrano,
> "Learn Your ABC's with Zoia!"

In fall 2017, Carbone taught "Archives and Art-Making" in the Department of Information Studies at UCLA to graduate and doctoral students specializing in archival studies and informatics and to undergraduates from UCLA's Department of Design Media Arts. The format of the course was similar to that of the CalArts course, except that students conducted research in and used materials from the UCLA Library Special Collections (LSC) for their art projects and did not have free rein in the archive. Instead, students worked with University Archivist Heather Brixton and Processing Archivist Angel Diaz to access and use archival materials in the LSC reading room.

While ideas from the archival studies literature greatly inspired CalArts students in their class discussions, written work, and art-making, at UCLA it was the humanities literature about the archival turn in contemporary art, and the occasion to engage viewpoints about archives from outside of the archival field, that galvanized the students. In particular, students were interested and eager to understand how artists approach, conceptualize, transform, and make meaning with archives. The humanities-based, outside-of-the-archival-field perspectives on archives provoked generative in-depth and critical class discussions about contemporary archival art-making, with students especially attracted to the diverse ways in which artists not only give new voices to, but also fill absences and silences in, records.

For their final projects, and like the CalArts students, the UCLA students created a variety of artworks in a range of media. These works included a short fantasy fiction ghost story that took place in an archive and a children's alphabet board book based on the personal papers of American librarian Zoia Horn. There was also a short video that featured a student plotting an elaborate plan to marry a well-known Los Angeles billionaire entrepreneur and philanthropist with deep ties to the art world and that incorporated photographs of the billionaire and architectural renderings for one of his buildings. Another student worked with a scrapbook compiled by A. Y. Owen containing an assortment of newspaper and magazine articles and photographs depicting the life and film and stage career of actor Lon Chaney. Moved by Owen's appreciation of Chaney and the "mental and emotional connection"[26] she felt toward Chaney that grew as a result of interacting with the scrapbook, the student created a shrine to the actor. The shrine consisted of numerous parts, including a mobile of black-and-white photographs of Chaney hung from the ceiling, votive candles with Chaney's image affixed to them, and framed photographs of Chaney in various silent film roles, such as Quasimodo from *The Hunchback of Notre Dame*. Finally, one of the students created a small zine that explored "the city as archive/the archive as city," and contained color photographs from former Los Angeles mayor Tom Bradley's official papers interspersed with the student's own color photographs of Los Angeles.

"Transformation" happened on several levels in this class. Besides the apparent transformation of archival materials into different shapes and considerations, which resulted in the records taking on new valences and significances, there were personal transformations as well. First, students found that the "practical" part of the class—doing research in the archives—filled a gap in their graduate coursework and the opportunity to combine their creative and academic selves in coursework gratifying. Second, students' conception of the archive transformed through their hands-on, creative practices with records; they came to understand the archive not only as a place for research but also as an "imagination chamber"[27] and site for creative investigation and experimentation. Moreover, students' experiences with archival art-making made very concrete how records can be (re) contextualized, a notion they—as archival and information studies students—read much about in the archival literature but often do not have the opportunity to experience firsthand.

Conclusion

Professional archival associations strive to raise the public profile and importance of the archival field and archival concerns, to increase and broaden uses of archives, and to better understand when and how the archival domain touches on that of other professions, disciplines, and community and personal endeavors. All of these require the parties involved to develop a greater and more nuanced understanding of the role and nature of archives and recordkeeping. Although further complexifying archival ideas, preoccupations and boundaries through courses such as those discussed here might seem to run counter to trends such as the standardization and streamlining of archival practices, it cannot be dismissed merely as an abstract theoretical exercise in the education of future professionals. It is what advances education beyond simply training by teaching students to think conceptually, critically, and deeply about records, the keeping of records, and the nature and effects of archives in and over time and across space, communities, and cultures. This kind of thinking and awareness prepares students for careers that will stand the test of time, technologies, and ideological shifts. It also prepares them to articulate and advocate for their professional concerns and expertise in environments where there is scarce mutual understanding and to connect with other fields where there are mutual interests.

Through our endeavors teaching to (and in) the fourth dimension, students *and* instructors together explored and experienced the potency of the Pluralize dimension and the myriad ways in which archives, records, and recordkeeping methods and systems (or lack thereof) can intimately touch people, transform the contents of archives, and open up or preclude pluralization possibilities. In each of these courses, the need for and interplay between all kinds and conceptualizations of archives—institutional, community, personal, embodied, and imagined—and people's affective and creative interactions with and responses to them became readily apparent. So too did the important possibilities of creating, locating, or discovering personal or societal meaning from very small aspects of an archive that could then grow or be grown into something much more extensive and intricate. This potential should be noted by archivists because students often found themselves working or attempting to work with archives and recordkeeping systems at a level that is much more granular and personally meaningful than archival practices currently take into account or may be able to support.

Both sets of courses demonstrably enhanced students' abilities to think "out of the box"; their orientation to detail; their awareness of gaps, inconsistencies, and anomalies in records; their desire to approach archival description and reference provision in new and different ways; their empathy for users of archives; and their awareness of how archival use traverses institutional and other boundaries. In addition, in approaching archival pedagogy in this way—engaging records and memory practices in social, interactive, experiential, and personally meaningful manners—we created courses that themselves contribute to pluralizing records. Teaching to the fourth dimension also constantly changed and informed participants' understandings of the other dimensions of the continuum, since most affective experiences in the fourth dimension arise from past actions (or lack of action) in one or more of the first three dimensions. In other words, the four dimensions of the continuum are tightly interrelated and have causal relationships with one another. While this is not a new observation, perhaps paying attention to fourth-dimension experiences with archives (physical, digital, embodied, or imagined) helps us to perceive more clearly what is lacking, wanted, needed, or in fact working well from many different agents' perspectives in the other three dimensions on the micro/local, as well as macro/global, levels.

As already noted, Ketelaar argues that it is important that archivists engage with disciplines that have made the archival turn but that rarely recognize what archival practice and theory can contribute to their discourse on the archive(s).[28] We realize that the kinds of educational innovation and transdisciplinary approaches described in this essay require a fluidity and flexibility in academic curricula and program structure that is not always possible in all educational situations, especially for programs that are tightly constrained by professional and accreditation requirements. It also requires a willingness on the part of other fields on a campus to participate by allowing their students to cross-enroll or by listing courses across departments, by their faculty serving as co-instructors, or even by designing similar courses within their own programs. Nevertheless, based on our own experiences we would strongly argue for both professional and disciplinary programs to consider ways in which they could incorporate similar approaches, especially if they wish to be responsive to the shifting epistemological paradigms, user needs, and the creative affordances of the twenty-first century.

Notes

1. In this essay, we take a broad view of records as encompassing the various understandings of the kinds of materials with which archivists and other recordkeepers are concerned, as delineated by Geoffrey Yeo in "Concepts of Record (1): Evidence, Information and Persistent Representations," *American Archivist* 70 (Fall/Winter, 2007): 315–343.

2. Anne J. Gilliland and Michelle Caswell, "Records and Their Imaginaries: Imagining the Impossible, Making Possible the Imagined," *Archival Science* 16, no. 1 (March 2016): 53–75, https://doi.org/10.1007/s10502-015-9259-z.

3. Sue McKemmish, "Recordkeeping in the Continuum: An Australian Tradition," in *Research in the Archival Multiverse*, ed. Anne J. Gilliland, Sue McKemmish, and Andrew J Lau (Melbourne: Monash University Press, 2017), 138.

[4] Chris Hurley, "About Me," Chris Hurley's Stuff, 2012, http://www.descriptionguy .com/about-me.html, captured at https://perma.cc/K49M-BFZV.

[5] McKemmish, "Recordkeeping in the Continuum," 139.

[6] Frank Upward, "Structuring the Records Continuum, Part Two: Structuration Theory and Recordkeeping," *Archives and Manuscripts* 25, no.1 (1997): 10–35.

[7] Gilles Deleuze and Felix Guattari, *A Thousand Plateaus: Capitalism & Schizophrenia*, trans. Brian Massumi (Minneapolis: University of Minnesota Press, 1987), 3–25 (emphasis added).

[8] Anne J. Gilliland, "From Keeping Records to 'Recordkeeping,' From Post-custodial Archives to Simply 'Archives': A Retrospective-Prospective Commentary on Cook's Electronic Records, Paper Minds," in *"All Shook Up": The Archival Legacy of Terry Cook,* ed. Tom Nesmith, Joan Schwartz, and Greg Bak (Chicago: Association of Canadian Archivists and Society of American Archivists, 2020).

[9] See, for example, Terry Cook, "Beyond the Screen: The Records Continuum and Archival Cultural Heritage" (paper presented at the Australian Society of Archivists Conference, Melbourne, Australia, August 18, 2000), http://www.mybestdocs.com /cook-t-beyondthescreen-000818.htm, captured at https://perma.cc/37PS-3BD3; Barbara Reed, "Beyond Perceived Boundaries: Imagining the Potential of Pluralised Recordkeeping," *Archives and Manuscripts* 33, no. 1 (May 2005): 176; Tom Nesmith, "Re-Exploring the Continuum, Rediscovering Archives," *Archives and Manuscripts* 36, no. 2 (November 2008): 34–53.

[10] Leisa Gibbons, "Culture in the Continuum: YouTube, Small Stories, and Memory-Making," PhD diss. (Monash University, 2014).

[11] Andrew J Lau, "Collecting Experiences," PhD diss. (University of California, Los Angeles, 2013).

[12] Kathy Carbone, "Artists in the Archive: An Exploratory Study of the Artist-in-Residence Program at the City of Portland Archives & Records Center," *Archivaria* 79 (Spring 2015): 27–52.

[13] Michelle Caswell, *Archiving the Unspeakable: Silence, Memory, and the Photographic Record in Cambodia* (Madison: University of Wisconsin Press, 2014).

[14] Eric Ketelaar, "Archival Turns and Returns: Studies of the Archive," in *Research in the Archival Multiverse,* ed. Anne J. Gilliland, Sue McKemmish, and Andrew J Lau (Melbourne: Monash University Press, 2016), 228–229.

[15] Marika Cifor and Anne J. Gilliland, "Affect and the Archive, Archives and Their Affects: An Introduction to the Special Issue," *Archival Science* 16 (2016): 1–6; Marika Cifor, "Affecting Archives: Introducing Affect Studies to Archival Discourse," *Archival Science* 16, no. 1 (2016): 7–31; Michelle Caswell, Marika Cifor, and Mario H. Ramirez, "'To Suddenly Discover Yourself Existing': Uncovering the Affective Impact of Community Archives," *American Archivist* 79 (Spring/Summer 2016): 56–81.

[16] Gilliland and Caswell, "Records and Their Imaginaries"; Michelle Caswell and Anne J. Gilliland, "False Promise and New Hope: Dead Perpetrators, Imagined Documents, and Emergent Archival Evidence," *International Journal on Human Rights* 19, no. 5 (2015): 615–627; Michelle Caswell, "Inventing New Archival

Imaginaries: Theoretical Foundations for Identity-Based Community Archives," in *Identity Palimpsests: Ethnic Archiving in the U.S. and Canada,* ed. Dominque Daniel and Amalia Levi (Sacramento, CA: Litwin Books, 2014), 35–55; Kathy Michelle Carbone, "Artists and Records: Moving History and Memory," *Archives and Records* 38, no. 1 (2017): 100–118, https://doi.org/10.1080/23257962.2016.1260446.

[17] Ernst Posner, *Archives and the Public Interest: Selected Essays by Ernst Posner,* ed. Ken Munden (Chicago: Society of American Archivists, 2006), 198–199.

[18] Archival Education and Research Institute (AERI), Pluralizing the Archival Curriculum Group (PACG), "Educating for the Archival Multiverse," *American Archivist* 74 (Spring/Summer 2011): 68–101.

[19] Anne J. Gilliland, Sue McKemmish, and Andrew J Lau, eds., *Research in the Archival Multiverse* (Melbourne: Monash University Press, 2016), http://www.publishing.monash.edu/books/ram-9781876924676.html, captured at https://perma.cc/9W6Y-YC6T.

[20] See, for example, James Lowry, ed., *Displaced Records* (London: Routledge, 2017); Ricardo Punzalan, "Archival Diasporas: A Framework for Understanding the Complexities and Challenges of Dispersed Photographic Collections," *American Archivist* 77 (Fall/Winter 2014): 326–349; Anne J. Gilliland, "A Matter of Life and Death: A Critical Examination of the Role of Official Records and Archives in Forced Displacement," *Journal of Critical Library and Information Studies* 2 (2017).

[21] For more detail about this course, Anne J. Gilliland and Hariz Halilovich, "Migrating Memories: Transdisciplinary Pedagogical Approaches to Teaching About Diasporic Memory, Identity and Human Rights in Archival Studies," *Archival Science* 17 (2017): 79–96.

[22] In this course, "case studies illustrate the problems of using and evaluating evidence on mass atrocities, the historical, ethical, and legal aspects of making justice for past abuses and the difficulties of making state leaders liable for human rights violations. New methods of (re)creating historical/human rights narratives from diverse archival sources are introduced, along with innovative digital systems of managing human rights information." Professors Iván Székely, András Mink, and Csaba Szilágyi, "Archives, Evidence and Human Rights," course syllabus, Central European University Department of Legal Studies, http://www.osaarchivum.org/files/Archives_course_AY2017-18_Syllabus.pdf, captured at https://perma.cc/5B33-7Y8J.

[23] Economic Research Associates, "Need and Concept," California Institute of the Arts Collection, Institute Archives, CalArts Library, 1966.

[24] To note, the contemporary art world's enduring captivations with archival things over the past several decades has resulted in a significant corpus of archival artwork and an abundant arts critical discourse about archival art practices. However, art critics, curators, theorists, and artists themselves rarely engage archival scholarship in their arts writing or practice. Another goal of this course was to examine the ways in which archival discourses and practices and arts discourses and practices might associate with and inform one another.

[25] We use the term "the archive(s)" here as an amalgamation to speak about, at the same time, archives (institutional repositories of collections of records), informal archives (historical materials found outside of institutional archives), and "the archive" (as concept or trope).

[26] Samantha Blanco, "Art Project Proposal: A Shrine to the Man of a Thousand Faces," unpublished manuscript, October 31, 2017.

[27] Jenny Sjöholm, "The Art Studio as Archive: Tracing the Geography of Artistic Potentiality, Progress and Production," *Cultural Geographies in Practice* 21, no. 3 (2014): 507.

[28] Ketelaar, "Archival Turns," 229.

9

Commentary
Ethics and Education

Alison Langmead

Each of the essays in this section is a rich exploration of its chosen topic, and each could be linked to another using any number of different, yet salient, trains of thought about archival ethics and education in the early twenty-first century. For the purposes of this text, I have chosen to focus on the ways that these authors offer their perspectives on the (changing) foundation of archival professionalism at this particular moment in time. In terms of a historical understanding of what archival professionalism has been until recently, all three essays take up and use, either latently or blatantly, the time-tested theories of Sir Hilary Jenkinson and his contemporaries, especially that generation's emphasis on the organic, "natural" accumulation of the archives and the critical importance of the impartiality of the archives and the archivist. Such impartiality is taken up directly by MacNeil, of course, when she notes, "for the first generation of archival theorists, . . . protecting the integrity of archival records as reliable evidence meant protecting their value as impartial witnesses to past events."[1] This type of impartiality, she rightly points out, is based on the rationalist empiricism of the Enlightenment and focuses, almost to an obsessive degree, on eliminating any contamination, or even perhaps infection, caused by the presence of the archivist in the records. This historical foundation of the archival profession prioritizes the erasure of the archivist from the archives.

Mattern offers a clear example of the ways that this historical emphasis on rationalist impartiality, as transmogrified by the archivists of the US government over the course of the twentieth century, has recently played out in the public sphere. Mattern notes that, when responding to concerns in 2015 surrounding then Secretary Clinton's use of private email servers, National Archives and Records Administration officials "consistently retained a neutral tone, hesitating to either offer criticism or to condone Clinton's reliance on personal email."[2] Indeed, NARA officials appear to have exerted a great deal of effort to ensure that they were seen as impartial arbiters of the guidelines, carefully setting themselves apart from the scandal by strictly maintaining a sense of impartial distance. This effort also ensured that they needed to speak little about the moral or ethical issues at stake and they could also deflect much of the blame for this problematic affair. As Mattern states, "[Their] talking points confirm that NARA officials were not interested in passing judgment on Clinton's email practices and instead wanted to focus on facts— namely, what NARA officials did in the wake of the discovery and what relevant guidance exists."[3] Their stance was clear: it was up to the State Department to set up their rules appropriately. NARA behaved appropriately, and no part of the blame for this recordkeeping debacle should come to the archivists.

The notion of an archival "neutrality" or "impartiality" can serve in this way to be just as much a blind, a defense that keeps the archivist clear from the messy reality of tending to archives, as it is a concerted effort to retain or maintain the pristine condition of the records themselves, as Jenkinson might have done. Indeed, the struggle to understand how any archival order could be "original"—a long-standing professional conversation that is mentioned by both MacNeil and Gilliland and Carbone—is a clear testament to this tension between an ideal world, where fonds are natural and organic, and the real world, where things are messy, embodied, and never truly orderly in any Enlightenment-worthy fashion. Jenkinson and his peers may have seen the mind and body of the archivist as a vector of probable contamination into this immaculately organized, never-possible world, but the authors of these essays show us a different world, one in which we are all in it together, the records and us, in the complicated soup of the real world. There is no way for archivists to effectively erase themselves, their choices, and their power from the archives.

Many archival theorists of the twentieth century have, of course, noted this state of affairs. Indeed, Gilliland and Carbone mention the arguments of Cook, Schwartz, and Ketelaar, who have all posited that "archivists play an active and power-laden role in shaping the record and how it is interpreted through their professional actions."[4] But have archivists ever wanted this power? With such power comes attention and the possibility of being accountable for choices in the archives. Archivists have direct knowledge of the power the archives can wield and have perhaps been afraid of it. They have long tried to maneuver their way out of any responsibility for how records are misused— although happy to take responsibility for providing appropriate access to appropriate people. Impartiality and neutrality can keep archivists safe, blinded, and disguised.

But to what end? Such erasure has never been truly possible, or, perhaps, desirable. MacNeil cites the work of historian Kathryn Burns, whose study of the notarial archives of sixteenth-century colonial Peru "illustrates one of the ways in which archival turn scholars have troubled the metaphor of records as evidence by positioning historical sources as constituent agents in reconstructing a particular conception of the past rather than as the unselfconscious remains of that past."[5] But this complex relationship between records and recordkeepers is not something that remains solely in the past. As MacNeil goes on to say, "if recordmaking practices are 'full of gambits, scripted moves, and countermoves,' so, too, are the archival practices associated with the management of historical records."[6] In this vein, archivists can become—or unavoidably are—as flawed and human as any records creator or records user. Indeed, they are as human as any public official trying to maintain their power and position.

The documentary history of the human race can do good and ill in this world, and its stewards cannot remain impartial, objective, or neutral, no matter how they try—and they have tried. And yet this strikes at the heart of the historical foundations of archival professionalism. As MacNeil notes, the ICA Code of Ethics directly connects the "objectivity and impartiality of archivists" with their "professionalism."[7] Following this line of reasoning, then, to resist objectivity and impartiality would be to undermine the foundations of the profession. And yet, here, in 2019, we are in a place where this objectivity and impartiality not only seem like a fool's errand, it seems impossible and deleterious to the status of archives on the global stage. In the wake of this transformation, these essays' authors suggest an alternative basis for archival professionalism in the twenty-first century: empathy and engagement.

For a number of years, archivists have been drawing themselves more and more into the narrative of the archives. Michelle Light and Tom Hyry's work on the importance of adding self-conscious, introspective annotations, including complete archival colophons, to finding aids and other descriptive instruments serves as the touchstone essay for this turn-of-the-millennium push for a larger presence of the archivist's voice directly in their work and in the archives.[8] Both MacNeil and Gilliland and Carbone assert the value of this aspect of the new archival professionalism, with MacNeil doing so proactively in her discussion of fonds as networked texts and Gilliland and Carbone doing so as a continuous claim underpinning their essay. As MacNeil notes, this approach

> uncouples integrity, as a quality of character, from impartiality and objectivity and expands the notion of accountability to encompass the ethical obligation of archivists to hold themselves to account for the actions and decisions they have taken with respect to the records in their care and, as much as possible, to make those actions and decisions known to users.[9]

The work of Light and Hyry's colophons can help to fulfill this mandate, and calls for such behavior urge archivists to forego their own physical and mental erasure and to proactively enter their thoughts and words into the record.

However, in these three essays, the authors call for the heightened presence of the archivist in the archives in ways that go beyond Light and Hyry's piece and that gesture toward a deeper, more open-hearted engagement. For example, in their discussion of the fourth dimension of the records continuum, Pluralize, Gilliland and Carbone note that

> This potential [for creating personal or societal meaning out of archives] should be noted by archivists because students often found themselves working or attempting to work with archives and recordkeeping systems at a level that is much more granular and personally meaningful than archival practices currently take into account or may be able to support.[10]

The notion of an archivist working with records in ways that are "personally meaningful" is particularly transformative, calling not only for the end of the bodily erasure of the archivist but of the archivist's full and active presence.

Indeed, for MacNeil, the heart of archival professionalism in 2019 is not founded solely on critical self-reflection ("the fonds as texts"); it is also a calling to proactively promote the promises of the records that we keep and to take active steps that make these documents do good in the world, using the metaphor of "records as narratives." This methodology "invites archivists to link archival integrity to a willingness to engage with and, to the extent possible, empathize with the particular needs of the individuals and communities who are seeking access to records."[11] Archival integrity and professionalism here becomes focused not just on a critical self-reflection appended to descriptive materials but, instead, emphatically on proactive engagement. Indeed, as Gilliland and Carbone suggest, the self-reflective colophon may be, in some ways, another shield, another blind, for archival detachment and erasure. In their discussion, they point out that "continuum thinking" underscores a fundamental point that is so often missed when archival ideas and practices are being taught—"that there are dynamics and a depth of complexity, change, and contingency associated with records and archives, and, as a result, there can be no two same archival moments within the continuum."[12] In this quotation, I hear these authors almost calling out for us to hear that we cannot write, describe, or use technologies to work our way out of this corner of self-erasure and partial irrelevance. Archivists are always present, always making a mark. Instead, archivists must engage directly, and humanely, with records creators and records users—that is, our fellow human beings. This is a more deeply engaged and thoughtful position—not just one step away from neutrality, objectivity, and impartiality, but many.

This transformation of approach is likely to be related to the shift in the notion of our archives as "laboratories of history" to places that are rightly inhabited not solely by historians but also by a host of people from genealogists and care leavers—those people who are directly looking for themselves and their own stories, rather than those, like historians, who tend to be seeking other people's narratives. What an utter transformation in archival principles it is to hear MacNeil suggest that archivists are to "actively support [care leavers'] efforts to identify and locate their care records from a stance of engagement and empathy rather than one of impartiality and objectivity."[13] It is a delight to imagine an archival profession truly devoted to the carework of the historical record of humankind.

With their emphasis on the role of education in the formation of new generations of archivists, Gilliland and Carbone put forward a pedagogy that emphasizes this engagement and subjective attachment to the archives, not a detachment or unselfconscious "neutrality." They report that their early attempts to integrate this approach have resulted in greater student connection with the field—indeed, some found the "opportunity to combine their creative and academic selves in coursework gratifying."[14] And yet the work that Gilliland and Carbone describe teaching is not traditional archival work. This emphasis on thinking through, with, and alongside these records is something that the archival tradition has distinctly, intentionally, and willfully tried to stay away from for more than a century. It is a part of our erasure. We are there, but we do not exist. This new pedagogy is a transformation of principles for a new generation of recordkeepers who are prepared to show up, be seen, and engage.

In her piece on NARA's role in the Clinton email scandal, Mattern opens a door to one possible way that even NARA—the most traditional of American archives—could move forward in this more empathetic and human-focused direction. In her concluding remarks, she argues that "in its training role, NARA should work closely with agencies to ensure that requirements and responsibilities for public employees are coherent and understood and to evaluate this training for efficacy."[15] Could it not be that the most effective way to implement this plan would be for NARA to focus on working with colleagues in the federal government with empathy and engagement? It may be a legacy of the Cold War that government officials are seen as cold, harsh, and unforgiving. But this cannot possibly be the lived reality of government service. It is difficult to keep the records of our government, and it is clear to see that these people do their work under intense pressure from all angles. Not just in their role as rules setters and standards arbiters but also in their role as fellow federal employees, the archivists of the National Archives and Records Administration could provide a great service to our country by allowing their empathy and engagement with their fellow administrators to infiltrate their actions and their policies on a proactive and public level.

Are records more rightly considered to be "evidence" when they belong to Secretary Clinton and "narratives" when they belong to the case files of care leavers? No, indeed. All of these records exist simultaneously and at once—a state of affairs so clearly embodied by the records continuum itself—in MacNeil's three metaphors of evidence, texts, and narrative. All of these documents, all of our archives, were produced by human beings and, as such, attend to the process of being human in their own ways.[16] However, seeing the records of the US federal government as emotionally connected narratives is not our tradition, or even our wont, and to change this state of affairs will take work.

Bringing difficult ideas such as these both to the archival profession and to the archival classroom is deeply important, and, as Gilliland and Carbone note, such work is "what advances education beyond simply training by teaching students to think conceptually, critically, and deeply about records."[17] Our desire to stay on the outside of our archives may also have allowed us to stay more easily on the outside of our pedagogies. But times are changing for the better. These authors urge us to become more wholly engaged with our world, our fellow human beings, our archives, and our classrooms. In the end, direct responsibility for our professional actions has always belonged to us, no matter how much we may have tried to shirk it. By focusing on empathetic and professional attachment, however, we find ourselves in a position where we can take responsibility for our engagement rather than our erasure.

Notes

[1] Heather MacNeil, "Records as Evidence, Text, and Narrative: Framing the Ethical Dimensions of Integrity," 87.

[2] Eleanor Mattern, "NARA and the Private Email Account: The Agency's Response to the Clinton Email Case," 116.

[3] Mattern, "NARA," 113.

[4] Anne J. Gilliland and Kathy Carbone, "Movement and Transformation: Teaching to the Fourth Dimension," 127.

[5] MacNeil, "Records," 89–90.

[6] MacNeil, "Records," 90.

[7] International Council on Archives, *Code of Ethics*, September 6, 1996, http://www.ica.org/sites/default/files/ICA_1996-09-06_code%20of%20ethics_EN.pdf, captured at https://perma.cc/Q2CC-TDE8, quoted in MacNeil, "Records," 85.

[8] Michelle Light and Tom Hyry, "Colophons and Annotations: New Directions for the Finding Aid," *American Archivist* 65 (Fall/Winter 2002): 216–230.

[9] MacNeil, "Records," 92.

[10] Gilliland and Carbone, "Movement," 140.

[11] MacNeil, "Records," 97.

[12] Gilliland and Caribone, "Movement," 127–128.

[13] MacNeil, "Records," 96.

[14] Gilliland and Carbone, "Movement," 139.

[15] Mattern, "NARA," 117.

[16] I include automatically or computer-generated documents in this category as well. Until we ascribe intentionality and meaning-making directly to automated processes, and not to the human beings who programmed or set those processes in motion, all documents are documents of the human condition.

[17] Gilliland and Carbone, "Movement," 139.

THEME THREE
Archival History

Richard J. Cox, *Navigating the Islands*, Oil on Canvas, 2015.

10

Representing the Others

Storytelling Dynamics in a Community Archives

Donghee Sinn

Introduction

Many community archives are initiated from commitments to promote
the community's stories and experiences that are often marginalized
or misrepresented in history. According to Andrew Flinn, the act of
archiving is a form of increasing the visibility of communities and their
history [1] and, in this sense, community archives are an "embodiment
of activism."[2] Such efforts can be driven by communities themselves,
and sometimes external impetus from formal archival institutions,
policies, or activist archivists' groups can initiate those activities.
There seem to be different challenges and dynamics in creating a
community archives, depending on how it is established and how
it interacts and responds to the social and political atmosphere. In
archival literature, many researchers have discussed various aspects
of how archivists work with communities, including, among others,
the importance of respecting communities' ethos and autonomy,
being cautious about the archivists' missteps of community's history
and memory, and the resistant attitudes of community partners for
mainstreaming their stories.[3] However, little research has focused on
how members of a community have developed the ways stories are

represented in response to the internal and external dynamics of the community. The approaches that a community chooses to challenge exclusion and misrepresentation demonstrates how a community's members contextualize their stories in the broader society. The decision-making processes for positions and approaches are likely determined by internal dynamics within the community. This notion seems applicable to the No Gun Ri community.

No Gun Ri Digital Archives began as a research project by academic scholars to create a digital platform for the memories of the No Gun Ri massacre. This setting allowed interesting observations, especially for the dynamics of how the members of a community unfolded their stories in the unique circumstances of Korean society. No Gun Ri materials had existed as independent and community-led efforts before this research project. The materials are the products of long-haul efforts to document and promote the community's stories. However, the No Gun Ri materials did not receive sufficient attention for archival management, and there is no place where diverse materials and oral testimonies are collected and preserved with professional care.[4] The intention behind this project was to offer a place where many No Gun Ri stories would be preserved virtually.

As part of the Digital Archives, the project conducted interviews with No Gun Ri community members. In this essay, I discuss the relationships between internal and external dynamics in No Gun Ri narratives as observed from the interviews. I do not address No Gun Ri's history and memories themselves or the relationship between the oral histories and archival materials.[5] Rather, I focus on the implicit or explicit wishes of the members of the No Gun Ri community about how their history is remembered and the center-periphery dynamics of their narratives under the particular circumstances of Korean society.

Mainstream and Marginalized Narratives

A massacre occurred in the early stages of the Korean War in the village of No Gun Ri in South Korea. The 2nd Battalion, 7th Regiment, 1st Cavalry Division of the United States Army was located there at the time. The massacre's survivors and families claimed that hundreds of civilians were killed under the twin railroad overpasses over four days following air attacks on the railroads. The survivors and victims' families put forth great efforts to publicize their stories, including submitting numerous petitions to the US and South Korean governments, writing a novel based on their story, meeting journalists and scholars, and even writing academic articles themselves. Finally, the No Gun Ri massacre was reported by the Associated Press (AP) in 1999, and the AP's report was wired by major news outlets around the world.[6]

The process of how the incident became known to the public, and how it was reported, investigated, and remembered also shed light on how a society reacts to an uncomfortable incident. The US government used an extremely narrow interpretation of military documents and oral histories in its investigation and concluded that the event was an unfortunate wartime accident rather than a war crime. Although the South Korean government's investigative report received criticism, that government provided recognition of the incident and supported the community. In 2004, the Special Act on the Review and Restoration of Honor for the No Gun Ri Victims was enacted. In 2009, the No Gun Ri Peace Park and Museum was established based on this Act, and it has served as a memorial basecamp for diverse cultural activities. The No Gun Ri community has been the driving force for all of these activities.

For almost fifty years, No Gun Ri was hidden from public scrutiny. Accusing US soldiers who shed blood for the freedom of Korean people against communists was not in accordance with Korean ideology, especially during the Cold War. Korea had a suppressive and rigid political atmosphere under the pro-American and pro-military regimes from the 1960s to the 1980s, and anything or anyone opposing South Korea and its allies' ideology could be considered pro-communist. Under these circumstances, a massacre by US soldiers was not an event to be proud of or to be included in Korean War history. Like many similar incidents during the Korean War, No Gun Ri was not actively remembered, if not forcefully silenced. In fact, Korean War history has been faithfully written to support and justify the ideology of each Korea (South and North).[7] Killings and violent incidents made public were usually those perpetrated by North Korean troops and used as propaganda by the South Korean government. The black-and-white logic of Korean War history was the major historical representation until the research of revisionist historians. Those alternative eyes from the revisionist perspective, however, are still based on the mainstream framework to overcome the nationalist narrative (North Korea as the evil "other") and often ignore (or oppress) other identities and narratives.[8]

The tension between mainstream and marginalized narratives seems to occur in multiple levels beyond the overall history of the Korean War. Such tensions may appear among similar tragic incidents. Once No Gun Ri became known to people, many similar incidents that had been silenced were reported. Korea had a democratic government in the 1990s and 2000s, and the case of No Gun Ri seemed to give survivors of similar incidents motivation to speak up. However, these stories did not have the same resonance in society as did No Gun Ri. No Gun Ri became a representative incident for those tragedies that happened during the Korean War,[9] and it seemed to be the center of focus among other marginalized incidents.

Research on hegemonic relationships in creating collective memory are not new in archival and historical literature. Archivists have acknowledged that traditional approaches in collecting lack the capacity to include all groups of society.[10] Archival thoughts evolve with changes in historical research trends from what Flinn calls "grander and larger narratives" to "new democratized and inclusive historical narratives."[11] Some efforts to bring marginalized stories into the mainstream discourses have been made with these new archival perspectives. But Ieuan Hopkins challenges the idea that when formal archival institutions are engaged in active inclusion of community archives, communities will be expected to participate. Often based on the agenda of universal access and inclusion driven by archival authority, the mainstreaming process is expected to be well justified and easily accepted, but it may not be always true.[12] In the relationship between majority and minority, or center and periphery, the majority usually takes control to include the minority via the mainstream framework. However, community narratives may not necessarily fit within the domain episteme, and thus they become decontextualized and recontextualize.[13]

Socially vulnerable groups, including sexual minorities, often experience ignorant or hostile responses from state or official policies and directions. Queer groups may find that mainstream archives are not a safe place to entrust their history.[14] Archives for those communities require a high level of security and anonymity and thus demand careful approaches for archivists to document their history.[15] Likewise, for cases involving human rights abuses, it is important that the communities that are being documented are placed in the center for the archiving project. They should have control over decisions for the records and documenting processes, regardless of the nature of the archiving body.[16] Communities' own independent archives could serve better to safeguard the community's history and memory and to further represent their identity. Those community archives will develop their own policies based on the community's demands and dynamics. The archives then will be shaped by community members' own perceptions of how they see their identity and desires about how they want to be understood from the outside. K. J. Rawson argues that the archival practices for a particular community archives could be different from standard archival practices and may frustrate researchers. Such frustration, however, may be needed to understand the very characteristics or identity of the communities.[17]

Dominant-minor relationships in narratives are not uncommon even within the history of a marginalized group. In LGBT history, gay male history is studied more than lesbian activism or bisexual/transgender activism is.[18] Black gay experiences are rarely discussed in either the black community or the gay community. In such cases, archiving for an individual group's identity and history is that group's activism in response to discrimination and directly related to political and social movements.[19] Flinn argues that clear political agendas and perspectives are important for communities to challenge and correct the falsely represented narratives and identity and to overcome exclusion.[20] Archival activism comes into play as a strong tool for cultural democracy and an attempt to seize the means to write history.[21]

Oral history provides a unique affordance for a community to document its past. In oral history, informants are the source of history, as well as the historians who will decide what and how to tell. This way, they can hold both means and ends, and thus oral history could be a powerful tool for non-hegemonic groups who do not possess their own tools to capture the experiences in their own terms.[22] Writing has been the tool of the ruling classes, but oral history has been a necessary condition of socially marginalized groups.[23] Oral history may not deliver facts, but it does bring imagination, symbolism, and desire of interviewees: it is a different kind of credibility as a historical source. Those testimonies are psychologically "true" and can reveal more than factually accurate accounts.[24] Due to these characteristics, oral history is a vehicle to include the community's own context in defining their history and identity.

Oral History of No Gun Ri

The oral history of No Gun Ri presents diverse dimensions about the community's experiences. The director of the No Gun Ri Peace Park and Museum (hereafter, the Park), Koo-Do Chung, a son of survivors, facilitated the process of conducting oral history interviews. Mr. Chung and his father, the late Eun-Yong Chung, have been the most active members of the community, spending their entire lives researching and publicizing No Gun Ri. Mr. Chung is not a professionally trained historian, but he is an activist and historian in his community. He has researched and published articles about No Gun Ri's history, and his authority in the knowledge of No Gun Ri has been granted through his time and efforts. Mr. Chung offered suggestions to the research team regarding who to interview and arranged the time and location of the interviews. His suggestions included the most active members of the community.

The interviews were conducted from March to August 2016 with five survivors (whom we designated as Survivor 1, Survivor 2, and so on), one family member (Family 1), and two employees of the Park (Staff 1 and Staff 2). The interviews were not rigidly structured. We encouraged the interviewees to speak freely regarding memories of No Gun Ri and their lives.[25] As a result, interviewees approached the interview differently. Some shared personal reflections and insights, while others spoke as if participating in a typical media interview. One interviewee took the opportunity to educate the team about the incident. No matter how each interviewee approached the interview, each story was presented in great detail for various aspects of No Gun Ri and participants' lives.

We heard about individual experiences with the incident and participants' life journeys with No Gun Ri memories. Not only that, we heard accounts of internal and external social and political dynamics of the community and with the society, including the

Korean political climate, the community's responses to such a climate, how the community viewed the incident within the context of Korean society, and the internal dynamics in the process of building No Gun Ri's memory. Alessandro Portelli's argument that the narrators' desires and symbolism could be captured from oral history seems applicable to No Gun Ri.

The individual interviews included personal experiences in the course of the No Gun Ri massacre, such as stories of the evacuation process from villages and seeking refuge toward the South, American soldiers' escorts onto railroads and subsequent air attacks there, shooting at the overpass tunnels underneath railroads for four days, and escaping at night from the tunnels. Also, the interviews went on to include how their lives have been after the incident: the hardship and anguish they have carried over the years, an extended fear of the vicinity of No Gun Ri, life as a person with disabilities, and ways in which they shared their stories with loved ones. In addition to the memories directly related to their experiences, interviewees had comments on their speculations of why the massacre happened and their difficult efforts in telling their stories in a politically conservative society.

The political climate in Korea from the 1960s to the 1980s was very rigid, and the military regimes had no tolerance for anti-Americanism or pro-communism. Such an atmosphere created direct influences (and consequences) on how the community reacted to the massacre. An interviewee (Survivor 2) noted that he was summoned by the police several times because he spoke about No Gun Ri, and for such behavior he was considered a communist sympathizer. He also believed that if the AP reporters had been Korean journalists trying to report in Korea, No Gun Ri would never have been made public. Thus, the No Gun Ri movement was extremely difficult under those circumstances (Survivor 5 and Family 1). Survivor 2 and Family 1 talked about the difficulty by mentioning that in the beginning only five people participated in this movement, and the late Eun-Yong Chung was one of them. Two among the original five are now deceased, and the interviews included the three surviving members of that early group.[26] The rigid political climate was the reason survivors took a detour by writing novels (Survivor 5 and Family 1). The No Gun Ri stories could be heard only after the civilian government had been elected in the 1990s (Survivor 3).

The community tried all possible methods to inform the public about No Gun Ri. In this process, they contacted progressive or radical journalists and had them report on the incident because other mainstream and conservative media did not show any interest at all (Family 1). However, they wanted to make sure that No Gun Ri's history was not told from a leftist perspective nor that their movement was associated with anti-Americanism (Survivor 1 and Family 1). Under the circumstances of Korean politics, positioning their stories away from the sensitive political framework seemed the strategy of the community. A family member mentioned:

> We should know the characteristics of No Gun Ri correctly. Some people say or have a prejudice that No Gun Ri is an anti-America movement because we talk about the uncomfortable truths about the United States. I would strongly say this is not true. . . . No Gun Ri is all about human rights and dignity of life. No Gun Ri shouldn't be considered anti-America movement or anything political. (Family 1)

There is another method in which members of the community contextualized their stories in a broader setting. Although not directly prompted, all interviewees but one spoke about lessons that they wish people would learn from No Gun Ri. The community members seemed to hope that their pain and suffering were remembered along with universal values, rather than in the context of a war crime or in the perspective of politics. Perhaps it is their way of understanding their hardship and that they did not suffer in vain. The lessons mentioned are mostly ideology-neutral and about universal values, such as peace and human rights (Survivor 5, Family 1, and Staff 2), that there should be no more war (Survivors 1, 2, 3, and 5, and Family 1), and that one should never forget his or her past (Survivors 1 and 5). Even for politically sensitive matters, a participant tried to express thoughts in a neutral fashion—for example, "one should act upon what one believes," "all people should work together to build a strong country," and "it is important to know the United States correctly" (Survivor 1). The No Gun Ri Peace Park and Museum seem to play a major role in delivering such desires of the community to the outside society:

> The No Gun Ri community requested that the government name the No Gun Ri park "Peace Park" rather than "Historical Park." . . . It is

because we should teach our future generations and world citizens why there is no place for war on earth. (Family 1)

What I want visitors [of the Park] to learn is how the violence of wars ruined our lives, and thus we should make every possible effort to stop wars. (Staff 2)

Park staff members shed some insights into the fact that the No Gun Ri community contextualized their stories for the common good.

I believe a historical event should be interpreted within the context of the present. . . . But I think that the name, "Peace Park," represents something pretty soft. . . . It seems a paradox to represent a harsh event with a soft label. I think this paradox is the compromise of the reality. . . . No Gun Ri is a place of pain. There was a brutal incident here. I feel the gap between violence and peace is way too big and deep. . . . I feel emptiness when talking about "peace" amidst pain as a device for effacement and oblivion. (Staff 1)

Some visitors mentioned that they could feel the pain and their heart became heavy. And they might not be able to come back. I was a bit terrified that this place is just a place for pain and sorrow. . . . So I began to think about how the Park can provide an opportunity for visitors to think and practice human rights and peace in daily life. This would be why people come visit the Park with their family. . . . I want the Park to be a place where you want to go, not a place you want to avoid. (Staff 2)

There may be a gap between the context that the community sets for No Gun Ri and the actual content No Gun Ri delivers to the public as described by the staff members. It may be the wish of community members that their anguish be sublimated into high values of peace, so that people can find it easier to digest the incident. Community members may think that such a goal is their assignment in history. Perhaps, when the war crime-related tragedy is linked to the universal value of human rights, No Gun Ri stories can be smoothly transmitted to mainstream discourses.

Being discussed in mainstream history was important to the No Gun Ri community. Community members wanted to contextualize their stories away from the political framework but close to mainstream historical discourses. It seemed that they felt the long period of denial and suppression paid off when their efforts were evaluated positively by authoritative entities such as governments and mainstream historians:

> No Gun Ri now appears in high school history textbooks. This tells that No Gun Ri is such an important incident in Korean history. (Family 1)

> A renowned scholar in Korean history, Man-yeol Lee, describes No Gun Ri as a war on history between Korea and the U.S. I agree with him that the past 50 years were the battles between Korean victims and the U.S. government. (Family 1)

They also thought that their efforts had made possible the recognition of the first historical event for which the US government made a "statement of regret" and later conducted an official investigation (Family 1). Family 1 further hoped that No Gun Ri set a model for other similar incidents. As such, the ways that community members contextualize their stories promote assimilation into the mainstream discourses: avoiding the political framework as radical movements, bypassing direct discussions of a war crime and its consequences (compensation), connecting the universal values of human rights and peace, and being recognized by a major historical authority as well as the mainstream political authority. They may have found that such strategies work in the Korean political atmosphere to deliver their stories to the broader society.

Since the No Gun Ri massacre had been silenced for about fifty years, it appears that community members have tried all possible methods to bring their stories to public awareness. Thus, another effective strategy for them was telling impressive and touching episodes of their experiences. It does not seem odd that stories with compelling narratives often receive higher levels of attention and are more memorable to the public. After all, it is impossible to talk about a traumatic and violent event like No Gun Ri without emotional responses. In the interviews, some extremely heart-wrenching episodes were mentioned repeatedly. Sometimes participants spoke for others and vicariously relayed experiences. Those stories included the episodes of a wife who was shot in her side with a bullet that traveled through her and pierced the heart of her son, who was on her back (Survivors 3 and 5); of a girl who lost her eye from the air attack (Survivors 3 and 4); and of a baby who was killed by her own father out of fear that her crying would draw the attention of soldiers (Survivors 2 and 3). In fact, these episodes have been covered in published works in great detail, including journalistic reports, books, a movie (*A Little Pond*), and other sources.

> Eun-Yong Chung's wife, she was about 25 years old. They had two kids, Koo-pil and Koo-hee. Koo-hee was killed at the tunnels. The wife fled by night from the tunnels with her son on her back. . . . During the escape, she ran into American soldiers. She begged for mercy. . . . But she was shot. On her side. Her intestines came out. The bullet also went into the heart of the baby who was on her back. The baby died. (Survivor 3)

> She was 13 years old. Now she is 79. A girl. A 13-year-old girl. She was on media a lot about her lost eye. Poor girl she was. . . . she was so scared and she was looking for her mom. But her mom was already shot. The eye was hanging, but her mom said "I got shot. I can't help you. You take it off yourself." . . . So the girl took it off herself and she has lived with an artificial eye. (Survivor 3)

> Imagine how terrible it would be to drown your own baby in the stream. The father went crazy and going around in rage then got killed after all. There is a statue of a father and a baby in the Park. That was to show this story. (Survivor 2)

All efforts to publicize participants' stories were rewarded as what happened at No Gun Ri was finally reported around the world. Because most of the interviewees are community leaders and have been involved in the activities for the No Gun Ri movement, they could proudly describe how and what they contributed over the years leading up to that moment. Survivor 2 stated that, in his capacity as a member of the town council, he had tried to preserve the bullet marks in tunnels from being covered up by cement during repairs. Interviewees mentioned traveling to Seoul to lobby parliament representatives for the No Gun Ri Special Act (Survivors 2 and 3). Survivors 2 and 4 were proud to confront American officials at the Pentagon during the US investigation to finally speak of this atrocity. A few participants mentioned that whenever possible, they happily spend time sharing their stories with visitors at the Park (Survivors

1 and 3). An interviewee was proud of his published research and the fact that he had supplied materials and evidence to journalists, including the AP reporters (Family 1). These individuals explained the moments of feeling proud and rewarded. There were also accounts of the Chung family and their commitment and endeavors throughout the No Gun Ri history-building process (Survivors 1, 2, 3, and 5, and Family 1):

> His [Eun-Yong Chung] perseverance was amazing. I think it all came from his anguish that he lost his children there. He tried and failed and tried and failed. He wrote letters to the U.S. Presidents. He wrote letters to Korean Presidents. But he didn't get any responses. . . . He continued to do whatever he could do. He struggled so much. But he didn't give up. . . . He was like "I will reveal the story to Americans and to the World even though I sacrifice myself." (Survivor 5)

> I think Eun-Yong did put his entire life into this and came through something that even the Korean government wasn't able to do. No one could. (Survivor 1)

The Chung family, the late Eun-Yong Chung and his son Koo-Do Chung, had never-failing perseverance and dedicated themselves to revealing No Gun Ri to the world. The community expresses great admiration for what they have done. Koo-Do Chung left his job and helped his father in the No Gun Ri research and movement (Survivor 5). As mentioned earlier, the Chung family were the de facto community historians, and they collected and used personal records and other historical materials for their research. The community depended greatly on them for No Gun Ri research. When asked about personal records related to No Gun Ri, most of them said they did not have any. Perhaps because community members depended on the Chung family for all this work, they might have neglected such activities on their own. As a result, individuals' personal records, except for the Chung family's, were not actively preserved within the No Gun Ri community. The endeavors of the active members created the greatest resonance in Korea, but the consequences might have been losing the diverse accounts in the community.

No, I don't have any [personal records about No Gun Ri]. When the Park was established, they collected any records or artifacts from the survivors. I was the secretary of the Survivors' Organization at that time, and I sent letters to the members. The government was going to pay for the records and artifacts, but the members didn't bring any. (Survivor 3)

The whole village was burned. Nothing much left. . . . Those my parents had were all gone. I was young, and I didn't know what's important. (Survivor 1)

Not at all. There used to be something, small pictures, but nothing was left. All gone. (Survivor 5)

The community has supported and depended on the Chung family's knowledge and endeavors. Many in the community did not have an opportunity for a high level of education, nor did they live an affluent life after the massacre. Korea was devastated physically as well as economically by the Korean War, and the No Gun Ri community experienced an even greater degree of destruction. Thus, individual members of the community may have had limited time and resources for No Gun Ri activities. The community's historical authority was placed on the shoulders of the Chung family. Eun-Yong Chung was a former policeman, and the Chung family holds a moderately conservative political position. Having individuals who devoted their lives for No Gun Ri was effective and economical in the community, and naturally these active members' activities, perspectives, positions, and narratives may have been established as a way that the community represents itself to the broader society.

In current cultural heritage institutions, diversity and inclusion have become greatly valued. Ieuan Hopkins states that formal authorities use diversity to empower individuals and communities and often intend to mainstream diversity for this reason.[27] In the No Gun Ri case, interestingly, mainstreaming efforts for their stories originated internally. Those mainstreaming efforts were made by intentionally positioning the No Gun Ri stories away from the political framework (especially from being tied with a leftist/progressive perspective) and close to universal values, selectively focusing on what the community considers important and major episodes of the massacre and following the community's historians'/activists' guidance. Such approaches may have further created the mainstream narrative of No Gun Ri within the community. And for the same reason the community may have not been able to actively discover and safeguard other voices that may have existed because distributing limited resources and energy would not have been as effective in moving their stories forward into the mainstream discourses in the particular Korean atmosphere.

Conclusion: Lessons Learned

The No Gun Ri oral history provides an opportunity to understand the internal and external dynamics of the community in its storytelling. Korean society has created a unique atmosphere for the No Gun Ri community, and the community's approaches to telling stories are somewhat different from other cases reported in the archival literature. From the interviewees, we could learn the ways in which the community's leaders place the No Gun Ri stories in the broader context of social and historical frameworks. The oppressive political climate in Korea in the past might have led them to follow a safer route to publicize their stories—fitting in with the mainstream discourses of Korean War history. This approach by the active community members might have been accepted widely in the community and finally shaped the community's symbolism and desires. In this process, minor voices (maybe those that would not bring wider publicity, those that do not fit in the acceptable political spectrum, or those from the members who had no education and/or resources needed to speak up) might have been marginalized within the community. By analyzing the content of the interviews, the research team realized that this project was not prepared for such stories, nor did it offer space to promote other possible dimensions in various No Gun Ri stories. The team learned how community members present their collective identity but may have neglected what would have been further marginalized or vanished from mainstream storytelling.

The archival and historical literature already alerts researchers about the dominant-minor relationships in historical narratives and the power of the intervention of archival authorities to represent a community's memories. Not only was the research team unable to perform its research to be intentionally inclusive for any minor accounts, but the whole process of the oral history project was conducted with major input from active community members.

The No Gun Ri Peace Park and Museum and the community historians, the Chung family, were extremely supportive throughout the research process, such as collecting archival materials to digitize, recruiting interviewees for oral history, and providing a comfortable work environment at the Park. The convenience and assistance that the team enjoyed motivated the team members and expedited the research process. Such supports contributed to the groundwork for the research, and therefore, the project was perhaps contextualized within the community's main framework.

Portelli argues that "the control of the historical discourse remains firmly in the hands of the historian: it is the historian who selects the people who are to speak; who asks the questions and thus contributes to the shaping of the testimony; who gives the testimony its final published form."[28] In this oral history project, the research team was not able to serve as an objective and independent historian in its research. In fact, the No Gun Ri research was conducted within the mainstream schema built by the active community members. Within a certain framework, it is difficult that archival documentation offers space to collect and preserve diverse stories inclusively and from outside the framework. For the No Gun Ri memory, the community and the No Gun Ri Peace Park do not provide room for such other stories, nor does the No Gun Ri Digital Archives project. Perhaps, some remedial approaches can be attempted. Even if the No Gun Ri oral history failed to document other possible accounts, its presentation could include the context of how the No Gun Ri narratives had been shaped and how and why other stories had not been actively preserved. In this way, users would be made aware of some possibility of hidden stories and that the particular representation of the No Gun Ri memory is what the community had selected to present as their stories.

If we could go back and collect the oral history for the No Gun Ri Digital Archives again, should we do it differently? How? The No Gun Ri community's efforts for their stories to be included in the mainstream Korean War history appeared to be their strategy to be recognized and obtain wider publicity in Korean society. That being said, within this community, minor voices might not have been honored intentionally. Due to the long history of being silenced, it was critical for the community to get the word out about the massacre, and thus community members might have felt that they could sacrifice other minor narratives. Although this could be just our speculation based on what we observed from the oral history, some questions here might be still relevant. Do archivists have a place in collecting and preserving inclusively even when archival documentation may not serve (or perhaps may be opposed to) the community's (or the active community members') intents? Archival scholars have argued that it is important for the community to have control over the archival decisions, and archivists should be careful about missteps into the community's memory and identity. Where is the balance in documenting inclusively for all voices of a community without crossing the line beyond what community members wish to present? If there are stronger voices and weaker voices in a community, is it archivists' responsibility to reach out to weaker voices? Would this not be the power intervention with archival authority to the community's memory and identity?

Notes

[1] Andrew Flinn, "Archival Activism: Independent and Community-led Archives, Radical Public History and the Heritage Professions," *InterActions: UCLA Journal of Education and Information Studies* 7, no. 2 (2011), https://escholarship.org/uc/item/9pt2490x.

[2] Diana K. Wakimoto, Christine Bruce, and Helen Partridge, "Archivist as Activist: Lessons from Three Queer Community Archives in California," *Archival Science* 13, no. 4 (2013): 297.

[3] John Erde, "Constructing Archives of the Occupy Movement," *Archives and Records* 35, no. 2 (2014): 77–92; Andrew Flinn, "Community Histories, Community Archives: Some Opportunities and Challenges," *Journal of the Society of Archivists* 28, no. 2 (2007): 151–176; Ieuan Hopkins, "Places from Which to Speak," *Journal of the Society of Archivists* 29, no. 1 (2008): 83–109; Sue McKemmish, Shannon Faulkhead, and Lynette Russell, "Distrust in the Archive: Reconciling Records," *Archival Science* 11, no. 3–4 (2011): 211–239; Mary Stevens, Andrew Flinn, and Elizabeth Shepherd, "New Frameworks for Community Engagement in the Archive Sector: From Handing Over to Handing On," *International Journal of Heritage Studies* 16, no. 1–2 (2010): 59–76.

[4] The No Gun Ri materials are physically located in the No Gun Ri Peace Park and Museum (No Gun Ri, South Korea). Our project team arranged and described the materials in the process of creating the Digital Archives and shared some basic archival practices and tools with the staff to use in their future archival management.

⁵ Alessandro Portelli states that oral history is a marginal source when comparing standard historical resources. Alessandro Portelli, "The Peculiarities of Oral History," *History Workshop Journal* 12, no. 1 (1981): 99.

⁶ Sang-Hun Choe, Charles J. Hanley, and Martha Mendoza, "GI's Tell of a US Massacre in Korean War," Associated Press, September 29, 1999.

⁷ Roland Bleiker and Young-Ju Hoang, "Remembering and Forgetting the Korean War: From Trauma to Reconciliation," in *Memory, Trauma and World Politics: Reflections on the Relationship Between Past and Present,* ed. Duncan Bell (London: Palgrave Macmillan, 2006), 195–212.

⁸ Henry H. Em, "Overcoming Korea's Division: Narrative Strategies in Recent South Korean Historiography," *Positions* 1 (1993): 450–485; Bleiker and Hoang, "Remembering and Forgetting."

⁹ Chan-Ho Eom, "For the Massacre of Civilians in the Korean War, Anger and Healing," *Human Sciences Research* 36 (2013): 585–607.

¹⁰ Flinn, "Community Histories, Community Archives"; Flinn, "Archival Activism"; Taylor R. Genovese, "Decolonizing Archival Methodology: Combating Hegemony and Moving Towards a Collaborative Archival Environment," *AlterNative: An International Journal of Indigenous Peoples* 12, no. 1 (2016): 32–42.

¹¹ Flinn, "Archival Activism."

¹² Hopkins, "Places from Which to Speak."

¹³ Hopkins, "Places from Which to Speak," 91–92; Anna Katharine Sexton, "Archival Activism and Mental Health: Being Participatory, Sharing Control and Building Legitimacy," PhD diss. (University College London, 2016), 68.

¹⁴ Riikka Taavetti, "A Marshall in Love: Remembering and Forgetting Queer Pasts in the Finnish Archives," *Archival Science* 16, no. 3 (2016): 294.

¹⁵ Taavetti, "A Marshall in Love," 294–295.

¹⁶ Michelle Caswell, "Toward a Survivor-Centered Approach to Records Documenting Human Rights Abuse: Lessons from Community Archives," *Archival Science* 14, no. 3–4 (2014): 308.

¹⁷ K. J. Rawson, "Accessing Transgender/Desiring Queer (er?) Archival Logics," *Archivaria* 68 (2010): 123–140.

¹⁸ Taavetti, "A Marshall in Love," 289–307.

¹⁹ Caswell, "Toward a Survivor-Centered Approach"; Andrew Flinn and Mary Stevens, "'It Is Nohmistri, Wimekin History.' Telling Our Own Story: Independent and Community Archives in the UK, Challenging and Subverting the Mainstream," in *Community Archives: The Shaping of Memory,* ed. Jeannette Bastian and Ben Alexander (London: Facet, 2009), 3–27; Andrew Flinn, Mary Stevens, and Elizabeth Shepherd, "Whose Memories, Whose Archives? Independent Community Archives, Autonomy and the Mainstream," *Archival Science* 9, no. 1–2 (2009): 71–86; Wakimoto, Buce, and Partridge, "Archivist as Activist."

²⁰ Flinn, "Archival Activism."

[21] Flinn, Stevens, and Shepherd, "Whose Memories, Whose Archives?," 71–86; Caswell, "Toward a Survivor-Centered Approach," 314.

[22] Alessandro Portelli, "The Peculiarities of Oral History," *History Workshop Journal* 12, no. 1 (1981): 105; Horacio R. Ramirez, "A Living Archive of Desire," in *Archive Stories: Facts, Fictions, and the Writing of History*, ed. Antoinette Burton (Durham, NC: Duke University Press, 2006): 124; Kyoko Aoki, *A Community of Narratives: Contextualizing the Archives Through Oral History*. PhD diss. (University of California, Los Angeles, 2012).

[23] Portelli, "Peculiarities of Oral History," 104. For this reason, the earlier initiatives to preserve the archives of working-class communities in the 1960s to the 1980s are associated with oral history movements. Flinn, "Community Histories, Community Archives," 153.

[24] Portelli, "Peculiarities of Oral History," 101.

[25] The interviews were conducted in Korean. The author translated the testimonies in English for this essay. The translation was done word for word as much as possible, but there are some places where expressions had to be interpreted due to the lack of words or expressions in English. Thus, there may be some gap between original Korean testimonies and English translations.

[26] Among the three surviving members, one passed away in September 2017. Thus, his testimony with us was his last interview.

[27] Hopkins, "Places from Which to Speak," 84.

[28] Portelli, "Peculiarities of Oral History," 105.

11

Makerspaces as Archives/ Archives as Makerspaces

Making and the Materiality of Archival Practice

Lindsay Kistler Mattock

Introduction

Makerspaces have come to be associated with public libraries, primary and secondary schools, colleges, and universities. They are places designed to spark creativity and innovation, sites where people come together to build, hack, tinker, invent, prototype, and create. In *The Makers Movement Manifesto,* Mark Hatch suggests that these activities are central to the human condition, arguing that "we must make, create, and express ourselves to feel whole."[1] In these spaces, makers do not simply read or learn about technology but, instead, think through and with the tools and materials used to create their own artifacts. Makerspaces flip the role of consumer and producer, reclaiming and demystifying the manufactured technologies that have become commonplace in our everyday lives. These are not just sites of creative practice but of critical making, a praxis that emphasizes material engagement and experiential learning through the iterative development of prototypes and artifacts. According to Matt Ratto, the focus is on the "act of making," the social and material aspects of the process of production, not simply the end product.[2]

Archives, too, are sites of making. They are made and constructed before being enfolded into the collections in institutional archives and then remade according to archival praxis. However, unlike makerspaces, archives fail to engage with the materiality of the records that constitute these collections. Framed as information artifacts, the material properties of archives are brought into focus during the functions of preservation and conservation but are otherwise considered secondary to the informational content inscribed onto these material forms. In this essay I explore making as a theoretical construct that can bring to light the significance of the materiality of archival collections. Using the archives of media collective and makerspace Paper Tiger Television, I will explore the material biases of archival praxis and propose a critical lens for the examination of the way that archival collections are arranged, described, and accessed.

Making and Materials

Many theories of making emphasize the social aspects of the process of making and the development of social bonds between makers. For example, media theorist David Gauntlett has used the concept of craft to explore the development of cultures of making from knitting groups to those building social spaces with Web 2.0 technologies such as WordPress, YouTube, and Flickr. Although he acknowledges making as an act of connecting "things," his focus is on the social interactions of makers: "Making things shows us that we are powerful, creative agents—people who can really *do* things, things that other people can see, learn from, and enjoy."[3] Gauntlett's conceptualization aligns closely with the discourse of participatory cultures that center on the collaboration afforded by online environments and social media technologies.[4] These theories of making are often rooted in the origins of the web, tracing the history of contemporary social media technologies through the first Bulletin Board Systems (BBS) to emerge on the budding web.[5]

Others have foregrounded the do-it-yourself or DIY movement that manifested from the counterculture movements of the 1960s. In this discourse, making is understood as a mode of empowerment, destabilization, and resistance. Matt Ratto and Megan Boler describe making as a "'critical activity' . . . that provides both the possibility to intervene substantively in systems of authority and power and that offers an important site for reflecting on how such power is constituted by infrastructures, institutions, and practices."[6] Practices as diverse as zine publishing, textile design, and guerrilla radio become sites for consumers of mass media and culture to become producers that generate new narratives. Making is a democratizing process and an inclusive practice that understands the creation of tools and objects as a means for empowering communities and sharing knowledge.[7]

Both bodies of literature foreground making as an overtly political act. While the social and material are brought into conversation, the social connections between humans are foregrounded. Paper Tiger Television's practices as a media collective could easily be framed through these theories of making. The collective's work through video and access cable channels is a purposeful choice that subverts mainstream commercial television and demonstrates to those consuming their media that they too can make media and tell their own stories. As a media collective, Paper Tiger Television is a community of makers, a group of individuals brought together through the act of making mediated through a particular technological context. But, in the collective's archives, we are left with the material. The records, media, and other artifacts of the archive are the residue of these practices. To understand the significance of the archive, we need a theory that attends to the interaction of the social and the material.

Building on other object- and material-centered theories, anthropologist Tim Ingold outlines a theory of making that accounts for both human and material, entangling technology, materiality, and human culture and society. The methodologies for studying material culture developed in the fields of anthropology, architecture, and art are reductive, Ingold argues, limiting the understanding of the influence of the materials in the process of making and reducing the artifacts that are studied to mere objects. The same is true of the process of making. Ingold observes that making is also reduced to an object, a *project*. Projects begin with ideation and raw materials to become artifacts. The raw materials may represent choices in the design process but are not actors in the process of creation. The resulting artifact is a static object in a completed state that can now be understood and studied as material culture.[8] Ingold's theory brings materials into correspondence with human and nonhuman actors that participate in the initial creation and continual use of artifacts, recognizing the influence of materials and matter in the human processes of making.

His analogy to architecture is perhaps the most apt for the comparison to archives. An "instance of architecture" is the understanding of a building as an actualization of a design, an object. An "ideal case" once finished, Ingold suggests, "should hold for all eternity to the form the architect intended for it."[9] But buildings are not static. They are part of the world we inhabit and, as part of this world, are continually affected by the passage of time, "of growth, decay, and regeneration, regardless of the most concerted of human attempts to nail it down, or to cast it in fixed and final forms."[10] The materials that make up the building, the humans that reside within, the infrastructures that support upkeep of the structure, and the environment surrounding it, are all part of the making of this artifact. The process of making does not begin and end with the initial construction of the building but continues into the past and future. Ingold argues that buildings, works of art, and artifacts from human cultures long past are not static; instead, they are forever changing and growing, becoming entangled and enmeshed in correspondence with one another and the human actors that encounter them. Making can be understood as a knot in an expanding meshwork of relationships between material, immaterial, and human. These knots are places where actors are not "joined up" but "joined with," acting in tandem to take the form of an artifact.[11] Ingold's knots take into account these dynamic relationships and the influence of materials in the creation of human artifacts.

Ingold's observations on the archaeological record provide insight into how this theory of making may be carried through to archival theory:

> For an entity of any kind to become part of the archaeological record, it must hold fast to a point of origin, receding ever further from the horizon of the present as the rest of the world moves on. Conversely, things that carry on, that undergo continuous generation or, in a word, that *grow* cannot be part of the record.[12]

Archival praxis, too, attempts to flatten archival records into these static objects, brought to the archives at the end of their life cycle; boxed, categorized, and preserved in controlled environments; and bound by the principles of provenance and original order. The past and future of archival materials are not acknowledged; archives are instead bound in time and space, reduced to mere objects of study on the shelf.

Media Myopia

The *creation* of records has played a central role in archival theory, but *making*—as a continual engagement with the materials of record creation—has not. In *Understanding Archives & Manuscripts,* James O'Toole and Richard Cox suggest that "successful understanding of the task [of archivists] rests on several fundamental things: the reasons for recording information . . .; the reasons for saving it . . .; the reasons for *not* saving it; the technology that supports records creation; and the characteristics and uses of recorded information."[13] Here, the rationale for records creation is emphasized rather than the material conditions under which records are created. The relationship of the record to recordmaking technology is, however, addressed. The authors reflect that it is the very shift from oral to written culture that predicated the need for archives. As societies began to inscribe information in fixed and tangible forms, these materials could be stored and reused to retrieve information. Archives are predicated on this cycle of creation and reuse of the resulting records. But archives here are conceptualized as sites for the preservation of "recorded information," with an emphasis on *information.* A record is similarly defined in relation to its written or inscribed content, having "fixed content, structure, and context."[14] Although *structure* refers to the physical form, it also relates to the intellectual organization of the information encoded in the record, not necessarily the materiality of the records. These physical properties are most commonly associated with artifactual, intrinsic, or symbolic value.

The artifactual value of a record extends from its symbolic value. This value does not derive from the material qualities of the object but from the material existence of the record and its symbolic function in culture. What O'Toole calls "impractical" reasons[15] for preserving the archival record emphasize the cultural value of the records, while the evidential value of the information contained within the record provides its archival value. Interestingly, arguments for the relevance of the materiality of archival records have been framed as a gap in archival knowledge.

In her discussion of nontextual materials, Joan Schwartz argues that archival praxis, specifically descriptive practices, have marginalized photographic records within repositories, blaming a "visual illiteracy" across the field.[16] She suggests the close material analysis of records offered through the practice of diplomatics as one way in which archivists can develop these interpretative skills: "By shifting attention away from the content of the photograph and focusing it on the functional context of document creation, diplomatics has the potential to shed new light on both informational and evidential value."[17] Archival scholar Ala Rekut mirrors Schwartz, arguing for a greater material literacy among archival practitioners, or the "ability to understand and interpret how meaning can be manifested in materials."[18] Offering a close reading of text-based documentation in archival collections, Rekut highlights the material properties of records that provide insight into the functional context of creation and use. Elsewhere, scholars have similarly argued for a more nuanced analysis of the material and aesthetic aspects of archival records, adding that, besides the format of records, the qualities of color and smell may also relay important information about the creation and use of the record and hold value for scholars.[19]

Each of these authors built their arguments through a material analysis of individual records, suggesting that the archival value of these records is not limited to the informational value of the message encoded in the form of image or text and that the material properties of records too contain information and are part of this message. Although these close readings elucidate the evidential value of various media in the archives through providing a detailed analysis of the material, social, and cultural context in which they were produced, these arguments become restricted to the analysis of specific documents rather than the archives in aggregate, contradicting standards of archival praxis. However, this close reading is necessary to bring to light the significant contextual information provided by an inclusion of the materiality of archival records in archival theory. Curator Steven Lubar emphasizes the entanglement of these individual records within the larger context of the archives, suggesting that these objects are "interactive." Mirroring Ingold's meshwork, Lubar suggests that "to understand them, we must consider their webs of interrelationships with other objects, with archives and printed materials, and with people."[20] It is the material practices of making that are illustrated here: the original making of the record as well as the remaking of the materials through their enfolding into institutional archives.

Decades before these material critiques of archival praxis, Canadian archivist Hugh Taylor reflected on the biases inherent in archival theory, arguing, "we have taken our records very much for granted while we have respected and sought to preserve their physical nature, we have regarded them simply as the neutral 'carriers' of messages or pieces of information, despite the fact that the nature of each medium does shape administrative systems."[21] Influenced by media theorist Marshall McLuhan, Taylor embraced the full "media of record" and a broader representation of the documentary record beyond text- and paper-based materials to include time-based media and representational forms of documentary art.[22] Taylor adopted McLuhan's mantra "the medium is the message" to suggest that information carriers supplemented critical contextual information regarding how records creators used different media to express their message. His perspective unified information and artifact, acknowledging this "interplay between the medium and the receiver . . . over and above the content of the message."[23] While the McLuhanian approach acknowledges the significance of representational forms apart from text-based records, these media are understood as "extensions of the human body"[24] rather than active agents, as in Ingold's theory.

McLuhan and contemporaries Walter Ong and Harold Innis were popular among archival scholars adopting the "total archives" approach. In 1979, Terry Cook sparked a debate in the pages of *Archivaria* with his critique of the administration of total archives in the Public Archives of Canada. Although the organization was collecting a broad representation of archives and manuscripts in a variety of media formats, the organization had divided the administration of the collections by media type. He argued that this artificial segregation of media "created a de facto fragmentation of the archival whole, as defined by the principle of provenance."[25] Maps, photographs, and other media were being separated from the associated text-based documentation or collected separately as representative of the history of the media. The rationale was that these different media formats required distinct preservation and conservation treatments and were thus placed within the custody of the archival professionals with expertise in these areas, a rationale that Schwartz would later argue continues to perpetuate the marginalization of such media. Cook concluded that it is only though the adherence to the principle of provenance that archivists maintain the integrity of archival collections, preserving the records as a complete archive and thus the context in which the various media had been created.

Archivists countering Cook's argument upheld the logocentric origins of the archival profession, observing that few archival collections contain nontextual media and that most "traditional historians" were trained to work with textual records. Those supporting the Archive's practices defended the intellectual division of collections among separate archival units and in the intellectual arrangement of finding aids as a useful practice for researchers who would otherwise find the extensive finding aids "unwieldy."[26]

However, Cook's supporters, notably audiovisual archivists, observed that these divisions lead to silos in archival practice that only serve to uphold the artificial distinctions between media formats.[27] In this scheme, they asserted, nontextual records become "supplementary," "stranded in a sort of archival limbo," serving the needs of specialized researchers and archivists rather than embracing the total archives.[28] Like Cook, they acknowledged that the only benefit to this practice was in the conservation of records, where the physical properties of the records necessitate specialized treatment.

Cook's argument was provenance-based: "it is the essence of the record and the context of its creation by the original agency, rather than the medium in which it is cast, that must remain paramount to the archivist."[29] Cook recognized that records creators make records in multiple media for different purposes and that uniting these materials in the archives under the principle of provenance preserves the archival value of the collections. While now decades old, this debate is significant, as it acknowledges the biases inherent in archival practice as they relate to the media of the record. In contrast to the item-level analysis of particular artifacts of Schwartz and Rekut, Cook argued that records of all media formats can be united under the fundamental principles of archival practice: provenance and original order. This does not suggest that the materiality of the archival record should be disregarded, instead, the interrelationship of these media should be preserved, acknowledging the way in which the materials work together to make the archives. The application of the founding archival principles is an engagement with the materiality of the record, not simply an intellectual exercise.

Emerging from Jenkinsonian ideals of the archives as unaltered accumulations of records transferred from the records creator into the custody of the archives, original order preserves archival context through maintaining the aggregations of records as they were generated and used by the creator. Nontextual records can seem to defy an original order as they are not often stored in file drawers alongside the text-based records created by the same individuals and organizations. While the principle of provenance unifies all media generated by a records creator into a single archive, original order acknowledges the internal relationships between the records to preserve their context and archival value. Although Taylor advocated for the unification of all media, he fell victim to the text-based origins of the field. Seeking commonalities between the linear organization of text-based records and nontextual media, he posited that audiovisual media possess an internal original order—sound film, for example, captures time at twenty-four frames per second.[30] Taylor failed to recognize the limitations of original order as conceived as the physical arrangement of text-based materials in paper-based organizational systems.

Embracing a materials-focused analysis, one can easily see the ways in which technologies of writing have shaped archival praxis. Informatics scholars Paul Dourish and Melissa Mazmanian observe that unlike information in oral societies, text is associated with "the emergence of properties such as persistence and durability" that bring "expectations of authenticity, accuracy, and legitimacy."[31] Archival praxis has been founded on these attributes of text. Further, they argue, "our ingrained assumption that historical and natural processes are, in fact, stable and linear, emerges from the technologies of written language."[32] Ingold's theory of making defies this linear logic imposed by text. The meshwork is nonlinear and nonhierarchical. The example that follows demonstrates how an archival praxis grounded in Ingold's concept of making can embrace the totality of the archival record, accounting for records of all media, from text to audiovisual, and analog to digital.

Makerspaces as Archives

Members of the nonprofit video collective Paper Tiger Television, which was founded in 1981, produce and distribute media through nontraditional media outlets, working in opposition to mainstream media corporations. The collective's members believe "that increasing public awareness of the negative influence of mass media and involving people in the process of making media is mandatory for our long-term goal of information equity."[33] Like contemporary makerspaces, making is at the center of Paper Tiger's mission. Members of the collective aim to create media that empowers its viewers to think critically about the media they consume and to make media of their own. Founder DeeDee Halleck explains that many early public cable access shows mimicked the aesthetic of commercial broadcasts, emulating news broadcasts or chat-show style interviews. Paper Tiger broke this mold, creating colorful handmade sets and props and allowing for other "transgressions" to be broadcast (e.g., sound cues and camera shots of the crew)—"cartoony backdrops, hand-held graphics, and the handmade feel are designed to inspire viewers to believe that they can make media too."[34] The DIY aesthetics serve as Brechtian means of breaking down the "fourth wall" and creating a space for viewers to think more critically about the production of media, while aiming to empower viewers to capture and distribute their own stories through the tools of video production.

Over the past three decades, members of the collective have included a rotating cast of video artists who produce shows challenging and critiquing commercial media outlets by creating programming focused on specific social issues and communities that may not otherwise be represented in the mainstream media. Programs are produced and distributed collectively, emphasizing Paper Tiger's nonhierarchical organizational structure, counter to the corporate hierarchies driving commercial media production. Paper Tiger Television is broadcast on local cable access stations in Manhattan and screened in community spaces and is available on the web. Throughout its history, members have also produced hands-on technology workshops, providing access to video technology to members of the community.

The Paper Tiger Archive thus reflects a statement on an early version of their website that, "the work of many prominent media scholars, activists, cultural critics, and artists, . . . but also that of activists from social justice movements whose struggle might otherwise have gone undocumented."[35] Members of the collective acknowledge their work as part of the larger history of public access television, video art, media advocacy, visual literacy education, and video activism and have thus maintained an active record of the organization and its productions since its founding in 1981. While the organization has not employed an archivist, its records demonstrate evidence of many efforts to preserve and catalog the growing collection of materials in the collective's Manhattan office.

The primary focus of the development of the Paper Tiger Archive, within the collective, is the preservation of the historical video productions created by members of the collective and productions that they continue to make; however, the extent of the textual records and artifacts from the history of the collective is evidence of the care that the organization has taken to maintain a comprehensive archive documenting the organization's activities since its founding. Before the collective had a permanent office, such papers and videos were cared for by individual members, including founder DeeDee Halleck.[36] The papers in the collection document the organizational meetings, grants, promotional flyers, publications, and other documents that are associated with the operations of the collective as an organization and the production of the collective's extensive media catalog.

In addition to these traditional archival materials, multiple generations of the videotapes documenting the collective's productions are preserved and cataloged in Paper Tiger's offices, from U-matic masters created in the 1980s to the digital formats used by the most recent collective members. The use of video is an active choice made by collective members, representing their decision to work within the boundaries of independent video production and Public Access Television. In addition, each successive generation of copied tapes in the archive reflects the successive changes in the technologies used by the archive and can serve as traces of the preservation and reuse of these works over time.

The materiality of the videotapes has been a particular concern for the collective's members throughout its history. As they adopt each new generation of production technology following changes in the standards for broadcasting and distributing their work, collective members must either migrate older material to new formats or continue to preserve the obsolete technology necessary to access the materials. The responsibility of cleaning, copying, and cataloging the videotapes falls to volunteers who are willing to sacrifice time for developing current productions to preserve those in the archive. Further, unlike paper materials, videotape must be preserved at temperatures well below room temperature to ensure continued preservation. Members recognize the lack of environmental controls in their offices that would prolong the life of the tapes and note the condition of the materials throughout the archive.[37] Throughout the 1990s, the collective's members raised funds to support in-house preservation activities, reviewed the growing body of preservation literature, contacted vendors about reformatting, and sought additional funding mechanisms to support the preservation of the growing videotape library.[38]

Figure 1. Paper Tiger Television Offices, September 2013. Photo by Lindsay Kistler Mattock.

In the custody of the collective, the materials in the archive were continually made and remade. Housed in the material space of the collective's offices, the original order reflected this material reality. Entangled in the collective's inner workings, members were responsible for the creation of new records and materials, but the archive also acted on the collective, shaping their engagement with video production and preservation. In this iteration, the archive is not a static object but a growing artifact always in the process of becoming. The nonlinear and nonhierarchical structure of the records, which were disbursed across the Paper Tiger office space, was representative of the nonhierarchical organizational structure of the collective itself. In this space, it is difficult to untangle the materials from the collective members, the human from the nonhuman. This archive thus represents how it was made.

With the growing concern for Manhattan offices' environmental conditions (see Figure 1), which were clearly unsuited for the videotapes in the archive, Paper Tiger donated the entire archive to New York University's Fales Library and Special Collections in 2010. At this point in time, the archive included the videotape masters from more than 200 Paper Tiger Television productions, as well as the collective's administrative records, publicity materials, photographs, props, and other production elements from Paper Tiger programs. The collection encompasses 60 linear feet of materials reflecting almost three decades of the Paper Tiger's history.[39] In this transfer of custody, the archive was remade, reflecting the material conditions of archival praxis rather than those of the collective.

Archives as Makerspaces

According to the finding aid, the Paper Tiger Archive was first processed in 2012.[40] The archive is arranged into ten different series, divided topically as well as by media type. The organization's posters and maps, photographs, video, digital media, and props each belong to a separate record series. The finding aid privileges the physical ordering and separation of materials within the institutional archive rather than an intellectual arrangement of the collection that would preserve the relationship between videotapes, associated administrative paperwork, production materials, props, and photographs.

Rehoused in acid-free Hollinger boxes and buffered file folders, the collection has been unmoored from the collective's filing cabinets, desk drawers, and shelves and carefully separated into numbered folders, each titled and dated to reflect the contents. Some folders show signs of minimal processing, containing multiple copies of the same document and blank sheets of notebook paper, while others appear to be artifacts of archival intervention, labeled and dated with the headings "Correspondence" and "Clippings." To guide the archival user through the dense collection of papers, several series are further divided into subseries following the standards of archival representation. For example, Series II, "Activities," is divided into four subseries—Programming, Exhibits and Installations, Workshops and Conferences, and Film Festivals and Screenings—clearly separating and segregating the paper materials corresponding to these activities within the collection. This seemingly benign classification simplifies the activities of the organization, suggesting no overlap between these four distinct categories. Further, the videotape materials, posters, photographs, and production artifacts are described elsewhere on the finding aid in separate series, intellectually separated from the related text-based materials in the archive.

Although the archive is maintained as a unified whole with the institutional archives, the actions of the archives in processing, preserving, and providing access to this collection have bifurcated the collection, emphasizing the distinctions across the record types rather than preserving the context of the records by maintaining the relationships between records, falling prey to the same biases that Terry Cook cautioned against in his critique of the practices at the Public Archives of Canada some decades before.

The relationship between the materials no longer reflects the original order but a re-ordering of the materials. These new arrangements are artifacts not of the original making of the archive by the collective but the remaking by the archivists. The Paper Tiger Archive now reflects the materiality of the archives and archival praxis. This new configuration is a reflection not of the original creation and use by the collective's members but that of the imagined new users of the materials seeking to easily navigate the breadth of the collection and find the records relevant to their research questions.

It is impossible and impractical for Fales Library and Special Collections to re-create the offices of Paper Tiger to reflect the original order and use of the collection. It can also be argued that the rearrangement and rehousing of the materials, along with the physical separation of materials of different media types, is necessary to ensure the continued preservation of the materials in the archives—one of the original aims of the donation. However, instead of mirroring the physical separation of materials in the archives, the finding aid could reflect the interrelationship between the materials by representing a different intellectual arrangement. As Terry Cook argued in the

1979 *Archivaria* debate referenced earlier, it is the preservation of
these relationships between records of all media types that gives the
collection its context and preserves the archival bond—the provenance
and original order. The inner workings of the collective cannot be
reduced to a linear process, so why do archival finding aids take this
linear form?

Ricardo Punzalan suggests a framework for distributed archival
collections that exemplifies ways in which archivists can begin to
respect the material realities of the collections in their custody.[41]
Reflecting on the reproducibility of photographic materials and the
social and cultural conditions under which they circulate, Punzalan
acknowledges the dispersion of multiple copies of photographic
materials across archival collections. Accounting for the temporal,
geographic, provenancial, and material dimensions of photographic
materials, his framework suggests a "better understanding of the
myriad layers of relationships between the scattered photographs
over space, time, formats, and entities."[42] Mirroring Ingold,
Punzalan's reconceptualization of the photographic archive affords a
comprehensive understanding not of a photograph as a singular artifact
but as an entanglement of the broader social, cultural, technical, and
material conditions of the photographs' creation as well as those that
continue to shape the way that these images circulate in archival
collections. Advocating for collaboration between institutions and
the establishment of linkages across collections, Punzalan illustrates
the ways in which archival institutions could reunify collections to
provide a more robust understanding of the way in which the records
were created, circulated, and continue to be used and studied.

While Punzalan's study is limited to a singular media type, he
signals the need to re-situate archival praxis within the material realities
of the media preserved in collections. Further, he demonstrates that
archives extend far beyond the boundaries of the artificial collections
housed in archives. In the custody of the collective, the Paper Tiger
Archive was a living artifact. However, within the archives, the
collection has been reduced to a static object, much like Ingold's
architecture example. The archive as remade within the context of
the institutional archives fails to acknowledge the interrelationship
between records, instead bounding the materials to record series
artificially segregated by media type and perceived function.

Paper Tiger's productions, like the photographs in Punzalan's study, exist in multiple copies, in personal collections, the stores of video distribution centers, the collections of museums and community centers, and in digital form on platforms such as YouTube and Vimeo, yet these materials were not included in the archive nor were they represented on the finding aid. Archival praxis has privileged the original master videotapes, while these copies continue to be managed by the collective. Ingold would argue that each successive generation produced as part of the collective's preservation activities are part of the materiality of the original. These copies are entangled in the history of the collective's preservation efforts and tied to the activities of the collective.

The Paper Tiger Archive is a dense collection comprising multiple formats that reflect the practices of the organization. Each record or aggregation of records represents a knot in the meshwork, the material conditions of the archive shaping the way that it was made, used, and reused. While the preservation of the materials at Fales Library and Special Collections have ensured that a piece of the Paper Tiger Archive will be preserved for the long term, archival praxis has re-made this collection, reducing it to a static artifact, a singular object of study, that fails to acknowledge the complex interrelationship of the records to the people, processes, and materials from which they were made. It is both the material and informational context of these records that link these collections and connect the collective to the larger technological and social histories that give the Paper Tiger Archive its historical significance. All archival collections belong to this larger meshwork of the documentary universe. Each document is connected—internally connected to the archive through the principle of provenance and externally connected through the way that the archive was made, reflecting these larger cultural, social, and technological influences.

Conclusion

Ingold's theory of making unveils new ways of looking at archives and the material influences on archival praxis, revealing material biases that are rooted in the textual origins of the archival field. As new media have been enfolded into the archive, archival praxis has stubbornly persisted in utilizing processing methods and representational tools grounded in a particular material logic. As the complexities of the Paper Tiger Archive have demonstrated, multimedia collections challenge these practices and afford new opportunities to rethink our tools. Digital finding aids and database software can be used to generate hyperlinks between records series described in archival finding aids and to even generate links to the content external to the institutional archives, such as the video continually managed on Paper Tiger's website and self-curated digital archive. But, the Paper Tiger finding aid reveals another blind spot of archival praxis. In the far reaches of the Paper Tiger materials, the access conditions for single series warns that "materials have not been preserved and are not available to researchers." This series contains the born-digital materials from the collective's archive encoded on digital disks and drives. These materials, like the other nonpaper materials, have been separated intellectually and physically from the archive, cast aside until a strategy for digital preservation and access can be implemented. Segregated on the finding aid, the media and the information that they contain are disconnected from the archive.

Paper Tiger's archive is not unique. Salman Rushdie's papers, preserved by Emory's Stuart A. Rose Manuscript, Archives, and Rare Book Library, has implemented a similar strategy to the arrangement, preservation, and access to the nonprint materials in the collection.[43] Similar to the Paper Tiger Archive, the materials, constituting 116 linear feet, have been arranged into thirteen series, including separate series for memorabilia, audiovisual material, and born-digital materials. This final series includes four separate computers, each described as a separate item in the inventory. The Library has "processed" a single machine, providing access to an emulation in the reading room,[44] but this object lingers on the finding aid disconnected from the analog materials in Rushdie's extensive archives. While the emulation represents the use of new technologies and digital methods to process a digital collection, the finding aid fails to reflect any advances in archival praxis. Instead, like the Paper Tiger Archive, the same material biases that Cook revealed almost four decades ago are perpetuated in contemporary practice.

The materials encoded on these machines do not follow the linear logic of the analog materials in the collection. File systems may emulate the files and folders of the analog archive, but databases, apps, and other digital objects follow the nonlinear, nonhierarchical logic of new media.[45] The material practices of archives must reflect the material conditions of these digital collections. An archival praxis centered on making can attend to the complexity of the variety of media represented in archives without becoming encumbered in the material analysis of individual records, can recognize the influence of the hand of the archivist and the tools of the archival field, and can represent the complex relationships between archives, culture, technology, and society.

Notes

[1] Mark Hatch, *The Maker Movement Manifesto* (New York: McGraw-Hill, 2014), 1.

[2] Matt Ratto, "Critical Making: Conceptual and Material Studies in Technology and Social Life," *Information Society* 27, no. 4 (2011): 253.

[3] David Gauntlett, *Making Is Connecting: The Social Meaning of Creativity, from DIY and Knitting to YouTube and Web 2.0* (Malden, MA: Polity, 2011), 244 (emphasis in original).

[4] Henry Jenkins, *Convergence Culture: Where Old and New Media Collide* (New York: New York University Press, 2006).

[5] Aaron Delwiche and Jennifer Jacobs Henderson, "What Is Participatory Culture?," in *The Participatory Cultures Handbook*, ed. Aaron Delwiche and Jennifer Jacobs Henderson (London: Taylor & Francis, 2012), 4–5

[6] Matt Ratto and Megan Boler, "Introduction," in *DIY Citizenship: Critical Making and Social Media,* ed. Matt Ratto and Megan Boler (Cambridge, MA: MIT Press, 2014), 1.

[7] Steven Mann, "Maktivism: Authentic Making for Technology in the Service of Humanity," in *DIY Citizenship*, 29–51.

[8] Tim Ingold, *Making: Anthropology, Archaeology, Art, and Architecture* (New York: Routledge, 2003), 20.

[9] Ingold, *Making*, 47.

[10] Ingold, *Making*, 47.

[11] Ingold contrasts the meshwork with Latour's actor-network theory. Latour's theory accounts for the relationship between human and nonhuman actors, demonstrating the influence of materials in human society, but the network analogy uses the concept of nodes to describe these sites of engagement—absolutes where actors connect rather than the fluid entanglement of the knot. Tim Ingold, "When *ANT* Meets *SPIDER*: Social Theory for Arthropods," in *Being Alive: Essays on Movement Knowledge and Description* (New York: Routledge, 2011), 89–94.

[12] Ingold, *Making*, 81 (emphasis in original).

[13] James O'Toole and Richard J. Cox, *Understanding Archives & Manuscripts*

(Chicago: Society of American Archivists, 2006), 8.

[14] Richard Pearce-Moses, "Record," *Glossary of Archival and Records Terminology*, https://www2.archivists.org/glossary/terms/r/record.

[15] James O'Toole, "The Symbolic Significance of Archives," *American Archivist* 56 (Spring 1993): 234–255.

[16] Joan M. Schwartz, "Coming to Terms with Photographs: Descriptive Standards, Linguistic 'Othering,' and the Margins of Archivy," *Archivaria* 54 no. 1 (2002): 143. See also Elisabeth Kaplan and Jeffrey Mifflin, "'Mind and Sight'": Visual Literacy and the Archivist," in *American Archival Studies: Readings in Theory and Practice*, ed. Randall C. Jimerson (Chicago: Society of American Archivists, 2000), 73–97.

[17] Joan M. Schwartz, "'We Make Our Tools and Our Tools Make Us': Lessons from Photographs for the Practice, Politics, and Poetics of Diplomatics," *Archivaria* 40 (1995): 42.

[18] Ala Rekut, "Material Literacy: Reading Records as Material Culture," *Archivaria* 60, no. 1 (2005): 13.

[19] Anna Chen, "Perfume and Vinegar: Olfactory Knowledge, Remembrance, and Recordkeeping," *American Archivist* 79 (Spring/Summer 2016): 103–120; Nancy Bartlett, "The Contemplation of Color in an Academic Archive," in *Controlling the Past: Documenting Society and Institutions*, ed. Terry Cook (Chicago: Society of American Archivists, 2011), 111–130.

[20] Steven Lubar, "Information Culture and the Archival Record," *American Archivist* 62 (Spring 1999): 11.

[21] Hugh A. Taylor, "The Media of Record: Archives in the Wake of McLuhan," *Georgia Archive* 6, no. 1 (January 1978): 1.

[22] Hugh A. Taylor, "Documentary Art and the Role of the Archivist," *American Archivist* 42 (October 1979): 417–428; Hugh A. Taylor, "Opening Address to the 'Documents That Move and Speak' Symposium," in *Imagining Archives: Essays & Reflections by Hugh A. Taylor*, ed. Terry Cook and Gordon Dodds (Lanham, MD: Scarecrow Press, 2003), 184–197.

[23] Hugh Taylor, "Media of Record," 1.

[24] Marshall McLuhan, *Understanding Media: The Extensions of Man* (1973; Cambridge: MIT Press, 2013).

[25] Terry Cook, "The Tyranny of the Medium: A Comment on 'Total Archives,'" *Archivaria* 9 (1979): 142.

[26] In her discussion of photographic records, Joan Schwartz argues that "if historians and other users of archives have persistently failed to appreciate the value of visual materials in the making and the writing of history, then archivists—through their ideas and standards, practices and actions, whether consciously or unconsciously, intentionally or unintentionally, overtly or systemically—are, in large measure, responsible." Schwartz, "Coming to Terms," 142.

[27] Ernest J. Dick, Jacques Gagné, Josephine Langham, Richard Lochead, and Jean-Paul Moreau, "Total Archives Come Apart," *Archivaria* 11 (Winter 1980): 224.

28 Dick et al., "Total Archives," 225.

29 Terry Cook, "Media Myopia," *Archivaria* 12 (Summer 1981): 148.

30 Hugh A. Taylor, "Documentary Art and the Role of the Archivist," *American Archivist* 42 (October 1979): 419.

31 Paul Dourish and Melissa Mazmanian, "Media as Material: Information Representations as Material Foundations," in *How Matter Matters: Objects, Artifacts, and Materiality in Organization Studies*, ed. Paul R. Carlile, Davide Nicolini, Ann Langley, and Haridimos Tsoukas (Oxford: Oxford University Press, 2013), 102.

32 Dourish and Mazmanian, "Media as Material," 102.

33 Paper Tiger Television, "About Us," http://papertiger.org/about-us/.

34 Paper Tiger Television Collective, *Roar: The Paper Tiger Television Guide to Media Activism* (New York: Paper Tiger Television Collective, 1991), 10, 31.

35 Paper Tiger Television, "Current Projects," https://web.archive.org/web/20131212204947/http://papertiger.org/current.

36 Interview with the author, August 21, 2013.

37 A memo dated March 15, 1995, reads: "URGENT—some tapes are in really bad condition. We need to locate these tapes and have beta masters made before there is no image left to reproduce." Paper Tiger Television Archive, MSS 276, Fales Library and Special Collections, New York University Libraries.

38 Video Preservation Project for the Collection Draft, February 4, 1999, Paper Tiger Television Archive, MSS 276, Fales Library and Special Collections, New York University Libraries.

39 "Guide to the Paper Tiger Television Archive, ca. 1981–2008, MSS.276," September 29, 2017, http://dlib.nyu.edu/findingaids/html/fales/pttv/admininfo.html.

40 At that time, the videotape materials were unprocessed and unavailable for research. Subsequent processing of the videotape collection in 2014 resulted in an expanded finding aid describing each of the titles in the archival collection. See "Series VII: Video Recordings," "Guide to the Paper Tiger Television Archive," http://dlib.nyu.edu/findingaids/html/fales/pttv/dscaspace_ref1655.html, captured at https://perma.cc/Y7KW-ZS8M.

41 Ricardo L. Punzalan, "Archival Diasporas: A Framework for Understanding the Complexities and Challenges of Dispersed Photographic Collections," *American Archivist* 77, no. 2 (2014): 326–349.

42 Punzalan, "Archival Diasporas," 347.

43 "Salman Rushdie Papers, 1947–2012," Stuart A. Rose Manuscript, Archives, and Rare Book Library, Emory University, https://findingaids.library.emory.edu/documents/rushdie1000/, captured at https://perma.cc/TDC9-MLW5.

44 See Laura Carroll, Erika Farr, Peter Hornsby, and Ben Ranker, "A Comprehensive Approach to Born-Digital Archives," *Archivaria* 72 (Fall 2011): 61–92.

45 Lev Manovich, *The Language of New Media* (Cambridge: MIT Press, 2001).

12

From Camp Pitt to Mississippi
Ten Years to a State Digital Archive

Patricia Galloway

Introduction

When I came to the Mississippi Department of Archives and History (MDAH) in 1979, I had behind me a BA in French from Millsaps College in Jackson, Mississippi, an MA and PhD in comparative literature from the University of North Carolina, and several jobs that I had held in Europe: as a medieval archaeologist for four years, 1974–1977, during which I learned a good deal about computers, and as a digital humanist for two years at the University of London, 1977–1979. I came to MDAH as a temporary hire to edit and translate a set of eighteenth-century French documents. Although I had used archives frequently for my own research, I knew almost nothing about what happened backstage. My initial exposure was as a behind-the-scenes researcher for the translation project. Luckily for me, in April 1980, MDAH contracted with the Society of American Archivists for their Basic Archival Workshop for new staff, and I learned what my colleagues were doing.

In addition, when I came to MDAH, I found that there were no computers in the building. Administrative staff dealing with expenditures were connected to mainframe computers operated by the Central Data Processing Authority (CDPA) for the state, but there were no other computers. In 1981, I was able to convince the Mississippi Historical Society (MHS) to purchase a microcomputer to run its mailing list. In the course of creating the request, I also prepared a five-year plan for MDAH's introduction of computers—a plan I submitted to CDPA, which had the authority to approve all computer purchases. Thereafter, I also became the acting responsible person for anything computer-related at MDAH. CDPA was eager to have some department serve as a guinea pig for the use of microcomputers, so the first request to buy one in 1981 was successful.

Creating a Digital Ecology at MDAH, 1981–1985

The Vector Graphic VIP machine with its two 5.25" floppy disk drives (see Figure 1) was purchased with a printer. It ran the CP/M operating system and it came with word-processing software. Database software was also acquired to use in managing the mailing list. Other employees wondered whether we might set up additional databases, such as in the library research room, where the staff wanted to be able to manage call slips (which yielded important statistics), while the archives wanted a database for tracking accessions. Some of these ideas came up as a result of the study of Mississippi state and local

Figure 1. Patricia Galloway with a Vector Graphic VIP machine that has two floppy drives.

archives that began in 1981 under a National Historical Publications and Records Commission (NHPRC) grant to the National Association of State Archives and Records Administrators (NASARA); in 1982 that study yielded a two-volume report by Henry T. Holmes, *The Management and Preservation of Mississippi's Historical Records: Problems and Potential.*[1] Holmes concluded that local records had the greatest need for archival attention, but there was also a section that pointed to the need to address the emergence of digital records in state recordkeeping.

The report led to MDAH attending the June 24–25, 1983, meeting in Atlanta of the twenty-seven states that participated in the first round of the NHPRC Assessment and Reporting Grants, together with federal representatives who were responsible for the grants, four consultants, and representatives of NASARA. MDAH representatives included Director Elbert Hilliard; the director of the Archives and Library Division, Madel Morgan; and the director of the Private Manuscripts Section, Hank Holmes Jr. At that meeting they participated in discussions about the way forward for states and met with the director of the Alabama Department of Archives and History (ADAH), Edwin Bridges, and with Richard Cox, who was in charge of local records at ADAH. The meeting resulted in a series of consultant reports on pertinent topics—Edwin Bridges wrote the report on state records and Richard Cox wrote the report on local government—which were compiled and published as *Documenting America: Assessing the Condition of Historical Records in the States: Consultant Reports Presented at the Conference of the National Historical Publications and Records Commission Assessment and Reporting Grantees, Atlanta, GA, June 24–25, 1983.*[2]

Back at MDAH, the interest in the first microcomputer in the building made it possible in 1983 to purchase a larger system that provided three terminals connected to one central installation. This system made the usefulness of computers for archival management apparent to more people. As one employee learned to use the word processor or database, others would seek information until they could use these tools for their own purposes. The first of the significant new projects that led MDAH into major file management by digital means was the cataloging of the WLBT Newsfilm Collection.

NHPRC and the Newsfilm Collection

The Newsfilm Collection came to MDAH as a gift. The collection of 220,000 feet of 16mm film, which was news footage shot from 1954–1971 by WLBT, an NBC affiliate in Jackson, had been preserved because it had served as evidence of censorship in lengthy litigation with the Federal Communications Commission (FCC) in a case over denial of the station's license. Materials from the cutting room floor showed how the station unfairly suppressed mention of the civil rights movement and the lives of black citizens of Mississippi. The original complaint was brought by Medgar Evers, the leader of the National Association for the Advancement of Colored People (NAACP) in Jackson, who finally was heard on the station in 1963 and was shot to death a few weeks later. The FCC's final ruling revoked the station owners' license. In 1979 a consortium that included black investors bought the station and restored the license, and on February 4, 1980, the consortium offered the film to MDAH's Private Manuscripts collection.[3]

In late 1983, MDAH received a grant from NHPRC to catalog the WLBT film collection, hiring an experienced film archivist who identified to the best of her ability all of the events and people found on all the pieces of film. One of the terminals of the new multiuser microcomputer system was dedicated to the project in order to manage the metadata generated by identifying the film clips. This project was supervised by Bill Hanna, who worked in Private Manuscripts. The documents were not digital, but what was constructed was a database that was used to create a searchable finding aid made from an index that drew on the body of metadata that was assigned to each film fragment. The printed paper catalog was completed in July 1985.[4] In addition, project archivist Lisa Buechele had presented a paper on the project at a joint meeting of the Society of Mississippi Archivists and the Society of Alabama Archivists in Tuscaloosa in 1985.

Minicomputers and Networking, 1985–1989

In 1985, MDAH purchased its first minicomputer, which would support up to eleven terminals, and a systems analyst was hired to work with me to take charge of the growing digital network. The search program written to search the Newsfilm metadata was later adapted to do the same for archival catalogs, and a "migration" program was written to transform word-processing files to the new system. The systems analyst also assisted in beginning to connect Records Management and Official Records catalogs for better control, working with both archivists and records managers. More elaborate databases would still be printed for patrons doing archival research; new practices were being introduced but they were not visible to patrons, although staff members were able to do more and faster as a result. Any PCs that came from small grants were integrated into the minicomputer system as terminals, including a typesetting workstation.

In 1989, MDAH, which was in need of additional terminals, expanded its network to include two additional minicomputers. We now had the ability to create local databases for single sections, while also being able to create centralized databases that would be shared. In addition, in February 1989 we established an Information Management Committee, consisting of division directors and an assistant from each division, meeting every month to discuss technology needs and to participate in long-range planning. Among the committee's first decisions was finding places for the new computers.

Camp Pitt and MDAH, 1989–1990 (Holmes, Hanna, and Harris)

At about this same time, another project came to fruition, one that had been planned and funded to carry out the task of educating state archival leaders about the digital world and how to plan for it. Although the project's official title was "Archival Administration in the Electronic Information Age: An Advanced Institute for Government Archivists," participants were nearly unanimous in referring to the meetings collectively as "Camp Pitt." The first reflection was from Richard Cox himself, writing after the first pair of institutes took place. Cox indicated that Camp Pitt had been inspired by grants to forty-eight states, which created studies in 1981 and 1983, but said that it was too early to judge the project's effects.[5] David Olson, who wrote the third grant proposal for Camp Pitt, echoed Cox in his 1997 review of the entire series in an *American Archivist* article. He also recounted the work of Edwin Bridges, director of ADAH, who pursued his idea of an advanced training for state archivists by gathering, in 1987, a steering committee consisting of Bridges, Larry Hackman (NY), and David Hoober (AZ).[6]

Richard Cox seems to have been Ariadne's red thread that made the initial Camp Pitt possible, and that same thread ran through Mississippi on two occasions. In 1979, while still working as City Archivist of Baltimore, Cox served as a local government consultant at MDAH under an NHPRC grant for a pilot records survey. In 1983–1986 he worked for Bridges as head of the Archives and Records Division of ADAH, when he attended the Society of Mississippi Archivists' Annual meeting in 1984 and offered "a national perspective on local government records problems" in the same session where local issues from the Mississippi Needs Assessment project were addressed. In 1988, he came to rest at the School of Information Sciences at the University of Pittsburgh, where he was a student and lecturer and, later, completed a PhD. He was influential in interesting Dean Toni Carbo Bearman in Bridges's notion of an institute for the states, and, with Cox's support, she provided the venue, while the Council on Library and Information Resources (CLIR) supplied two years' funding for the first two meetings.

Possibly because of the fine reception of the 1982 report on Mississippi archives, as well as the participation by MDAH staff members Hilliard, Morgan, and Holmes in the Atlanta meeting follow-up to the NHPRC reports, archivists from Mississippi were invited to participate in the first iteration of Camp Pitt in 1989.[7] Holmes, who was by then director of the Archives and Library division, and William Hanna, by then director of Records Management, went to the first institute, which lasted just under two weeks, from June 4 to 16, 1989. Liisa Fagerlund from the World Health Organization served as moderator and Cox served as *rapporteur*. Bridges introduced the background and Toni Carbo Bearman introduced the program, which consisted of lectures on the emergence of recordkeeping technologies and an introduction to strategic planning development. By the first Friday, the schedule fell into a morning discussion of a technological topic followed by an afternoon session on the various elements of a strategic plan. On the second Wednesday the two themes were brought together through a discussion of policy leading to the development of a model strategic plan. On the final Friday, Fagerlund and Cox led the review of the whole institute. This general pattern would hold good through all the meetings from 1989–1998.[8]

The attendees were meant to go home and apply what they had learned on their home turf. By May 1990, Holmes exchanged a report on strategic planning with other members of the team they had participated in, including representatives from Arizona, Minnesota, North Dakota, North Carolina, and Georgia. That report was a detailed review crafted by Holmes and Hanna of how Mississippi stood with respect to digital records and what it had to do going forward. In it, they analyzed stakeholders, external environment (generally promising, apart from gubernatorial tendencies to privatization), and internal environment (generally promising because of good relations with CDPA and recent staffing up with the systems analyst at MDAH). It also targeted situations that needed to be tackled quickly so that MDAH would not be trapped in policies that it did not introduce. Clearly, Camp Pitt had done its work in Mississippi to encourage further serious thinking and, especially, initial planning for how to address coming problems.

Dwight Harris, then Archival Program Supervisor in the Archives and Library Division, attended the second institute in 1990—Holmes only attended for the first week—on behalf of MDAH. After that meeting, Harris participated in the creation of a NAGARA document, *A New Age: Electronic Information Systems, State Governments, and the Preservation of the Archival Record,* which appeared in initial form as Appendix 3 of the 1990 report.[9] A group of eleven archivists, including Harris, revised that text to create the pamphlet, made available to anyone for free.[10] The pamphlet urged all state archivists to agree on the major principles for the management of public records, to work toward a coordinating body for state information policies, and to reach agreement on the requirements of digital records preservation.

Although MDAH archivists did not attend any additional meetings of the institute as it continued, this early participation influenced the Archives and Library Division and the Records Management Division to move toward alliance. Certainly Holmes, Hanna, and Harris took the lead in several aspects of MDAH's trek into the world of digital archiving. Many MDAH projects had prepared the participants for Camp Pitt (e.g., the management of the Newsfilm Collection by Hanna), and later projects were influenced by their experience as computerization of different aspects of archival work proceeded.[11] Like the WLBT Newsfilm Collection, the next project that required digital management was driven by social justice and the civil rights movement.

The Mississippi State Sovereignty Commission Papers

The Sovereignty Commission project had its roots in the paper recordkeeping of a state agency, the State Sovereignty Commission, which had been created by the Mississippi legislature in 1956. Its aim was to call a halt to the civil rights movement in Mississippi, which it did using various methods, depending on the governor of the era.[12] Its funding was removed by Governor Bill Waller in 1973, and in 1977, after arguments against destruction of the records by both MDAH and several strong supporters in the legislature, the commission was dissolved and its records turned over to MDAH, under legislation requiring that they not be opened until 2027. Litigation to open them began almost immediately and continued until 1989, when the United States Court of Appeals for the Fifth Circuit declared the sealing of the files unconstitutional.

Although relatively passive up to that time, MDAH worked with the court toward a digital solution to preserve the records without physical redaction, proposing a virtual database in 1993. The court was persuaded by the idea of not harming the documents. A vendor was contracted in 1994, but the task was complex; at the time there was no such thing as an out-of-box system that would permit virtual redaction that could be selected on the fly by classifying the user. The vendor, who had plenty of experience with the digitization and management of local court records, agreed to work with MDAH to achieve what had been proposed to the presiding judge.[13]

Scanning and indexing began in 1996 and continued into 1997, after which MDAH placed advertisements in major newspapers across the United States to find the victims of the Sovereignty Commission's activities in order to offer them the option of having their identities redacted or being permitted to include a comment on any records that referred to them by name. The Sovereignty Commission records were opened in 1998 as a redacted, digitized database, such that researchers could come to the archives and search by names or by the classifications used by the Sovereignty Commission itself, on two workstations in the research room. Although for this project MDAH had to digitize paper documents to enable virtual redaction for privacy, this process meant that MDAH had to fully manage the virtual collection by being able to reach documents through the metadata grid that was created for each document and in a live environment. This project, which overlapped a repository project, thus took MDAH that much closer to managing born-digital objects.

An NHPRC Grant: The Digital Repository

At about the same time, MDAH took on a project that amounted to the creation of a digital archives, using what MDAH staff had learned in making the department's activities increasingly digital. It was especially important that the three MDAH employees who had gone to Camp Pitt had risen to positions of influence and were directly involved in the project: Henry T. Holmes was director of Archives and Library, Bill Hanna was director of Local Records, and Dwight Harris was director of Records Management. Archives and Library had its own systems analyst, Linda Culberson. Since 1983, I had headed Special Projects, which included among its mandates creation of automation for the work of MDAH and had accrued one systems analyst as well as a programmer. Through cooperation with other Mississippi government agencies, MDAH had gained recognition as an agency that had a fifteen-year relationship with what had been the CDPA and was now Information Technology Services (ITS)[14] in the maintenance of the MDAH digital environment. In 1991, I had been recognized by an invitation to NHPRC's Working Meeting on Research Issues in Electronic Records.[15]

Once it was decided that MDAH could not go forward without preparing to preserve the digital records of the state of Mississippi—as the contributions of Holmes, Hanna, and Harris to Camp Pitt argued—and after a 1996 amendment to the public records law that placed electronic records under the law,[16] the next question was monetary support. The Mississippi Legislature appropriated grant-matching money at $98,270[17] and was willing to establish four new positions to create an Electronic Records Section at MDAH—at the same time that it had agreed to raise bond money for a new archives building. The Mississippi Department of Health (MDOH) was willing to work with MDAH as a case study (it had a broad range of types and formats of records). Meanwhile MDAH had established a presence on the government-wide Electronic Records Study Committee, and testimonial letters from the ITS as well as other important agencies proved to be persuasive, along with the MDAH grant proposal, to win a two-year grant from NHPRC from 1997–1999, which was funded in December 1996. The Electronic Records Initiative (ERI) was designed to build a repository and a set of policies that would be acceptable to state agencies in general.

In February 1998 a questionnaire was sent out to IT staffs in Mississippi state government. The questionnaire queried the presence of digital records and their setting in terms of hardware and software. We chose 63, or 44.37%, of state agencies, boards, and commissions for the sample and received responses from 86%. The survey's overall message was that electronic records management was an emerging issue and that many agencies wanted to see MDAH take an active role in helping them with methodologies and guidelines.

In April and May of 1997, the Electronic Records Initiative hosted Luciana Duranti of the University of British Columbia, who had been hired as a consultant on digital recordkeeping for her work on capturing government records upon creation for the US Army. James Allan from the University of Massachusetts Amherst then addressed the ERI team on access and information retrieval. In June and July, the team was introduced to MDOH's database system, PIMS, which ran all of the agency's county health offices, and we visited one of the health clinics to observe how PIMS was used in the field.

In January 1998, I was made director of the project, taking over from Linda Culberson.[18] As the next step, the ERI team inventoried the MDAH Administration Division for hardware, software, and the born-digital files present on those machines. Records Management, directed by Harris, evaluated the standing of digital records being produced by the Administration Division, together with their retention periods, while Official Records reappraised the digital records so that we could carry out exercises on automating retention. This practice made a neat model demonstrating how Official Records and Records Management would work together in the future. The ERI team also worked with Records Management to develop new scheduling forms that reflected electronic records concerns. In June, David Pilcher joined the team from the Sovereignty Commission project and Anna Schwind was hired from Delta State University to serve as technologist on the project.

In May MDAH began the case study in partnership with MDOH, beginning by working again with Official Records and Records Management to understand what the existing MDOH collections contained and what action was needed on the agency's digital records. With that done, we began meetings with the MDOH records manager and the agency's IT staff. We decided to investigate the PIMS patient-service database (which had many tentacles within MDOH), as its contents were being ported to a new archival system called SAR. During that process, we were allowed to use the dummy testing data for SAR to experiment, while we considered how to manage this database from a noncustodial or delayed-custody model. We learned just how much constant attention to the existence of electronic records, with their continuous and often extended use, is necessary for the proper care of permanent records derived from databases.

As we began to look toward the set of guidelines we planned as part of the project, we set up an Electronic Records Advisory Panel to assist us with regulation, advice, and comment on the guidelines we were developing. The guidelines document that was created in 1999 covered four kinds of data: email, desktop applications as found in a typical suite, enterprise databases, and websites. For email, we collaborated with MDOH, experimenting with having the staff tag official emails with specific tags to see how well this would work (from hindsight, not well). For desktop applications, we recommended a choice from the DoD 5015.2 standard of systems that would sit on a network and capture outgoing and incoming files, coupled with our notion of escrow archiving, whereby agencies could turn over archival materials to MDAH to manage while retaining privileged access to them. For databases—still to this day a problem—our work with MDOH's PIMS database and its SAR archival brother led us to consider the notion of conditional schedules, a form of noncustodial (but supervised) archiving, that could change when appraisal or formats changed. For websites, we adopted the practices of an NHPRC-sponsored Syracuse study and discussed with staff members of the Mississippi Library Commission the possibility of partnering with them to take all changes to archival websites, to which they would provide access.[19]

After the end of the grant period, the ERI became the Electronic Records Section (ERS) of the Archives and Library Division, led by David Pilcher, while the Information Technology Section that had been spun off from Special Projects was explicitly taken into the Administration Division and continued to support the new Electronic Records Section.[20] In early 2000, agencies with many digital records began asking the ERS to further their scheduling process. This provided the section with opportunities to develop more fine-grained practices adaptable to each agency than had been the case with the overall NHPRC-funded project. Finally, and perhaps ironically, the ERS was able to archive ITS's paper and digital records relating to their actions to deal with the Y2K bug that had been present on many computers.

Shortly after the end of the grant period, the ERS accessioned its first full-fledged digital collection, which consisted of the records of outgoing Governor Fordice—and that office had not been appraised.[21] But we took from that lesson that digital recordkeeping scheduling ought to be a serious part of any appraisal effort, and the ERS technical specialist ought to meet formally with the technical officer responsible for the computing infrastructure of each agency. Another lesson learned manifested itself in plans for the new Archives building: the walls that enclosed the ERS, which was on the same floor with processing of all other kinds of records, were designed to come down as digital recordkeeping began to dominate government work.

Tracing the Implications of Camp Pitt

The implications of Camp Pitt for the ultimate creation of a digital archives for the state of Mississippi fall into two categories: planning expertise and the difficulties around technological knowledge, already outlined by Edwin Bridges and Richard Cox in *Documenting America*, which led to Camp Pitt and the development of digital recordkeeping, not only within state agencies but within the archives themselves.

In Bridges's eyes, Mississippi had been relatively successful when it came to state records. He saw the state as one of five that "seem to be mounting aggressive, newly invigorated programs" and further said that "in some of the good reports, such as those of Mississippi and New York, one can sense an urgency, a commitment, a depth of analysis, and clarity of focus."[22] When it came to the treatment of local records, Cox reflected that few states had much good to say about local recordkeeping, but he pointed out that Mississippi had

> visited every chancery and circuit clerks' office in the eighty-two counties and had professional archivists complete survey questionnaires. The state records personnel in Mississippi believed that such an approach was necessary because the assessment and reporting project was the first information gathering process of this kind, and they report that the results of this approach were a "very positive" response from the clerks and a time of "renewal" for the state's archival profession. "Through the opportunities of the Assessment Project, the archival constituency has been identified."[23]

Further, Cox said of Mississippi that the state had straightforwardly laid the task at the door of the state archives, calling for "the establishment of a local government records study commission appointed by the governor and supported by state funds."[24]

The NHPRC-funded Assessment Project had brought forth for Mississippi a thorough effort carried out by Holmes, Morgan, and Hanna; shortly thereafter the state also made a serious effort in the direction of local records, bringing local recordkeepers into the archival fold and setting up trainings and periodic meetings to brief them on new issues, including digital ones; this was directed by Hanna. And Camp Pitt provided a planning agenda that was clearly very useful in tackling the digital records problem for the entire state.

What seems obvious to me—from my perspective as digital archivist at MDAH from 1979 to 2000—is that dealing with the Camp Pitt planning agenda locally required continuity and a layering of activities. By the time of Camp Pitt in 1989–1990, three young archivists, Holmes, Hanna, and Harris, had begun to take strong roles at MDAH. All three were active in the three cases I mentioned above: Holmes as head of Private Manuscripts had edited the pre-Camp Pitt 1982 NHPRC-supported review of state archival problems and as head of Archives and Library sponsored and helped write the NHPRC digital archives proposal; Hanna in Private Manuscripts shepherded the Newsfilm Collection, led the new Local Records section, and firmed up the Records Management Division; and Harris in Official Records took responsibility for the security of the Sovereignty Commission records as they were being digitized and then as head of Records Management organized the reappraisal of records from MDAH's Administration Division and MDOH that were becoming newly digital.

A second group of archivists coming along behind them took over the infrastructure work that was called for as MDAH moved into the grant-funded origins of its new digital archives. Linda Culberson became IT manager of the Archives and Library Division under Holmes; David Pilcher, previously a member of Official Records, moved from leading the Sovereignty Commission project to joining and eventually leading the Electronic Records Section; and several of the other partners in the Electronic Records Initiative did excellent work that allowed MDAH to create a digital archives at the completion of the NHPRC project.[25]

One other thing needs to be said. We must remember that, in Mississippi state government, MDAH pioneered the use of small computers that made customized, department-specific practices possible, while CDPA ran mainframe computers that were doing large-scale tasks for all of state government. During the 1980s, minicomputers became the most economical way to allow multiple people to make use of a single computer, and MDAH adopted them. During the 1990s, MDAH adopted personal computers and turned its minicomputers into servers, joined together in a network just in time to make use of the internet at a time when most people were learning computers at their workplace but before it became so important to the everyday activities of the general public.

But MDAH, as in most other states, began with staff members who had never used a computer, which meant that they began their usage at work, at a time when MDAH's activities were not, by and large, being done on computers—that meant the agency had to pioneer. This was the case in each one of the projects I have outlined in this story, but once staff members were familiar with using computers to do their work of archivy—and familiar with figuring out how to do that—it was time for them to feel confident in dealing with digital records from state agencies, which brought along their own complexities to be solved. It is important that there was continuity among MDAH personnel so that the same people could apply new knowledge. I have argued elsewhere that a place of digital archivy needs to be a place where experimentation is at home. I think that to a significant degree Camp Pitt helped engineer that kind of work-group attitude, and, at least for me, that is a major reason why it deserves to be remembered.

Notes

[1] Henry T. Holmes, ed., *The Management and Preservation of Mississippi's Historical Records: Problems and Potential*, 2 vols. (Jackson: Mississippi Department of Archives and History, 1982).

[2] The outcome of that project for the first twenty-seven states was Lisa B. Weber, ed., *Documenting America: Assessing the Condition of Historical Records in the States, Consultant Reports Presented at the Conference of the National Historical Publications and Records Commission Assessment and Reporting Grantees, Atlanta, GA, June 24–25, 1983* (Albany, NY: National Association of State Archives and Records Administrators, 1983). Mississippi's contribution would be praised, along with those of New York and Wisconsin, in Bruce Dearstyne's review of the report, "*Documenting America*: Report Assesses the Management of the Nation's Historical Records," *Government Publications Review* 12 (1985): 315–320.

[3] See Kay Mills, *Changing Channels: The Civil Rights Case That Transformed Television* (Jackson: University Press of Mississippi, 2004).

[4] The catalog for the project was published as Lisa F. Buechele, ed., *Newsfilm Index: A Guide to the Newsfilm Collection, 1954–1971* (Jackson: Mississippi Department of Archives and History, 1984). Details of the digital processing required for both the work on the catalog and its index were provided in an appendix written by Patricia Galloway, "Newsfilm Project Software Details," 541–542. A favorable review of this publication by Alan Lewis, a film and videotape archivist for CBS News, appeared in *American Archivist* 50 (Winter 1987): 119–120. The proper name of the collection is WLBT Newsfilm Collection—MP1980.01, and it is available on the Mississippi Department of Archives and History's website at http://www.mdah.ms.gov/arrec/digital_archives/newsfilm, captured at https://perma.cc/QA52-TBA2.

[5] Richard J. Cox, *The First Generation of Electronic Records Archivists in the United States* (New York: Haworth Press, 1994), Chapter 5, "The NAGARA Institute: An Evaluation of its Effectiveness as a Form of Advanced Archival Education," 163–188.

[6] David J. Olson, "'Camp Pitt' and the Continuing Education of Government Archivists: 1989–1996," *American Archivist* 60 (Spring 1997): 202–214.

[7] Cox indicates that Camp Pitt was indeed inspired by the grants to forty-eight of the states to create studies in 1981 and 1983: "This institute . . . grew out of the state assessment and reporting grants funded by the National Historical Publications and Records Commission in the early to mid 1980s." Cox, *First Generation*, 170.

[8] Olson, "'Camp Pitt,'" 205.

[9] The National Association of Government Archives and Records Administrators' original report, *Archival Administration in the Electronic Information Age: An*

Advanced Institute for Government Archivists (Pittsburgh, Pennsylvania, June 3–15, 1990) (Albany, NY: Pittsburgh University, 1990), is available from ERIC as ED331470 and IR01482; Appendix 3 (https://archive.org/details/ERIC _ED331470), created by the state government issues working group of which Harris was a member, is on pages 39–43.

[10] This pamphlet, *A New Age: Electronic Information Systems, State Governments, and the Preservation of the Archival Record*, was published in 1990 by the Council of State Governments and included endorsements from both NAGARA and NASIRE.

[11] We set up a computer locator system to manage movable shelving that was installed in 1992–1993; we learned how to migrate databases so that we could continue to use systems we had developed. An increasing number of employees became conversant with our systems; by 1995, most typewriters had disappeared.

[12] For a summary of the governors and their attitudes toward the Commission, see Sarah Rowe-Sims, "The Mississippi State Sovereignty Commission: An Agency History," *Mississippi History Now* (September 2002), http://mshistorynow.mdah .state.ms.us/index.php?id=243, captured at https://perma.cc/9UWD-6EFY.

[13] The vendor was Robert Wilson's Syscon, a small concern from Alabama that was willing to work with us to determine how to make the virtual redaction work. See Sarah Rowe-Sims and David Pilcher, "Processing the Mississippi State Sovereignty Commission Records," *The Primary Source*, 21, no. 1 (1999), https: //doi.org/10.18785/ps.2101.02. See also Sarah Rowe-Sims, Sandra Boyd, and H. T. Holmes, "Balancing Privacy and Access: Opening the Mississippi State Sovereignty Commission Records," in *Privacy & Confidentiality Perspectives: Archivists & Archival Records,* ed. Menzi L. Bernd-Klodt and Peter Wosh (Chicago: Society of American Archivists, 2005), 159–174.

[14] Shortly before, CDPA had changed its name to Information Technology Services.

[15] Reported in *Research Issues in Electronic Records, Report of the Working Meeting* (St. Paul: Minnesota Historical Society, 1991). This meeting was called by the Minnesota Historical Society, on behalf of NHPRC, as a first step in advancing a research agenda in digital recordkeeping and preservation that NHPRC would fund.

[16] This amendment had been discussed and put forward by the Electronic Records Study Committee (a working group of information managers from Mississippi state government, including MDAH, and private entities) of the Information Resource Council (a group of influential agency directors who advised ITS on information policy).

[17] It also appropriated $73,117 for the second year.

[18] Culberson had drafted the NHPRC grant but had to turn to planning for digital recordkeeping and its location in the planned new building. She remained a consultant to the project that she had helped frame and that would be under her guidance at the end of the grant.

[19] The Syracuse study report was Charles R. McClure and J. Timothy Sprehe, *Analysis and Development of Model Quality Guidelines for Electronic Records Management on State and Federal Websites· Final Report,* January 1998 (Washington, DC: National Historical Publications and Records Commission, 1998), https://files .eric.ed.gov/fulltext/ED422907.pdf, captured at https://perma.cc/4223-WVG7.

[20] The final report to NHPRC can be found at Patricia Galloway, *Mississippi Electronic Records Initiative: A Case Study in State Government Electronic Records, Final Report,* May 2000, https://www.ischool.utexas.edu/~galloway/pkghome_website /FINREPT.pdf, captured at https://perma.cc/8FNC-EJSB.

[21] Fordice was the first Mississippi governor to serve two terms in a row, or eight years, during which there had been great changes in how records were kept.

[22] Edwin C. Bridges, "State Government Records Programs," in *Documenting America,* 9, 11, respectively.

[23] Richard J. Cox, "Local Government Records Programs," *Documenting America,* 24–25.

[24] Cox, "Local Government Records Programs," *Documenting America,* 25–26— although he pointed to several other states that had called for a similar process. Mississippi was well placed to carry out such a task, since the chair of the board of trustees of MDAH, William Winter, had served as governor from 1980 to 1984. Further, in 1984, Ray Mabus (auditor, but was to be elected governor for 1988– 1992) was interviewed by the Society of Mississippi Archivists for *The Primary Source* (Volume 6, issue 2, page 10; https://doi.org/10.18785/ps.0602.01) about the management of digital records—and Richard Cox spoke in the same session.

[25] Today, as Mississippi state government is carried out mostly digitally, the second generation has taken the lead, as Pilcher is director of Archives at MDAH.

13

Commentary
Archival History

Robert B. Riter

Introduction

Richard J. Cox's intellectual contributions to archival studies include a unique commitment to the development of a mature, rigorous, and comprehensive body of archival history scholarship and a consistent argument for its necessity in supporting and contextualizing archival thought and practice. This commitment was present at the outset of his archival career in Maryland. His early writings explore the state's archival history.[1] In his later writings, he continued to explore American archival history, broadly defined. His historical research is instructive in demonstrating innovative uses of outside literatures and sources and particularly well illustrated by his investigations of Lester J. Cappon, which are informed by careful examinations of Cappon's diaries and related institutional records.[2]

Cox has also been a leading and consistent critic of writings on archival history, at regular intervals commenting on their weaknesses, needs, strengths, and possibilities. This is exemplified by two essays.[3] His 1983 analysis, "American Archival History: Its Development, Needs, and Opportunities," was the first comprehensive review of the archival history literature. In it he makes a rigorous argument for the necessity of historical knowledge in supporting the development of the archival profession and the daily work of archivists, writing that "it is vital that we know as much as possible about the development of the profession to aid our continued self-study, reevaluation, and progress, especially in time of unusual stress and change."[4] Though critical—he says that his assessment "reveals an uneven coverage in both quality and subject"—the essay reflects a quiet optimism for the future of archival history scholarship, concluding with a set of recommended research directions.[5]

In 2000, he revisited this assessment in "The Failure or Future of American Archival History: A Somewhat Unorthodox View," the first comprehensive assessment of the historical literature published since his own 1983 review. While noting "promising signs," Cox is again careful to identify weaknesses and needs.[6] His 1983 recommendations, which included "a need for extensive state histories, institutional histories, regional histories, and a single-volume synthesis," remained unaddressed. He offers an additional recommendation for scholars of archival history to look outward to other disciplines, where significant archival history activity had taken place.[7]

Again, Cox expresses optimism, identifying the innovative use of methods, increased use of archival sources in supporting historical arguments, and a broadening scope of examination as encouraging trends. He concludes his assessment with the comment that "my own sense is that we will see a growth in the historical study of records and recordkeeping because of the modern sensibility about their importance."[8] It is with the same spirit of intellectual engagement that I offer my remarks on these essays and their relationship to the practice of archival history.

Defining Archival History

The essays by Sinn, Mattock, and Galloway reflect Cox's stated optimism for the future of archival history as a disciplinary area. These investigations, varied in their institutional contexts, objects and structures of analysis, and methodological frameworks, are indicative of continued growth and the potential for further disciplinary maturity. Collectively, they are illustrative of an archival history practice that includes a variety of subject areas, objects of analysis, and disciplinary approaches.

Sinn provides a multifaceted examination of initiatives to preserve and communicate No Gun Ri narratives. Using the development of No Gun Ri community archives initiatives—specifically, the development of its oral history project as a departure point—Sinn offers an investigation at the intersection of community, institution building, and the dynamics of narrative construction and communication.

Mattock provides a history of archival transformation and of the dynamics that inform how archives are formed and transformed by institutions. The Paper Tiger Archive, as a site of examination, offers a significant institutional history but also provides a history of archival relationships. Mattock isolates a critical archival relationship—that between archivist and artifact—and reveals in this episode how archival perceptions and valuations of the materiality and physicality of records informed their treatment and presentation.

Galloway's investigation of the development of the computing and electronic/digital records infrastructure at the Mississippi Department of Archives and History (MDAH), its early involvement in electronic records initiatives, and the maturation of these activities offers institutional, computing, and technical histories. In drawing attention to the relationship between the activities at MDAH, Camp Pitt, and national state electronic records initiatives, Galloway also documents the emergence of communities of practice and professional networks. This essay aids us in considering the varieties of archival infrastructure, processes of institution building, and community development.

Though distinct in their subjects and approaches, read collectively, these essays are thematically cohesive. Each addresses themes relating to infrastructure, construction, materiality, and community. Methodologically, each model varied practices of archival history. These pieces contribute to our understanding of archival thought, practice, and consequence, and can aid in contextualizing contemporary archivy.

Investigating Archival Infrastructures

The possibilities and limits of archival practice are informed by the nature of archival infrastructure. Archival infrastructures are themselves historical evidence, reflecting the technological, professional, sociopolitical, intellectual, and institutional climates from which these structures emerge. These essays draw attention to the varieties of archival infrastructures, the processes by which those infrastructures emerge, and the consequences of their particular constructive legacies.

Sinn, Mattock, and Galloway all comment on a critical point: the historical study of infrastructures involves identifying and critiquing intersecting, but distinct, structures. Their investigations critique community as infrastructure, archival ideas as infrastructure, archival equipment and architectures as infrastructure, and values as infrastructure and demonstrate how, as amalgamations, they form institutions, policies, professional communities, technical and social networks, and bodies of thought—all of which are themselves infrastructure. In teasing out these distinct elements and elucidating their formation and construction, this complexity is clarified.

These are histories of archival formation, influence, and consequence. What factors inform how our institutions, professional bodies, thoughts and ideas, and practices are formed? How are our contemporary institutions, thinking, actions, and decisions informed by the contexts of their building? Through historical engagement, these questions can be understood.

Mechanisms of Archival Construction and Translation

Archival thought and action results in processes of construction and translation. Ideas and concepts are formulated, and later reshaped, by generations of archival thinkers and professionals aligning their demands of their archival eras. Technical and representational systems are developed and formulated—later to be redeveloped and reformulated. Records, collections, and their associated narratives are made, remade, circulated, and recirculated as they are preserved and communicated.[9]

These essays offer histories that document these acts of construction and translation. Galloway details the development of technical infrastructure as burgeoning structures into formalized archival units and professional networks. She describes the impact of a grant-funded initiative on a formal archival unit. Embedded within this structural narrative is the process of constructing a community that contributed to the development of professionals capable of imagining, arguing for, designing, and implementing networks, spaces, and policies. Similarly, Sinn reveals a history of community dynamics that informed how community narratives were gathered, generated, communicated, and maintained. As Sinn also indicates, community-focused archival history is a form of political history. How do group dynamics emerge? How are agendas set? How do leaders emerge? What are the consequences of these dynamics and the construction of these narratives and their presentation?

Mattock places a material examination of the Paper Tiger Television Archive within the larger context of the discipline's evaluative frameworks, demonstrating the relationship that exists between archival ideas, archival actions, and the resulting archival outputs. The physical manifestation of collections, and their representation and communication, is the result of translating archival ideas into archival actions. As Mattock reveals, conceptions of material value—or in this case the absence of these conceptions—informed organization and description practices that did not reflect a concern with the material subjects of the archives. This point is also revealed in the discussion of how archives are formed and transformed with communities. The Paper Tiger Television archives, as originally maintained, and its later formulation as the Paper Tiger Archive in the Fales Library and Special Collections, reflect distinct constructions. Archival history methods can aid in critiquing archival production.[10]

Sinn's material investigation of the construction of oral histories offers insight into the processes by which narratives are constructed, communicated, and mediated within community-based initiatives. As a case, this clarifies the individual elements that contribute to narrative construction and the processes by which individual narratives become framed as community narratives and private narratives become public narratives. In identifying the dynamics of influence, community member participation, agenda setting, and the role of external factors, Sinn documents an ecology of narrative construction.

Creating and Managing Communicative Structures

Archival investigations are examinations of communicative forms, practices, and structures. Professional networks established by archivists can also be read as communicative structures. In evaluating professional networks, Galloway's analysis parses the emergence of intersecting professional networks and scholarly communication channels. MDAH, and its pioneering digital archivists, are placed within the larger context of national discussions regarding state management of electronic networks. From this analysis, we understand the factors that informed the development of internal professional networks, the emergence of regional and national networks for collaboration and discussion, and their intersecting initiatives and collaborations.

Sinn's examination of the No Gun Ri archival initiatives provides a nuanced examination of these themes within a community archives context. Organizationally, community dynamics are revealed, drawing attention to how gatekeeping operated within this community discussion in terms of the construction of narratives. The analysis of oral history construction also draws attention to how narratives were viewed as communicative structures, particularly at the intersection of communication, community, and politics. Intention is isolated and examined, discussing how the goals and objectives, in terms of outcomes, informed the nature of narrative content and dissemination.

In drawing attention to the materiality of communication, Mattock offers an analysis of artifacts and of the access structures that community and institutional repositories developed. In analyzing the diverse documentary forms contained in the Paper Tiger Archive, Mattock comments on the relationship between the material history of objects (how they are generated, their material composition) and their communicative potential. Potential is the critical point. Materiality is a physical and social condition. Mattock's analysis demonstrates how archival recognition and valuation informs how objects are positioned institutionally and descriptively.

Conclusion

Individually, these essays offer histories of origins: of communities, infrastructures, collections, narratives, and ideas. Collectively, they provide insight into dynamics of archival construction across a plurality of documentary forms, institutions, practices, geographies, and sociopolitical environments. The examinations of institutions, professional networks, collections, and narratives performed by Sinn,

Mattock, and Galloway elucidate how infrastructure, process, and practice can be clarified and critiqued. All demonstrate the varieties of historical data that can support archival history—archival records, archival writings, personal/institutional oral records, lived experiences, and archival infrastructures read as records.

I return to Professor Cox's critique and optimism. These papers reflect a maturing archival history domain, where diverse conditions are investigated through innovative methods and provide additional bodies of evidence for understanding and reflecting on our practices.

Notes

[1] Richard J. Cox, "A History of the Calvert Papers, MS.174," *Maryland Historical Magazine* 68 (Fall 1973): 309–332; and Richard J. Cox, "Public Records in Colonial Maryland," *American Archivist* 37 (April 1974): 263–275.

[2] Richard J. Cox, ed., *Lester J. Cappon and the Relationship of History, Archives, and Scholarship in the Golden Age of Archival Theory* (Chicago: Society of American Archivists, 2004); Richard J. Cox, "Lester J. Cappon and the Creation of Records: The Diary and the Diarist," *Archivaria* 75 (Spring 2013): 115–144; Richard J. Cox, "Lester J. Cappon and the Publishing of Modern Documentary Editions," *Journal of Scholarly Publishing* 46 (April 2015): 224–250.

[3] Richard J. Cox, "American Archival History: Its Development, Needs, and Opportunities," *American Archivist* 46 (Winter 1983): 31–41; Richard J. Cox, "The Failure or Future of American Archival History: A Somewhat Unorthodox View," *Libraries & Culture* 35 (Winter 2000): 141–154.

[4] Cox, "American Archival History: Its Development," 31.

[5] Cox, "American Archival History: Its Development," 31 and 41.

[6] Cox, "Failure or Future," 142–143.

[7] Cox, "Failure or Future," 143 and 148–149.

[8] Cox, "Failure or Future," 149.

[9] Borrowing from historian Robert Darnton's communication circuit, which models the reception of printed books, we can describe this process of creation(s), representation(s), and presentation(s) as an *archival circuit*. See Robert Darnton, *The Kiss of Lamourette: Reflections in Cultural History* (New York: W. W. Norton, 1990), 110–113.

[10] Lisa Darms, "The Archival Object: A Memoir of Disintegration," *Archivaria* 67 (2009): 143–155.

THEME FOUR
Memory

Richard J. Cox, *Spruce Head Maine*, Oil on Canvas, 2015.

14

Fiesta Videos
Living and Producing
Social Memory of El rancho

Janet Ceja Alcalá

Introduction

In the small Mexican town of La Plaza del Limón (La Plaza), there
is no archives, museum, or library catering to the formal keeping of
records, objects, or texts. In their place is a great deal of storytelling
and vast opportunities to explore the past. A visit to any of the many
tienditas (corner stores) on any given block could easily lead to the
possibility of engaging in casual chatter or a serious discussion about
almost anything relating to the town's current events or local history.
Through everyday encounters, people engage in highly social and
communal moments that privilege both the present and past over
documented facts seeking to prove something to someone.

Although I grew up in California, quite removed from La Plaza, I
knew of it and its people through stories. My parents were born there
and talked about their hometown all of the time, and through their
memories I came to identify as a part of this imagined community.
The Mexican American identity as a bicultural phenomenon means
that we retain parts of our Mexican heritage as we adapt to American
society. As expected, we assume our locality's temporality and official
notion of the past—but not without question. In the United States,

the past manifests itself as myth based on white European settler colonialism, whether it is represented through the English pilgrims or Spanish missionaries. Our hybrid identities and our "double consciousness," as W. E. B. Du Bois wrote about black communities, are not represented in these seemingly heroic and grand historical narratives we learn about in school. When we do attempt to exhume our histories, we are oftentimes positioned in historical temporalities that are framed as critical or ruptured. In these historical breaks, our identities exist as silences without voice, or they are invisible like gaps.

In this essay, I use an ethno-biographical approach to "recover" and document one aspect of *la memoria popular* in La Plaza. I do this by privileging a rather modest technological advancement in the town—commissioned fiesta videos produced by local videographers. These videos are important transmitters of our community's social memory.

Social Memory

Social memory focuses on memory linked to specific social contexts, which is a slightly different take on the active meaning making that sustains community identity as collective memory. The emphasis is on the *social* dimension of memory, as opposed to the "internalization of group identities" that get passed on and remembered.[1] Shared narratives that reference a group's past in specific social circumstances cannot only help maintain cultural cohesion but also can highlight interesting tensions that are situated through interactions. The disciplinary training and philosophical position of the scholar embarking on this transdisciplinary subject—memory—also makes a difference in its interpretation. Sociologists Jeffrey K. Olick and Joyce Robbins describe the social memory phenomenon as "a matter of how minds work together in society, how their operations are not simply mediated but are structured by social arrangements."[2] In this sense, social memory is not static, and its configurations change over time to reflect different cultural and political realities.

Because of the social and economic arrangements that push people out of their countries of origin, largely the consequence of neoliberalism in the late twentieth and early twenty-first century, diasporic communities must find creative ways to return to their homelands. Commissioned videos act as symbolic objects representing this journey back home through memory—not to mention that this act literally depends on the physicality of the videos and their ability to be sent easily across national boundaries. Scholars have described this type of techno-based remembering as a spatial view of memory because of how it flattens time.[3] Temporal frames of reference become obscured by information technologies that help coordinate relationships across space rather than time. This has been the case for many people in La Plaza who for more than fifteen years have been watching commissioned videos of themselves at any given moment in the comfort of their homes. The videos are instrumental in encouraging the town's local and diasporic community in the United States to maintain intimate, albeit highly mediated visual connections to their place of origin. To unpack some of these connections, I explore how one videographer's work in documenting Our Lady of Guadalupe's fiesta is represented through production practices motivated by the diaspora and those living in La Plaza. I then describe how this co-constructed narrative about who they are is a highly mediated representation of how the locals wish to be remembered.

Approach

During the years from 2011 to 2013, I conducted an archival ethnography in La Plaza to understand how, in the absence of an official town archives, the community's fiesta honoring Our Lady of Guadalupe was preserved by the town's local and diasporic community. I also sought to learn more about my own cultural history in the process.

My approach to social memory and its implications for archivists follows some of the ideas put forth by Richard J. Cox, Brien Brothman, Terry Cook, and Francis X. Blouin, ideas that can be summarized as the need to consider other ways of understanding the past in order to be able to develop new archival theories that extend these modes of knowing into our everyday practice.[4] Commissioned fiesta videos serve as an example of records that represent and evidence this nontraditional view of archival value.

In many rural localities in Mexico, historical information is not customarily documented or published; instead, it is orally transmitted. While orality is indeed a valuable source of information, much also goes unspoken and lost for generations of people who have been affected by migration and acculturation in new environments. Videography presents an interesting way of leveraging a multi-sited community's voice and vision as both memory and record.

Historian Luis González has written about the lack of documentation that exists in rural Mexican communities. While he acknowledges the importance of oral sources in gathering information, he also argues that this information must be treated critically and in relation to what sources do exist about the locality, whether written, archeological, or representative of other phenomena.[5] Indeed, there are few original sources available about La Plaza, so I conducted several interviews, including one with Oscar Nieto,[6] one of three local videographers; I have drawn heavily on his interview and 2011 DVD production of the town fiesta. In addition, I consulted secondary sources that contextualize the history and politics of the region. Finally, I have incorporated my own accumulated experiences as a second-generation member of the town's diaspora into my analysis.

La Plaza del Limón

With a population of about two thousand inhabitants, La Plaza sits nestled in a quiet valley greeted by picturesque hills in the state of Michoacán (see Figure 1). The locals refer to the town as "La Plaza" or "El rancho," both of which reference the colonial history and spatial layout of the Mexican hacienda. The word *plaza* refers to a central square, and the town's name suggests that the land occupied by the people of La Plaza would have been at the center of a hacienda's ranch or farmland.[7] This theory is supported by the fact that the settlement in which La Plaza exists saw many *hacendados* (hacienda owners) from the seventeenth century up to the early part of the twentieth century, when the hacienda system was legally abolished.[8] La Plaza's name thus remains a marker of its colonial past and ongoing present condition under the influence of globalized neoliberal policies that have transformed it into an agricultural center with an international market. Ironically, this agricultural viability has also increased the migration of its inhabitants to the United States.[9] Some leave to find the money to keep cultivating their land even as it is increasingly costly to do so and government policies continuously undercut farmers' labor—not to mention the plight of those who do not own land and must financially subsist as farmworkers with low wages. This region in particular ranks as one of the highest in all of Mexico for the number of temporary workers who travel to the United States and for the amount of remittances that it receives from migrants in the United States.[10]

Figure 1. Landscape of La Plaza del Limón. Photo by Janet Ceja Alcalá.

Remittances have been especially useful in helping La Plaza undergo major infrastructural developments. For instance, it boasts paved roads, a large Catholic church with an attractive adjoining public plaza, and the recent construction of a chapel, in great part due to contributions from the diaspora. One can see these infrastructural changes in videos produced by videographers who for almost two decades have been documenting fiestas and other social events in this region (see Figure 2). It is likely that no one person from La Plaza has as thorough a collection of fiesta videos as these videographers do. Studying and documenting how their works contribute to the memory-making traditions of small rural communities in Mexico is especially important as video devices have become more ubiquitous and are further affecting how these communities interact with video technology. Therefore, amateur videographers demand our attention during this shift toward the latest visual media-based culture; they are the unexpected keepers of significant and quickly aging records documenting rural populations in Mexico.

Figure 2. Fiesta videos documenting La Plaza del Limón.
Photo by Janet Ceja Alcalá.

Commissioned Fiesta Videos

Three independent videographers service La Plaza, but, for the purpose of this essay, I focus on Oscar Nieto's productions because of his collaborative approach to video making. Nieto began documenting fiestas in La Plaza in the year 2000 and claims to have been the first to do so. Originally from the neighboring municipal town of Ixtlán de los Hervores, he began recording the fiesta by invitation from the locals. Today, videographers no longer need an invitation; they simply capture and compile their footage into DVD sets.

Nieto's general experience with videography work actually dates back to 1990 when an elderly neighbor sold him a camcorder. The neighbor's family members, who lived in the United States, had given it to him, but he decided that, at his age, he had no interest in using it. Nieto went on to establish his videography business, and since then he has purchased other cameras and equipment for his productions. Although consumer-grade camcorders and video formats from the 1990s to the present have changed dramatically, Nieto's process has not. He continues to record local festivities and produces DVD copies to sell to his customers. Launching an online business or even uploading samples of his work to social media platforms are out of the question. This is in part due to a lack of information literacy and access to technology that support these types of entrepreneurial efforts. His dependency on creating physical copies of the videos is thus a generational production trend and one that goes beyond La Plaza.

Filmmaker Rebecca Savage recounts that while conducting a visual ethnography in San Francisco Tetlanohcan in Tlaxcala, Mexico, she learned that commissioned copies of videos of quinceañera fiestas (fifteenth-birthday parties) are sent abroad to migrant family members in the United States who could not attend the fiestas.[11] For a fee, these videos, along with other goods, are delivered by *paqueteros* (delivery persons) who are able to cross borders freely and legally. Another filmmaker, Antonio Mendéz Esparza, demonstrates how this type of audiovisual-based remembering has become habitual among migrants through a poignant scene in his film *Aquí y Allá* (*Here and There*, 2012). In the scene, a family in a small Mexican town gathers around their television to watch a fiesta video. Suddenly the husband asks his wife why she had not sent him the video while he was living in New York (see Figure 3); as a musician, he wanted to keep up with musical trends happening in his homeland.

Figure 3. A Mexican family watching a fiesta video in the film
Aquí y Allá *(*Here and There, 2012*).*

Such commissioned video productions are not limited to Mexico. Journalist Sarah Maslin Nir documents a similar phenomenon with diasporic Jamaican communities in Jamaica, Queens, Bedford-Stuyvesant, Brooklyn, and the Bronx. In this case, the diaspora is keen to visit local convenience stores and buy Jamaican dancehall party videos that capture the latest in fashion, dance, and slang.[12] These videos can be up to six hours long, and because they capture dancehall parties held in specific Jamaican localities, diasporic viewers watch attentively, looking for family and friends.

These examples demonstrate how amateur videography provides a highly local and popular source of information that incites social memory and produces new visual and technical aesthetics that transgress mainstream genres and practices. As film scholar Patricia R. Zimmerman has affirmed of amateur productions, it is "not simply an inert designation of inferior film practice and ideology but rather is a historical process of social control over representation."[13] As we shall see in La Plaza, this social control over representation is enacted through novel video production practices developed to appeal and attend to local and diasporic publics. However, before discussing the dynamic of fiesta videos as a source of social memory, it is important to describe some basic elements of Our Lady of Guadalupe's fiesta in La Plaza.

The Fiesta's Social Structure

Catholic fiestas typically stem from religious rituals. One such ritual is the *novena*, which includes prayer services recited for nine days to honor and make requests to special entities, such as saints and Marian figures. In La Plaza, Our Lady of Guadalupe is the divinity observed and celebrated. Her celebration takes place every year at the end of January, which is different from the official observance date on December 12. This is done to accommodate those living abroad and in other parts of the country who are unable to make the pilgrimage home for the official celebration date. The locals often joke that there are now more of them living in the United States than in Mexico,[14] and this change to the official religious holiday demonstrates the impact that globalization has had on this locality.

The local priest oversees Our Lady of Guadalupe's fiesta, and he is tasked with delegating a great part of the organizational labor to community leaders. His strategy is to have nine organizing committees each lead and carry out one of the nine days of the novena. While each committee approaches its organizational tasks differently, they all have to raise funds to support the church's expenses and other secular activities. This includes supporting the cost of celebrating two daily Masses (e.g., church decorations, candles, honoraria, etc.) and coordinating a church procession that takes place each day immediately before the evening Mass. Coordination of the procession entails looking for volunteers to carry religious banners, hiring folkloric performers and musicians, and preparing trucks with religious scenarios, among many other activities. The townspeople who participate in the day's events might do so to fulfill personal acts of piety or as their religious obligation, though not all have the means or desire to contribute. All committees must satisfy the financial baseline of fundraising to support the church's expenses, and they all go above and beyond that baseline. Secular activities have been naturalized into each committee's work and are expected by the townspeople as a part of the celebration. Two major examples of these activities include pyrotechnic displays and musicians playing live music.

In 2011 the committees listed in Table 1 were responsible for coordinating and carrying out the fiesta. Each committee had a representative from each of the social groups listed, which span representation from the local trades and describe gender roles and age groups. These social groups not only embody and structure the fiesta, they also reveal local hierarchies of power displayed through the devotional labor[15] enacted. This labor is manifested through each committee's ability to carry out its day's festivities. The fiesta, then, is a performance on many levels. It is a religious performance in which the townspeople display their piety; a performance of the town's normative identities; and a performance that displays each committee's social status based on its members' ability to successfully curate the novena. Videographers have been able to capture this social structure and changes to the fiesta for more than fifteen years now.

The Fresero's Day

Specific scenes that Nieto shot of the freseros' day (strawberry farmers) illustrate his production approach and how the townspeople influence his practice. In addition, members of La Plaza are involved in co-creating content with Nieto and, as such, help shape the video's narrative and, consequently, what is remembered.

Nieto's freseros' day footage opens with exterior shots of the old parish chapel, church, and plaza. Black and lime green text overlaid on the images includes the event's date and a short quote in Spanish from the *Nican Mopohua*, an early text documenting Our Lady of

Day	Name in Spanish	Name in English
1	Las señoras de La Plaza del Limón (Día de la Divina Providencia)	The Day of the Divine Providence, led by the women of La Plaza del Limón
2	Los ecuareros, albañiles, y Banda Limonera	The Day of the Ecuareros (self-sustaining farmers), Construction Workers, and the Limonera Band
3	Los señores de la maquinaria	The Day of the Machinery, led by large-scale work equipment owners (e.g., tractors, trucks, etc.)
4	Los freseros	The Day of the Strawberry Farmers
5	Los comerciantes	The Day of the Merchants
6	Los chiveros y ganaderos	The Day of the Goat Herders and Livestock Ranchers
7	Los jovenes	The Day of the Youth
8	Los hijos ausentes (Día de los emigrados)	The Day of the Absent Children, led by the émigrés or diaspora
9	Los ejidatarios	The Day of the Ejidatarios, led by shareholders of communal lands

Table 1. Our Lady of Guadalupe's Novena in 2011 by day.

Guadalupe's apparition in the indigenous Náhuatl language (see Figure 4). The quote, which was adapted for this specific novena committee, states "When Juan Diego entered with the Virgin [imprint on his cloak], he bowed and knelt before him [the bishop]; he [Juan Diego] immediately gave him the message that our Lady from heaven. . . ." This is followed by the text that that has been adapted, in addition to credits for the day:

> The *freseros* also bow before
> God to give thanks for all
> the generous blessing he provides.
> Headed by:
> Eduardo and Francisco Zaragoza and Jesus Rios
> Accompanied by:
> The catechists and all of the parish children
> Celebrated by:
> Father Armando Estrada

These poetically imagined credits are meant to honor the committee heads and recognize their piety in relation to the sacred words of the *Nican Mopohua*. In the background, Nieto has placed and edited various shots of the rancho's plaza and the surrounding atrium. On this day in particular there is a massive concert stage that blocks a part of the church's façade. This juxtaposition is symbolically telling of the fervor for the secular evening activities that will soon take precedence over the religious ones. Besides the visual footage that sets up the day's activities, there is traditional music synced with sounds of music bursting with cheer. The song, "Las mañanitas," usually sung on someone's birthday or saint's day, helps put viewers in a celebratory mode.

Figure 4. Opening scene of a fiesta video highlighting the freseros' day with an excerpt from the Nican Mopohua. *Image from Solemnes Fiestas en Honor de La Virgen de Guadalupe (Solemn Feasts in Honor of Our Lady of Guadalupe, 2011).*

Nieto's camera continues to take the viewer through the town and, specifically, its main architectural structures until an abrupt edit signals the poor technical integration of the opening scenes with the rest of the video. Because Nieto doesn't have editing software, he outsources the opening credits to a video production store in the nearby city of Zamora. The new scene introduces another music track; this time it is *banda*, which is popular Mexican brass band music. The song is an immigrant ballad titled "México ya regresé" ("Mexico, I've Returned"). The lyrics tell the story of a male Mexican migrant who left his homeland to work in the United States. Although he has the good fortune of returning to his pueblo, presumably with the means to provide for his family, he wishes never to return to the United States. Given its topical nature, this song has the power to move and perplex diasporic viewers as they identify with the song's lyrics and watch footage of what they have left behind. As such, the soundtrack is an aural grammar used to convey emotion and guide viewers through musical storytelling.

The camera, which up to this point had been surveying the exterior of the church and surrounding plaza, settles on and zooms in on a poster of Our Lady of Guadalupe hanging on the church façade. This image dissolves into a superimposed framed image of Our Lady of Guadalupe located inside the church. The camera then slowly zooms out, and the interior of the church becomes the center of the frame. The camera continues to move around the church and capture various objects and religious statues with a mix of medium shots and close-ups. Nieto uses these camera techniques throughout his production so as to not bore viewers with standard medium shots of a location. When the tour of the church has ended, he cuts to an exterior close-up shot of a mesquite tree with bean pods located in the plaza's gardens. This is an element worth appreciating because people from La Plaza will immediately recognize this legume, which many would have enjoyed as a local treat. These intimate touches of linking La Plaza's diaspora to the built and natural environment of their hometown are not found in other locally produced fiesta videos.

After shooting the mesquite pods, Nieto cuts to more footage in the immediate proximity of the church. He then uses a long shot to capture a street and cuts to a medium shot of an elderly couple. The footage is at first inconspicuous because it focuses on the street, and since he has already spent a great deal of time shooting exterior spaces, it appears as though the viewer is now touring La Plaza's streets. It is not until there is a close-up of a plaque engraved with a family's last name and a sudden cut to an elderly man opening the door to his home that it becomes apparent that the footage is a bit out of the ordinary (see Figure 5). This and a few seconds of the subsequent footage revolve around the family's home and a few shots of the family (see Figure 6). Nieto then cuts to long shots of the town's streets with passersby that help transition the video away from the focus on the family just observed.

This part of the video has been staged in collaboration with the family because whereas Nieto no longer receives novena committee invitations to record specific days of the fiesta, he does receive individual requests from locals to capture footage of them at any point during the fiesta. He claims to get anywhere from fifteen to twenty such requests per day, and oftentimes he fulfills them by spontaneously staging special screen time for people. For instance,

Figure 5. An elderly man opening the door to his home.
Image from Solemnes Fiestas en Honor de La Virgen de Guadalupe
(Solemn Feasts in Honor of Our Lady of Guadalupe, 2011).

Figure 6. Long shot of the elderly man's home.
Image from Solemnes Fiestas en Honor de La Virgen de Guadalupe
(Solemn Feasts in Honor of Our Lady of Guadalupe, 2011).

while panning during a procession, he may focus the framing on local townspeople who have made such requests. These requests also come from the diaspora living in the United States. For example, this may involve having Nieto shoot special footage of relatives or of a recently built home. Remittances sent to Mexico are frequently used toward investments in the built environment, such as the construction of homes, and capturing these structures on video is evidence that they have been built. It also demonstrates the growth of a new social migrant class transforming their economic capital into tangible investments that change the cultural and social dynamic of migrant communities. Scholar Jesús Gil Méndez notes that members of the diaspora who leave the country have a recurring cultural pattern of returning to their homeland due in part to the maintenance of and expansion of assets and property, such as homes and plots of land.[16] Nieto's production practices creatively weave this relatively new sociohistorical phenomenon into the video's structure.

Along with the inclusion of special footage requests, there is also censorship. In particular, men often request that Nieto avoid capturing them on record when they are dancing with women or drinking alcohol because these images could compromise them with their significant others. This is another way in which Nieto's customers help determine what is included in his videos. He describes this process in reference to dancing as follows:

> First, I review [the videos] and when I see [the men in the videos I say to them] "you showed up like this and like that—is this a problem?" [They might say:] "No, yes," or "You know what, yeah it's better to remove it, remove it!" . . . So the amount of footage I can gather is limited and during the dance parties I'm on the look out [for these men], and I say [to myself] I better shoot from this angle instead because it's true that [in the United States] they will see them dancing and get caught. Others tell me "Look, when I raise my hand like this [makes hand gesture] it means 'no' [don't record], okay?" And we agree and sometimes they tell me the same thing if they're drinking alcohol with friends.[17]

These types of occurrences reinforce macho and womanizer stereotypes that get scripted out of the video. Social complexities that could affect the family structure are thus excluded and a veneer of proper social norms gets reinforced. In addition, if these men are to remain a customer base, Nieto must reckon with their desire to be forgotten. It is important to note that just because Nieto censors this content, it does not mean that other videographers do the same.

We continue to tour La Plaza, and the camera casually introduces more townspeople while gut-wrenching banda ballads narrating the immigrant experience in the United States play in the background. More and more people appear, standing around, sitting, and casually socializing as they wait for the evening procession to make its way through the street. Nieto's sensibility in capturing the routine, people's ordinary gestures, and integrating sentimental sounds into his videos demonstrate his ability to identify with the populace he serves. When I asked him why he enjoyed videography work, he explained,

> It's a job from which one feels satisfaction because besides recording the event, well, you really get to know people, meet more people, become familiar with more places and you make more friendships. . . . Almost always during fiestas, because kids are present, I feel like they talk to me, you know, and I see them and get to know them and the elders, too, who see the videos or who see me around recording.[18]

The relationships he builds with people work to his advantage because as he gains their trust, they become invested in his work, as opposed to that of other videographers. Nieto's history and relationships have thus allowed him to develop a unique aesthetic that is for the community, albeit in association with an exclusive customer base. The major challenge Nieto faces with his participatory-oriented video work is finding a balance that can accommodate a communal vision and many personal interests. In addition, this creates a tension in his productions. Some make it a point to tease and criticize him for fulfilling personal requests for screen time. He playfully impersonates them: "Hey, you recorded those drunkards way too much, don't shoot them anymore . . . and you shot [so and so]. How much did he pay you? Because you recorded him like he paid you to do it! What's up with that?" According to Nieto, he satisfies these requests at no extra charge: "They are included with the purchase of the video," he states. At the same time that he is criticized, he is also complimented: "There is a person there from La Plaza and [what she said] stuck with me, well, a little, because she said to me 'I like to watch your movies because you know what we want to see.'"[19]

Nieto's interest in getting to know the locals has helped him produce a unique narrative of La Plaza's fiesta. His interpretation of the celebration is highly influenced by the townspeople, whether representative of a local family with new money or of men who want to be forgotten.

Not all members of La Plaza place the same value on commissioned videos. One person I spoke to said that he did not care much for videos or photographs of La Plaza's fiesta because it was the experience of being present in his hometown that mattered to him the most. This sense of place and being with family and friends was something that resonated with many of the people with whom I spoke. Above all, the fiesta brings families and friends together to celebrate their faith, sometimes after years of separation, and although this experience of being home cannot be replaced with a video, these objects are experiential surrogates for those who cannot visit their homeland for financial or legal reasons. In this sense, fiesta videos can bring people together to celebrate and re-create an experience that defines their past and that can help trace their cultural identities.

Conclusion

On returning to La Plaza for the next fiesta, I was immediately taken aback by the widespread use of people recording the event with their smartphones and tablets. This observation points to a transition from a handful of videographers having a monopoly on recording technology to a stronger democratization of means in recording one's own experiences. Today, we see this all around us with social media sites, video applications that help us make movies, and the ease of posting videos on YouTube. For the time being, though, videographers still have a place in La Plaza, because it is one thing to be able to shoot raw footage of an event and upload it to YouTube and another to actually compose a coherent visual narrative more than a few minutes in length. Videographers' production skills and abilities still grant them an exclusive storyteller status; yet, as more people become their own storytellers, La Plaza's video history may very well become more informal and fragmented. Still, the goal is the same, to audiovisually remember La Plaza's fiestas together.

The value of commissioned videos comes from the social memory they incite by displaying communal practices with family and friends; these lived cultural experiences are what help lend authenticity to these videos. Moreover, if La Plaza's fiesta videos gather authenticity from the diaspora's ability to "be present," both literally and metaphorically, then as archivists we ought to study and question how archives can be designed to facilitate such a presence for diasporic communities. In some parts of the world, community archiving and the pluralization of archives has brought much-needed attention to these issues by focusing on the sociocultural aspects and politics of archiving. In Mexico, however, governmental policies still drive archival work, and archival education in Mexico is largely motivated by administrative recordkeeping functions that focus on governmental, legalistic, and fiscal matters.[20] These recordkeeping priorities create an interesting problem in a country with populations whose cultural diversity and ways of constructing the past have existed outside of the formal archival threshold. As has been discussed here, there are other literacies and recordkeeping practices that exist and function under different principles and material conditions than what official archives have historically represented. Therefore, we must continue to explore how archival theory can support pluralistic episteme to address how different knowledge ways and the social memories they produce can be framed as viable records in the global archival repertoire.

Notes

The author dedicates this chapter to her PhD advisor, Dr. Richard J. Cox.

The section "Commissioned Fiesta Videos" is a revised version of a section of the author's dissertation. Janet Ceja, "Informal Records and the Autochthonous Preservation of the Fiesta of Our Lady of Guadalupe in Rural Mexico," PhD diss., (University of Pittsburgh, 2013).

[1] Scot A. French, "What Is Social Memory?," *Southern Cultures* 2 (1995): 9.

[2] Jeffrey K. Olick and Joyce Robbins, "Social Memory Studies: From 'Collective Memory' to the Historical Sociology of Mnemonic Practices," *Annual Review of Sociology* 24 (1998): 105.

[3] Brien Brothman, "The Past That Archives Keep: Memory, History, and the Preservation of Archival Records," *Archivaria* 51 (2001): 63–64.

[4] See Richard J. Cox, "The Concept of Public Memory and Its Impact on Archival Public Programming," *Archivaria* 36 (1993): 122–135; Brothman, "The Past That Archives Keep"; Terry Cooke, "Remembering the Future: Appraisal of Records and

the Role of Archives in Constructing Social Memory," in *Archives, Documentation, and Institutions of Social Memory: Essays from the Sawyer Seminar*, ed. Francis X. Blouin and William G. Rosenberg (Ann Arbor: University of Michigan Press, 2000), 109–101, and Francis X. Blouin Jr., "Archiving, Mediation, and Constructs of Social Memory," *Archival Issues* 24 (2010): 101–112.

5 Luis González, "El arte de la microhistoria," in *Otra invitación a la microhistoria* (México: Fondo de la Cultura Económica, 1993), 45–46.

6 The videographer's name has been changed for the sake of anonymity.

7 In addition, Ramón Rodríguez Barrera, a La Plaza native, was documented stating that La Plaza was once a part of El Limón, a neighboring rancho. La Plaza's name implies that geographically it would have been at the head of El Limón, and indeed it is. See María Antonieta Delgado Tijerina, "Valgo por la tierra. Procesos agrarios y cultura campesina en una zona de la Cíenega de Chapala, Michoacán," master's thesis (El Colegio de Michoacán, 2001), 64.

8 See Heriberto Moreno García, *Haciendas de tierra y agua en la antigua Cienaga de Chapala* (Zamora, Michoacán: El Colegio de Michoacán, 1989); and Miguel Jesús Hernández Madrid, La comunidad autoritaria: estudio de las estrategias de vida en un ejido de Ixtlán De Los Hervores, Michoacán (Zamora, Michoacán: El Colegio de Michoacán, 1990).

9 See Jesús Gil Méndez, "La migración como factor de cambio en el espacio agrícola de localidades rurales ubicadas en el Valle de Ixtlán, Michoacán," *Revista de Investigaciones México-Estados Unidos CIMEXUS* 2, no. 2 (July–December 2007): 59–81; Jesús Gil Méndez, "Actividad agrícola y migración internacional en localidades rurales del Valle de Ixtlán, Michoacán," *Textual* 54 (July–December 2009): 49.

10 Fundación BBVA Bancomer y Secretaría de Gobernación, Anuario de Migración y Remesas: México 2017 (México, Distrito Federal, 2017), https://www.bbva .com/wp-content/uploads/2017/07/1707_AnuarioMigracionRemesas_2017.pdf, captured at https://perma.cc/WFW9-T8FS; Gil Méndez, "Actividad agrícola y migración internacional en localidades rurales del Valle de Ixtlán."

11 Rebecca Savage, "Towards the Ethnography of Filmic Places: Video-Based Research and Found Footage Filmmaking in the Anthropological Investigation of Mexican Migrant Event Video," PhD diss. (University of Westminster, 2012), 5–6.

12 Sarah Maslin Nir, "Jamaicans Get Party to Come to Them, via DVD," *New York Times*, March 31, 2013.

13 Patricia Zimmerman, *Reel Families: A Social History of Amateur Film* (Bloomington: Indiana University Press, 1995), xv.

14 Census data substantiate this claim by showing a correlation between the region's slow growth and migration trends, specifically during two major time periods. The first period, from 1940–1980, was due to the US Bracero program, which recruited large portions of temporary workers in rural parts of the state of Michoacán from 1955–1963. The second major migration period took place from 1980–2000, along with changes in birth and mortality rates. Still, as noted earlier, migration

patterns in the region remain high. Gil Méndez, "Actividad agrícola y migración internacional en localidades rurales del Valle de Ixtlán," 35.

[15] I adopt the term "devotional labor" from Elaine A. Peña's work in which she uses the term to describe faithful practices and offerings in the form of pilgrimage, prayer, song, dance, and shrine maintenance among other religious activities that create and preserve spiritual linkages between people and spaces, and histories and traditions, across geopolitical, social, and institutional boundaries. Elaine A. Peña, *Performing Piety Making Space Sacred with the Virgin of Guadalupe* (Berkeley: University of California Press, 2011), 10.

[16] Gil Méndez, "La migración como factor de cambio en el espacio agrícola de localidades rurales ubicadas en el Valle de Ixtlán, Michoacán," 75.

[17] Simplified interview excerpt from Ceja, "Informal Records," 160.

[18] Ceja, "Informal Records," 159.

[19] Ceja, "Informal Records," 165.

[20] Kelvin L. White, "Meztizaje and Remembering in Afro-Mexican Communities of the Costa Chica: Implications for Archival Education in Mexico," *Archival Science* 9, no. 1–2 (2009): 47–48, 50.

15

Where There's a Will

On Heir Property, African American Land Stories, and the Value of Oral Records in American Archives

Tonia Sutherland

Introduction

Twenty years ago, in 1998, archival scholar Richard J. Cox published an article titled "Archival Anchorites: Building Public Memory in the Era of the Culture Wars," in which he explored the role of cultural diversity in how archivists evaluate the value of records and develop policies around records retention. That same year, on the other side of the globe, *South African Archives Journal* published an article by archival scholar Segomotso Masegonyana Keakopa, "The Role of the Archivist in the Collection and Preservation of Oral Traditions," in which she stressed the importance of the archivist's role in collecting and preserving African oral traditions.[1] These two articles, which appeared in the archival studies literature at the same moment—albeit in vastly different contexts, reveal concomitant concerns about the need for archivists to liberate narratives, support accountability, and document and preserve subaltern histories and cultures. In "Archival Anchorites," Cox asserts that "although archivists constitute a small profession, their importance in preserving evidence of the past and hence their role in determining the nature of society's memory is substantial."[2] In her article, Keakopa echoes this sentiment, expressing deep concern about the determinations of societal and historical memory made by postcolonial archivists in African nations who ignored the cultural, historical, and societal value of oral traditions—which they did not understand and of which they did not approve. She argues that "post-colonial archivist[s] . . . preserved an inaccurate heritage, one that largely ignored the oral traditions which formed the basis of African history."[3] Noting that archives, as cultural heritage repositories, "reflect the complexities of the societies they inhabit," Cox suggests that what should "galvanize the public is why certain records are deemed to be worthy of long term maintenance or preservation, and [others] are not."[4] Keakopa similarly asserts that decisions made by archivists are sometimes violently problematic:

> Archival holdings [do] not necessarily reflect [history] accurately . . . mainly because records were written by people whose culture was foreign and whose civilisations were different. Their perceptions of African societies were influenced by their own interests and norms, and their attitude towards African oral traditions generally unfavourable, mainly because they came to Africa with preconceived notions about black people and their way of life.[5]

Considered collectively, the compelling—and interrelated—arguments made by Cox and Keakopa are particularly applicable to discussions about African American history and records: slavery-era practices kept many enslaved Americans of African descent intentionally and functionally illiterate, leading African Americans to simultaneously revitalize, celebrate, and re-inscribe the oral traditions rooted in their ancestral African culture. As Keakopa notes, however, state-sponsored archival institutions lack systematic strategies to collect and preserve oral records, oral testimony, and oral traditions, and where such strategies do exist (such as in Keakopa's Botswana), they tend to do so "on the basis of individual interest and enthusiasm."[6]

Oral tradition, also called orality, is the first known—and most continuously widespread—mode of human communication. Oral traditions are the means by which societies without written records preserve memory, past, and identity. In addition to being a mode of communication, oral tradition is arguably a methodology indigenous to the African continent. As a form of scholarship, oral tradition is frequently used to study social groups that do not maintain written records. In the context of African national archives, this methodology is particularly useful; in postcolonial African nations, the primary function of many archives was to preserve records inherited from colonial administrations. Because the records were created by people whose cultural norms and attitudes toward Africans were in direct conflict with Afrocentric norms and attitudes, these colonial records do not reflect an accurate or unbiased history of the nations or peoples concerned. Keakopa asserts that,

> whereas oral traditions are particularly important in documenting those societies without written records, throwing light on historical, social, economic and cultural development, they also articulate the voices of those who are hidden in history giving the voiceless a voice in a fast-changing world. Included in this category would be the less-privileged, ethnic minorities and women, etc. Oral traditions explore crucial areas that are scarcely touched on by written records, and by so doing help to fill the gaps in the documented colonial records that today make up early African history and form the basis for most African archival collections.[7]

African Americans, whose histories are directly tied to this legacy of colonialism, also do not have a past free from colonial interpretations. Culturally, African American traditions evolved from African traditions and were similarly devalued by European settler colonialists in the Caribbean and the Americas. In the present-day United States, African American historical documentation and archival representation is inextricably tied to chattel slavery, Jim Crow, and other forms of racialized violence. What is at stake for African Americans in US archival repositories is historical knowledge free from the same colonial and white supremacist interpretations that deny any meaningful African American past outside the colonization of the African continent and enslavement on the American one. For African Americans to read their own history and identity against the grain of white, colonial, American archivy, alternate forms of epistemology are necessary.

Many organizations throughout the United States record oral history interviews to document individual experiences for future generations. Presidential libraries, for example, have long collected oral histories, and the National Archives' first attempt to document its own history through oral interviews began as early as 1969. However, although institutions like the National Archives and the Society of American Archivists have a long record of strong oral history programs, oral history is not the same as oral tradition, and the two do not produce the same kind of documentary record. Oral histories follow specific guidelines and rules that stand counter to the narrative and mnemonic memory devices used in oral tradition. The overwhelming majority of oral history projects in the United States reflect similar goals: to codify institutional memory, to document specific historical moments and movements, and/or to gather individual histories. For example, the National Archives History Office was specifically created in 2013 to collect the historical experiences, insights, and perspectives of current and former staff members in an attempt to help the agency understand its culture, work practices, decision-making processes, historical actions, and events.[8] Oral histories do not serve a mandate to maintain the cultural and communicative narratives inherent in oral traditions or produce records that remain in their original oral format; rather, they are meant to produce fixed responses to predetermined questions. While oral histories are extraordinarily valuable tools for documenting history, it is also true that archivists in the United States remain uncomfortable with record formats that do not easily lend themselves to archival fixity. Embodied experiences such as live performances, rituals, festivals, and oral traditions that produce embodied records remain outside the archival corpus, and so, too, do the communities and cultural practices they represent.

In "Archival Anchorites," Cox suggests several possible avenues for archivists interested in creating what we might now call more inclusive or representative archives: pursue the meaning in the evidence found in records, trying to stay out of debates; seek to gather records that document myriad social groups and viewpoints; serve as passive recipients of records from those wishing to donate to archival repositories; focus on the "crucial aspects" of society; and, finally, *create new spaces where the archival memory of the marginalized can be protected.*[9] In her article, Keakopa argues that "[o]ral traditions . . . can contribute to the writing of an African history free from distorted colonial interpretation" and that "research based both on oral memory and documentary evidence helps in reevaluating secondary sources and brings a fresh approach to the writing of . . .

history."[10] Cox argues for the creation of new spaces while Keakopa's argument suggests that oral traditions have the power to facilitate the emergence of a richer and more accurate picture of African—and, by extension, African American—history. In this essay, I use land stories and heir property in the southeastern United States as a case study to argue that developing a liberatory vision for an African American future pivots on creating new spaces for the inclusion of oral records, oral testimony, and oral traditions in the American archival corpus.

Heir Property

Typically involving landowners who died intestate—or, without a written will—the term *heir property* refers to the informal succession of inherited land and real estate.[11] In cases in which there is a written will to serve as documentary evidence, land rights issues are relatively uncomplicated; when a landowner dies intestate, however, the state decides who inherits the land. In 2007, the US Department of Agriculture (USDA) estimated that by 1910 African American land ownership reached its peak of about 15 million acres. USDA reports suggest that land ownership continually decreased after 1910, declining to 2.3 million acres by 1992—an even grimmer estimate than that of the Uniform Law Commission.[12] Because of the significant impact heir property has on land loss—and because of the significant impact land loss has on African American wealth—African American land loss prevention organizations consider heir property one of the most pressing ongoing concerns for African American communities in the American South. African American land ownership and retention is of particular importance because for generations of African Americans, especially in the rural South, land ownership has symbolized a step toward racial equality and self-sufficiency. Reversing the land loss trend remains an important objective for African American families and communities.

Heir property divisions follow a simple—but often confusing—fractional interest real estate formula in which each party's percentage of ownership represents a fraction of the value of the property. For example, if a deceased property owner had three descendant heirs, each would inherit one-third of the property. If those three descendant heirs produced a total of six additional descendant heirs, each of the nine descendant heirs would be entitled to an equal portion (one-ninth) of the property. With the addition of each descendant heir, the amount of land belonging to each individual fractional owner decreases. Frequently, with tenuous relationships to written records and so many in-common custodians of the land, government records are difficult to keep track of and maintain—which also leads to property loss. For example, it is difficult to uphold state records requirements for property taxes, birth and death records, marriage licenses, and zoning change records when land is held in common by multiple members of multiple generations and passed by verbal bequeath.

Throughout the United States, but particularly in the Southeast and Hawai'i, heir property is commonly passed from generation to generation by verbal bequeath and without written legal paperwork. In South Carolina alone, there are at least seven counties representing a minimum 47,000 acres of heir property, and, per South Carolina law, an oral will is not analogous to a written will. Rather, Last Will and Testament documents must be drafted by an attorney, signed, and witnessed to be considered a legal record. Verbal bequeaths, or oral wills, are not legally enforceable in the United States—in no small part because there is no system, through design or contrivance, for oral testimony, oral records, or oral documents in the US documentary universe.

There are other concerns to consider. For example, banks and other financial institutions require collateral for mortgages; without a systemic recognition of the oral records that prove the nature of land ownership or custodianship, tenants-in-common are frequently determined to not be legal owners of the entire property and therefore cannot transfer property titles or get loans for home improvements. This means that even though heirs as in-common owners are required by law to pay property taxes, they retain no equity in the property they own. It also means that without a written deed, heir property owners are unable to access government assistance or relief. In Houston and other areas of Texas, African American heir property owners faced difficulty when trying to access federal recovery funds in the months and years following hurricanes Ike and Dolly in 2008.[13] Survivors of Hurricane Katrina in New Orleans were faced with similar concerns in 2005.

Heir property generates other problems for African American property owners. Developers eager to capitalize on attractive or profitable properties have been known to purchase a single share of fractional ownership—becoming the newest "member" of the family—and then attempt to force a sale. Because heir property typically sells quickly and for less than market value, these sales rob African Americans of what is sometimes their only source of inherited wealth. This is particularly true in urban areas (heir property holdings are not always large rural or agricultural land parcels). It can be especially difficult to establish heir property titles in cities, where small, single-family parcels cannot be physically divided.

In Alabama, based on laws of intestate succession, all owners hold a fractional interest in a whole estate. If the land remains undivided, all owners get equal access to the entire property. Because land varies geographically throughout a parcel, it cannot be assumed that each acre is equal in value. However, oral testimony and oral records can frequently account for these discrepancies. A land custodian or property owner telling an oral "land story" gives many cues and clues about divisions of property, such as tree lines, bodies of water, building structures, and so on. These oral traditions endure in African American communities, despite being systematically devalued, both as cultural expressions and as legitimate documentary sources.

In African American communities, heir property succession stems from the Reconstruction era, when African Americans first gained property rights in the United States. At that time, African American families did not create written wills to establish formal ownership or stewardship of property for future generations, primarily because they were denied access to, did not trust, or could not afford to use the legal system. Compounding the problem, the legacies of slavery and Jim Crow impacted literacy among African Americans in the southeastern United States, prompting a continuing reliance on oral traditions. As recently as 2003, the National Assessment of Adult Literacy (NAAL) indicated that document literacy rates for African Americans across the United States were significantly behind those of their white counterparts.[14] Because African Americans are historically, culturally, and societally bound to orality and oral records, it can be argued that American archivists, in the interest of creating more inclusive and representative archives, should and must develop the political will—the motive force that generates political action—to (1) design mechanisms to appraise, preserve, and provide access to these records; (2) adopt advocacy measures encouraging the amendment of state and federal records laws to include oral testimony and oral records; and (3) create new spaces, as Cox suggests in "Archival Anchorites," where the historical memory of African Americans can be protected.

To be clear, this redress does not require reinventing the proverbial wheel. On the contrary, examples of these practices already exist in other nations; these existing practices can be amended and adopted for American archives. In 1998, Segomotso Masegonyana Keakopa, in her writing about African archives and oral traditions, noted that oral tradition had already been identified as one method through which the precolonial African past could be accessed and the postcolonial African record corrected. In practical terms, this shift toward the oral specifically involved the establishment of new archival institutions as well as a commitment to the continuous collection of oral traditions. These long-extant practices can and should be embraced by American archivy—it is time for archivists to engage thinking that identifies as part of the archival mandate an obligation to preserve and maintain oral testimony, oral records, oral documents, and other oral traditions.

African American Land Stories

The way the story was given to me was that Sallie lived on The Ridge. Sallie and her brother lived together, and they owned slaves. During the war, Sallie's brother wanted to help Southerners, so he and his slave traveled on horseback to Virginia, where Sallie's brother was killed. Luckily, the slave made it back to The Ridge and told Sallie what had happened to her brother. There was great concern that the Yankees would come and do whatever they wanted with the land, and so Sallie decided she would divide the property herself and give the land to all of her slaves. After a while, Sallie moved to the next town over and got married, but her slaves kept her name and the land that she had given them.

Macon County, Alabama, is home to many black land stories. It is home to the stories of enslaved African Americans brought to clear and settle colonial Alabama and their freedmen descendants. It is also home to Tuskegee University and the storied black churches where unsuspecting men were duped into enrolling in the infamous United States Public Health Syphilis study. These stories exist at a crossroads, intersecting with the ancestral land stories of the Mvskoke (Muscogee) peoples. Before European encroachment and the forcible removal from their ancestral land, the Muscogee tribe spanned the southeastern United States. The Muscogee people constructed large ceremonial complexes of earthen pyramids along the rivers of this region and later built expansive towns within these same broad valleys that now lie in the states of Alabama, Georgia, Florida, and South Carolina.[15] In what is now southeast Macon County, Alabama, the Muscogee established a footpath along a long, narrow, raised strip of land. This land ridge footpath, simply known as "The Ridge," now exists in a stretch of Alabama land known colloquially as the Black Belt. Coveted by European settlers, this 50-mile-wide strip of rich, fertile, dark soil stretches across south-central Alabama, beginning in Macon County and ending at the Alabama/Mississippi border. After the Indian Removal Act of 1830 forced or coerced the relocation of Indigenous peoples in the Southeast, colonial European settlers arrived in the region in large numbers, bringing with them (or importing via the slave trade) enslaved Africans. As a result of this textured past, the Black Belt conjures a long and layered history of the Indigenous tribes, enslaved African Americans, colonial planters and traders, and their many descendants who have inhabited the land. So named in part as an homage to the rich blackness of the topsoil, and in part as a reference to the enslaved African Americans who toiled there, Alabama's Black Belt is a collective *lieux de mémoire*—a rich site of collective memory.[16]

The land story of Sallie and the enslaved people of The Ridge is an heir property land story shared with me by Aisha, whose ancestors inherited Sallie's land.[17] Aisha shared the land story of Sallie Who Lived on The Ridge in the storytelling spirit of an oral tradition, incorporating repetition, building, and mnemonic techniques. Aisha's land story, given by oral testimony, is the only existing record of Aisha's family homestead, its history, and what will hopefully be its future. Aisha is next in line to be the steward of Sallie's land, which has remained in the custody of her family since just after the Civil War. Stewardship of the land has been passed much like the story—through oral records, oral testimony, and oral traditions. As I have already suggested, while in various countries around the world orality and oral traditions are essential aspects of intangible cultural heritage in which gesture and ritual repetition are imbued with deep cultural meaning and relevance, engaging with embodied memory practices in the United States continues to present sociocultural, political, and policy problems. The Western epistemologies that form the basis for these problems privilege the material authority of written texts over the validity of the speech-acts embodied in oral documents. It is undeniable that this privileging of the written text (alongside the privileging of colonial narratives) has had disproportionately devastating consequences for African American communities around issues of family, community, property, and inherited wealth.

Land, particularly homeland, is linked to identity formation as a site of memory. For African Americans, land stories often reflect long-term generational investments in the land by people both previously enslaved and who were early tenants of the land throughout the first half of the twentieth century. I would like to argue that when a person's relationship with a site of memory changes—an unbidden change in the stewardship or proprietorship of heir property, for example—ontological and epistemological understandings of self can be disrupted. This disruption often results in what Maria Yellow Horse Brave Heart calls "historical trauma." Defined as a cumulative emotional and psychological wounding, over the life span and across generations, and emanating from massive group trauma experiences, historical trauma is also a form of transgenerational trauma.[18] In the United States this suffering refers to the experiences of particular groups of people and their descendants, including Holocaust survivors, Japanese American survivors of WWII internment camps, Indigenous peoples whose land, languages, and cultures have been colonized, and enslaved African Americans.

Such is the case with the descendants of the once-enslaved people who still inhabit The Ridge in Macon County, Alabama. For many to whom the land stories of this region belong, the historical trauma is complex, layered, and multifold. African American descendants of enslaved people made their home on appropriated sacred Muscogee ancestral land, which was then deeded—typically without the legal documents required by the systems devised and sustained by European colonizers and enslavers—to the once-enslaved people who had toiled the land and for whom the land is linked to the historical trauma of human ownership. It bears stating directly that in the United States, enslaved people were considered property and, as such, could not themselves own property. Once free, African Americans were legally authorized to exist politically and economically; one of the ways this new freedom was expressed was through acts of ownership. Owning things was a means by which to prove one's existence, to work against the notion that a person could have so little economic control as to effectively disappear.[19]

Valuing the Oral

Archival scholars have long argued that archives—explicitly included among Pierre Nora's *lieux de mémoire* (sites of memory)—are sites of power, identity, and collective memory.[20] However, as Terry Cook writes, "memory is notoriously selective—in individuals, in societies, and, yes, in archives."[21] Referencing legislation, official mission and mandate statements, annual reports, and positions taken by senior archives officials, Cook argues that archivists have the power to assign value to memory, deciding what is and is not "worth remembering." Archivists and lawmakers, Cook suggests, "continually refer to the archival role in preserving the 'collective memory' of nations, peoples, institutions, movements, and individuals; or they refer to appraising, selecting, acquiring, and then preserving records of 'significance,' or of 'value,' or of 'importance' which, put another way, means preserving those [deemed] worth remembering, worth memorializing."[22] The assignation of cultural value and worth, as it falls to the archivist, is central to both Cox's argument in "Archival Anchorites," that archivists might create new spaces where the historical memory of African Americans and other marginalized people can be protected, and to my argument here about the need for archivists to increase oral literacy and establish archival mandates to document and maintain oral records, oral testimony, and oral traditions.

The oral traditions utilized in Indigenous and African American land stories that act as primary documents and historical records related to heir property, as well as the heir property itself as a physical site of collective memory—as exemplified in the heir property land story of Sallie and The Ridge—stand in sharp contrast to the current limitations of American archivy. There are, however, archival scholars whose work is useful to consider in making an argument for orality in archives. Archival scholars Jeannette Bastian and Eric Ketelaar have both identified the limitations of traditional archival formats and emphasized the need to transcend those limits. Building on Bastian's work, I have argued that the evidentiary properties of records supersede their format and, more specifically, that the evidentiary properties of records supersede their need to be text-based.[23] Similarly, archival scholar Margaret Hedstrom has argued that archives should be "sources for the potential discovery or recovery of memories [or sites of memory] that have been lost."[24] These arguments, taken collectively, are critical to expanding archival thinking, theory, and practice to account for oral records—such as African American land stories—in United States archivy, and by extension, the people for whom those land stories are both primary source documents and vital historical records.

Standing in sharp contrast to US archival practice, as early as 1947, Marguerite Verdat, a Senegalese paleographer and archivist, began collecting oral traditions, deeming it essential "to save elements of history that are menaced with disappearance before having been written down."[25] The Cultural Archives of Senegal continued Verdat's mission to document Senegalese ethnic oral cultures. Methodologically, this was accomplished by representative data being collected and recorded by specialists who knew the language and culture of the ethnic group. As Saliou Mbaye wrote in the *American Archivist* in 1990:

> In general, for each month in the field it takes three months for the cataloging and transcription of the recorded data. Each tape is transcribed and eventually translated into French. Each inquiry is cataloged in the following way:
>
> - the name of the ethnic group
> - the heading (scenes of planting, healing, baptism, etc.)
> - the subject covered (history, religion, art, education, etc.)
> - the genre (myths, legends, stories)
> - the date of the document
> - an indication of the place
> - the group to which the document belongs
> - the title of the document
> - the type of recording device[26]

Mbaye's description of process is simple, elegant, and straightforward. It is not that it is not possible to develop policies and procedures for oral records, oral testimony, and other oral traditions; rather, many archivists in the United States lack the political will to conceptualize and enact more inclusive and representative archival practices; to create space for marginalized voices in archival institutions by developing or adopting new archival practices; or to develop and codify practices that serve more than the dominant historical, social, and cultural needs of a white, Western society.

As white American archivists have failed to act—in striking contrast to both the processes employed by the Senegalese Cultural Archives and the archival practices described by Keakopa in "The Role of the Archivist in the Collection and Preservation of Oral Traditions"—on behalf of African American traditions and thereby also on behalf of authentic African American histories, it is also worth noting the cultural and racial overlay endemic to principles of whiteness in American archival theory and practice. Writing in 1998, Richard Harvey Brown and Beth Davis-Brown argued that archival work has inherent political motivations and ramifications. I have also argued, in other writings, that archivists enact a dangerous and violent *archival amnesty* when they extend white supremacist attitudes and behaviors into the present by failing to collect, preserve, and make available materials that document the lived experiences of—and the human rights abuses that have been enacted against—marginalized peoples.[27] These two arguments—taken alongside Cox's argument in "Archival Anchorites"—that "the pioneering Southern state archives were part of the effort to reestablish a Southern white hegemony, requiring the reinvention of the past among other things"—speak to specific concerns about the legacy of archives and archival practice in the American South and the broader refusal of many American archivists to document and preserve anything other than the history of white supremacy, including an authentic African American cultural heritage, one not solely viewed through the lenses of colonialism and chattel slavery.[28] Developing archival theory and practice around oral and other embodied records is one way to amend the historical record and allow for richer, more robust African American narratives to emerge.

Conclusion

Records that account for the nuanced and complex African American land stories; evidence of historical traumas; evidence of rights of ownership, stewardship, or custodianship; and representations of cultural beliefs have fallen into the gaps and vagaries of American archivy. Although Cox advances the idea in "Archival Anchorites" that some "militant multiculturalists argue that their cultures and their contributions should always be treated as equal or superior influences on society, even when historically that might not be the case," I contend that our contemporary understandings of history warrant challenges—particularly those that emerged from the ultimately hegemonic voices of colonial empires.[29] I further maintain that decolonial interpretations of history do not constitute a singular, stagnant reading of the past but rather multiple and ever-evolving ones. These aspirational quests for alternative narratives demand methods of historical investigation both independent of history books and relevant to African American cultural contexts.

Cox argues that "members of racial, ethnic, religious, or cultural minorities understand that records documenting their past must be preserved and available for use"; I would extend this argument to suggest that members of these communities also know best which records—as well as which record *formats*—should be preserved and made available.[30] Although archivists might continue to resist the need to expand archival thinking and practice to include oral records, oral testimony, and oral tradition, there are certainly other archival interventions for heir property cases that currently do not exist. Existing record types—such as family artifacts, photographs, census records, land surveys, and diaries that reflect the history of the property and/or the history of the people that have lived on the land—could also bolster African American legal standing in heir property cases.

Toward this end, it is noteworthy that, in "Archival Anchorites," Cox eventually turns to documentation strategy, calling on records creators, custodians, and users to collaboratively identify what should be documented and which records would best suit those documentation purposes. While versions of documentation strategy have been employed with varying levels of success in North American archivy, a strong case can be—and has been—made by practicing

African American archivists, community archivists, and community engagement scholars that communities should be empowered to take the lead in directing documentation efforts. For African American land stories and other oral records, this means looking to African American communities as experts in their own right.

Some archivists have argued that the kind of archival practice for which I am advocating here—archival practice that is community engaged, decolonial, inclusive, and Afrocentric in every process from appraisal to access, and informed by every theory from provenance to archival custody—falls outside the purview of American archivy. Many archivists still argue that archives can and should be neutral and uncontroversial. Indeed, quoting Edward W. Said's 1994 book, *Representations of the Intellectual*, Cox notes in "Archival Anchorites" that archivists tend to think about appraisal as a simple aspect of professionalism:

> something you do for a living, between the hours of nine and five with one eye on the clock, and another cocked at what is considered to be proper, professional behaviour—not rocking the boat, not straying outside the accepted paradigms or limits, making yourself marketable and above all presentable, hence uncontroversial and unpolitical and "objective."[31]

Cox goes on to argue, however, that

> since nearly every major political and other controversy surfacing . . . somehow relates to records, it would be difficult for the archivist not to be controversial, even though we rarely hear from archivists in the highly visible debates involving records as crucial evidence or as contested evidence. Given that the archivists often make the final determination that something will or will not be saved . . . how can the archivist shy away from controversy?[32]

Without controversy, chance, courage, and experimentation, archivists would never have prevented the destruction of records during World War II. Likewise, archivists in Cambodia, El Salvador, and South Africa would not have documented war crimes and other human rights abuses, and that documentation would never have led to transitional or restorative justice. And in that vein, the Protocols for Native American Archival Materials would never have been developed. It is not a matter of the ability of archivists to innovate and design new systems, policies, protocols, and practices—it is a matter of will. Rather than asking a minority ethnic group in the United States to alter cultural modes of communication to end the practice of oral wills, might the expert archival community not exert the considerable political will it has already demonstrated, this time in service of a community that has already sacrificed tremendously at the hands of an oppressive dominant culture? As rich sites of collective memory, archives might also serve with intentionality as models for other *lieux de mémoire* as archival outreach often includes community workshops and resource sharing initiatives, many of which could incorporate similar techniques to capture oral records as the Senegalese Cultural Archives has done for decades.

Cox's final note in "Archival Anchorites" is a fitting end here—the assertion that archivists need to engage in broader discussions of how public memory is constructed, whose memory is included, and how that memory is culturally situated:

> Ordinary records can become extraordinary symbols when they are moved to the archives. . . . What should be deemed important . . . is the evidence these archives provide for all of us to understand our past and present.[33]

Notes

Author's Note: I am grateful to Dr. Allison Upshaw, who, along with Dr. Richard J. Cox, served as inspiration for this work.

[1] Segomotso Masegonyana Keakopa, "The Role of the Archivist in the Collection and Preservation of Oral Traditions," *S. A. Archives Journal* 40 (June 1998): 87.

[2] Richard J. Cox, "Archival Anchorites: Building Public Memory in the Era of the Culture Wars," *Multicultural Review* 7, no. 2 (June 1, 1998): 53.

[3] Keakopa, "Role of the Archivist," 98.

[4] Cox, "Archival Anchorites," 52.

[5] Keakopa, "Role of the Archivist," 98.

[6] Keakopa, "Role of the Archivist," 98.

[7] Keakopa, "Role of the Archivist," 98.

8 Jessie Kratz, "Building on a Tradition of Oral History," *Prologue Magazine* 48, no. 2 (2016), https://www.archives.gov/publications/prologue/2016/summer/historian-oral.html, captured at https://perma.cc/2CGP-ZJBE.

9 Cox, "Archival Anchorites," 59 (emphasis added).

10 Keakopa, "Role of the Archivist."

11 *Heirs' property* is land that is held "in common" by a group of people. A family, for example, might inherit heir property via informal succession. Because there are multiple owners, they are considered tenants-in-common of a piece of heirs' property. Tenants-in-common are especially vulnerable: any individual tenant can force a partition or property sale, and too frequently real estate speculators acquire a small share of heirs' property in order to file a partition action and force a sale. Using this tactic, an investor might acquire the entire parcel of land for a price well below its fair market value—and deplete a family's inherited wealth in the process.

12 National Archives and Records Administration, "Heir Property," *Federal Register,* January 10, 2007, https://www.federalregister.gov/documents/2007/01/10/E6-22102/heir-property, captured at https://perma.cc/H2DT-ELE5.

13 Sarah Breitenbach, "Heirs Property Challenges Families, States," Pew Charitable Trust, *Stateline,* July 15, 2015, http://www.pewtrusts.org/en/research-and-analysis/blogs/stateline/2015/07/15/heirs-property-challenges-families-states, captured at https://perma.cc/7HZP-KA29.

14 US Department of Education, Institute of Education Sciences, National Center for Education Statistics, "1992 National Adult Literacy Survey," June 2000, https://nces.ed.gov/pubsearch/pubsinfo.asp?pubid=199909, captured at https://perma.cc/7D6P-S8GN; US Department of Education, Institute of Education Sciences, National Center for Education Statistics, "2003 National Assessment of Adult Literacy," March 2007, https://nces.ed.gov/naal/pdf/2007464.pdf, captured at https://perma.cc/HCW9-9EVC.

15 The Muscogee (Creek) Nation, "Muscogee (Creek) Nation History," 2016, http://www.mcn-nsn.gov/culturehistory/, captured at https://perma.cc/2DAH-8XX3.

16 See Pierre Nora, "From *Lieux de Mémoire* to Realms of Memory," in *Realms of Memory: Rethinking the French Past* (New York: Columbia University Press, 1996), xvii. Heir property is, in many ways, a collective memory concern. In 1925, French sociologist Maurice Halbwachs argued that while individuals are memory-bearers, the collective (family, community, nation) decides what is of value to remember. Linked to collective memory and identity formation, *lieux de mémoire* (sites of memory) were popularized by French historian Pierre Nora, who argued that *lieux de mémoire* exist because there are no longer any settings in which memory is a real part of everyday experience.

17 The name of the storyteller has been changed for privacy and other ethical reasons.

18 See, for example, Maria Yellow Horse Brave Heart et al., "Historical Trauma Among Indigenous Peoples of the Americas: Concepts, Research, and Clinical Considerations," *Journal of Psychoactive Drugs* 43, no. 4 (October 2011): 282.

19 In the United States, one cannot talk about the concepts of property and property rights without also talking about the historical and contemporary geopolitics of power, including colonialism and globalization. It is important to note here

that while notions of land custodianship are aligned with Indigenous beliefs and practices, the idea of ownership must be cast in contrast to the Muscogee people's relationship to the same land. To what extent African American heirs in the southeastern United States should feel bound to honor Indigenous cultural frameworks requires a much broader discussion than is possible here, but it would be tremendously irresponsible not to acknowledge and reinforce an Indigenous cultural standpoint and positionality in regards to these native ancestral homelands.

[20] Pierre Nora, "Between Memory and History: *Les Lieux de Mémoire*," *Representations Special Issue: Memory and Counter-Memory* 26 (Spring 1989): 7–24.

[21] Terry Cook, "Memory, Identity, Evidence, and Community: Four Shifting Archival Paradigms," *Archival Science* 13 (2013): 101.

[22] Cook, "Memory, Identity, Evidence, and Community," 101.

[23] Jeannette Bastian, "Reading Colonial Records Through an Archival Lens: The Provenance of Place, Space, and Creation," *Archival Science* 6, no. 3–4 (2006): 267–284, and Eric Ketelaar, "Sharing: Collected Memories in Communities of Records," *Archives and Manuscripts* 33, no. 1 (2005): 44–61. See also Jeannette Bastian, "'Play Mas': Carnival in the Archives and the Archives in Carnival: Records and Community Identity in the US Virgin Islands," *Archival Science* 9 (2009): 113–125. I have also written about the need to develop more robust archival theory and practice for embodied records. See, for example, Tonia Sutherland, "From (Archival) Page to (Virtual) Stage: The Virtual Vaudeville Prototype," *American Archivist* 79 (Fall/Winter 2016): 392–416, and Tonia Sutherland, "Restaging the Record: Opportunities for Collaboration in Event-Based Archivy," in *Annual Review of Cultural Heritage Informatics,* ed. Samantha K. Hastings (Lanham, MD: Rowman and Littlefield, 2015), 17–38.

[24] Trond Jacobsen, Margaret L. Hedstrom, and Ricardo L. Punzalan, "Invoking 'Collective Memory': Mapping the Emergence of a Concept in Archival Science," *Archival Science* 13, no. 2–3 (June 1, 2013): 217–251.

[25] Saliou Mbaye, "Oral Records in Senegal," *American Archivist* 53 (Fall 1990): 568.

[26] Mbaye, "Oral Records in Senegal," 569.

[27] Tonia Sutherland, "Archival Amnesty: In Search of Black American Restorative and Transitional Justice," *Journal of Critical Library and Information Studies* 2 (2017).

[28] Cox, "Archival Anchorites," 54. Although I am specifically addressing archives in the American South here, it should be noted that this problem is pervasive throughout the United States.

[29] Cox, "Archival Anchorites," 55.

[30] Cox, "Archival Anchorites," 53.

[31] Edward Said, *Representations of the Intellectuals* (London: Vintage, 1994), 74, quoted in Cox, "Archival Anchorites," 56, https://www.academia.edu/15713641/Said_Edward_-_Representations_of_the_Intellectual.

[32] Cox, "Archival Anchorites," 56.

[33] Cox, "Archival Anchorites," 60.

16

The Road to Memory
Beyond Touchstones and Triggers

Jeannette A. Bastian

Introduction

In this essay, I explore the expanding and changing place of memory in archival work. Variously characterized as corporate memory, touchstones of memory, memory triggers, or houses of memory, memory has always played a part—although often a minor one—in the full understanding of records. But, while the analog mechanisms of memory (paper, photographs, etc.) tend to keep memory at a distance as reflectors or reactors to records, memory in the digital realm has assumed a more compelling and immediate role within the archival realm.

A Tale of Two Memories

In a 1993 article in *Harper's Magazine*,[1] Thomas Mallon tells the story of finding boxes of his father's cancelled checks in his mother's attic thirteen years after his father's death. As he leafs though the boxes, the carefully noted expenditures trigger Mallon's memories of his father and his own boyhood growing up in suburban Long Island in the 1950s. Through the checks, Mallon reconstructs his father's life and, as he does so, uncovers clues about his own boyhood and adolescence, things that he never realized at the time. The checks—including a final one for the refilling of oxygen tanks—are revelations as well as reminiscences to the younger Mallon as he pieces together his father's life, now understanding family struggles that he never realized as he was growing up.

Although this story is about Mallon's father and the young Mallon, it is also about records and their power to evoke memory. The word *archives* never appears in this article, yet the archival elements are easily recognized—order, provenance, transactions, evidence. The author himself acknowledges the archival nature of the checks, even foreshadowing a more complex relationship between records and memory when he writes, "these checks were not merely a record of my father's transactions with the world; they were the transactions." Recognizing their collective value beyond the personal, Mallon observes that, "like the grid of streets in the suburban development on Long Island, New York, where I was born, my father's neatly stacked checks map a whole postwar way of life."[2]

Mallon and the boxes of numbered and dated checks create a compelling archival story, one that speaks clearly to the power of records to conjure memory. When Mallon observes that "what was never meant to be saved, like what was never meant to be overheard, is usually what contains the truth," he articulates a view that formed the base of archival activity throughout the twentieth century when archives were primarily thought of as memory evokers, triggers, and houses of memory that store our past.

But that was then. And this is now.

In a 2018 article in the *Atlantic*, Amir-Hussein Radjy, an author based in Cairo, writes movingly about a collection of crowd-sourced videos compiled by an independent media group, Mosireen. The videos, recorded on smartphones, document the 2011 revolutionary protest against the Egyptian regime of Hosni Mubarak at Tahir Square. Mosireen had hoped to use these videos in a trial against the regime as evidence of the brutality of the security forces. But the political situation in Egypt changed rapidly in the other direction. The trial never happened. Instead, Mosireen used the videos to create a virtual "resistance archive," which its members named 858 (the amount of footage). Radjy writes that "the collection includes footage shot during the revolution by both members and non-members (many of whom choose to remain anonymous). When I spoke with members of Mosireen, they described the act of assembling their video archive as a defense of the revolution's memory against the regime." Radjy further notes that "in a society where dissent has become dangerous, Mosireen's archive is an exercise in the subversive power of memory."[3]

The archive consists of 1,662 video images, each capturing and witnessing a particular moment of the eighteen days of the Tahir Square revolution. The images are searchable by keywords and in the aggregate are powerful visual testimonies of the event.[4] The author notes that "the power to photograph, film, and broadcast protests across the Internet in real time seemed to prove the emancipatory power of technology."[5] But the subsequent use of these videos as documents of a political moment that has been suppressed seems to indicate that in addition to or complementary to its "emancipatory" power, digital technology has also released a new "memory" power.

With the immediacy of a smartphone, an image captured in real time becomes an instant memory, and a moment is documented almost simultaneously with its memory-creation. Through this instant creation, memory itself suddenly has a new agenda because while this technology might memorialize and document an action, it also becomes a witness, memorializing and sustaining a concern for social justice.

In *The Era of the Witness*, Annette Wieviorka examines memory through the prism of the oral testimonies of Holocaust victims. She movingly and vividly recounts the oral testimony of the first hesitant Holocaust survivor at the Adolf Eichmann trial in Jerusalem in 1961, a testimony that opened the floodgates of previously repressed and ignored memory. She writes, "testimonies, particularly when they are produced as part of larger cultural movements, express the discourse or discourses valued by society at the moment the witnesses tell their stories as much as they render an individual experience."[6] As the Tahir Square videos suggest, the ability to instantly record and share the moment has become today's witnessing, recording a perspective in the immediacy of the individual experience. Technology has changed our relationship with memory. "Memory," notes media scholar Abigail De Kosnik, "is now the basis of a great deal of cultural production."[7] No longer merely triggers and touchstones, our records have become our memories, our memories have become our records.

Memory and Records

This essay owes much to the insights of Richard Cox, whose scholarship has always considered memory as a critical component of recordmaking and keeping. Early on, he identified a seismic shift in the connections between memory, the people and communities who create memory, and the ways in which those connections impact the relationship between memory and records in a postmodern, socially constructed world. In his 2003 book *No Innocent Deposits*, Cox stated that "whatever comes into the archives and how it gets there might be beside the point because archives are a symbolic way station on the road to collective memory,"[8] offering a prescient glimpse of an expanded and significant role for memory in archival production, moving the discussion from the personal to the collective and suggesting a seamless transformation of records into memory and vice versa. Since 2003, memory as both an archival process and a societal product has continued to evolve. Side by side with this theoretical evolution have been the rapidly evolving tools of memory. Through technological affordances, such as smartphones, tweets, Instagram posts, and Facebook likes, memory has moved center stage, a dynamic component of our lives as society relentlessly records and shares itself, demanding and creating instant memory.

How might this "instant" memory affect and transform the archives/memory relationship? Although memories are always driven by the technologies that capture them—be they photographs, letters, memorials, or performances—the internet, with its multiple evolving social media tools, represents a new type of engagement, one that conflates actions, disrupts sequences, and encourages movement, simultaneously producing both the record and the memory. No longer distanced, re-centering memory within the archival sphere suggests strategies for documenting the immediacy of our personal and global "transactions," engaging with communities, and creating dynamic archives that are at once memories of the past and memory-making in the present.

Modeling memory streams that conflate the memory/archives equation extends Cox's construct of archives as a "symbolic way station on the road to collective memory." In this essay, I consider this equation by focusing on the potential impact of current tools and strategies to refashion and rethink connections between archives and memory. Considering the power of technology to mingle action, transaction, record, and memory, I stress the affordances of that power to reimagine the relationships between and within communities of records and memory in the context of a living dynamic archive where the archive and the memory are one.

Memory Studies and Archives

Beginning in the latter quarter of the twentieth century, memory—specifically, collective or social memory—began to enter academic discourse and became a focus of concern for historians, sociologists, anthropologists, and others, including archivists, in the social science and humanities disciplines. This discourse took as its starting point Maurice Halbwachs's essential insight that not only do we see the past through a lens of the present, but each lens is that of a group rather than an individual. Halbwachs wrote that "while the collective memory endures and draws strength from its base in a coherent body of people, it is individuals as group members who remember . . . every collective memory requires the support of a group delimited in time and space."[9] This recognition of the centrality of memory was primarily fueled by the recognition that the Holocaust and other extreme human tragedies of the twentieth century could not be understood solely through traditional documentation and archival evidence alone. Testimonies, witnessing, trauma, and personal and collective memories were critical windows for fully comprehending these terrible events in human terms. Studying memory offered the potential of understanding communities and cultures in new holistic ways that were not possible through conventional historical sources.

Thus was the beginning of the "memory boom" of the 1980s, leading to the development of the "memory studies" of today, an interdisciplinary scholarly field that continues to gain in importance and influence in the academic world, producing journals, conferences, articles, books, and all the paraphernalia of scholarship.

In their introduction to *The Collective Memory Reader*, editors Jeffrey K. Olick, Vered Vinitzky-Seroussi, and Daniel Levy offer a broad social perspective on the wide net cast by memory:

> The new insight of memory studies is . . . not merely that memory is omnipresent but that it is at once situated in social frameworks (e.g.,

family and nation), enabled by changing media technologies (e.g., the Internet and digital recording), confronted with cultural institutions (e.g., memorials and museums), and shaped by political circumstances (e.g., wars and catastrophes). Social frameworks and historical circumstances change over time. . . . Studying (and theorizing) memory allows us to shift our focus from time to temporalities, and thus to understand what categories people, groups and cultures employ to make sense of their lives.[10]

In other words, studying memory opens windows into understanding history, communities, cultures, and events in ways that may not have been possible through traditional documentation. A group of sociologists and psychologists debating in 2009 about whether an interdisciplinary field of memory might be viable noted that:

it is difficult to imagine an area of one's life that is not shaped profoundly by memory, from our most personal and intimate recollections of the past, our sense of self and our ability to execute daily routines, to the ways in which remembering communities construct the past through language, ceremonial and mundane practices, political policy, and physical structures. Yet our respective disciplines are limited in addressing this complex nexus of questions due to methodological or theoretical constraints.[11]

Importantly, memory also points toward social justice. As the images of Tahir Square illustrate, memory is not simply an academic exercise. Layers of memory intermingle with documentation to add meaning to a profoundly personal but also communal event—one that, through the affordances of memory, we can understand with our hearts as well as our heads, one that both validates and humanizes the evidence. Memory in a sense annotates the text and sustains it. But the "archive" of Tahir Square also heralds a further advance in memory studies. No longer solely the province of academics, memory is now a societal as well as social activity. Crowd-sourced, citizen-inspired, technology-driven, memorializing has become a critical activity both for the collective and the individual, a matter of identity and community as well as justice.

Memory has always had a natural and obvious affinity to archives, yet archival scholars are only beginning to explore memory as a theoretical lens for explicating complex archival and societal relationships.[12] This emerging scholarship by archivists, in addition to the turn toward memory in many disciplines, suggests that memory and its complex relationship to archives and archival concerns be considered as an archival focus in its own right, one that leads to new practices in the use of memory to explicate and document.

Archivists have long claimed a special relationship with memory. Australian archivist Michael Piggott reminds us that Sir Hilary Jenkinson may have had the first word on that relationship when he accorded "archives a memory role from the moment they exist as records."[13] In his *Manual*, Jenkinson writes:

> The official or responsible person . . . who has to preside over any continuous series of business functions, the manager of a small estate at one end of the scale, the controller of a kingdom's finances at the other, relies for the support of his authority on memory: so soon as writing becomes general in use he adopts the preservation of pieces of writing as a *convenient form of artificial memory* and in doing so starts a collection of Archives.[14]

The linking of memory and archives as part of the archivist's responsibility has continued within the archival sphere. The records kept in "houses of memory" are declared as national memory, sharing an implicit and significant relationship. For example, the National Archives of Australia describes itself as "the memory of our nation—collecting and preserving Australian Government records that reflect our history and identity,"[15] while the US Library of Congress called its online website of primary sources "American Memory."[16]

Although the characterization of "houses of memory" as the treasures of our past contained within archival institutions, where archivists are the holders of the "keys to collective memory,"[17] is a persistent one in the archival mythos, archivists have many other connections to memory. Corporate memory or organizational memory is probably the memory trope most familiar to archivists. But memory and archives have been linked together and seen as sharing an implicit and significant relationship in many other aspects of archival processes. Not only do archivists collect, manage, and preserve the "stuff" of memory, but through appraisal, they participate to a great extent in determining its continuity and perpetuation. Cox writes that "it is my contention . . . that archivists need to reconsider the implications of public memory for the function and act of archival appraisal leading to the formation of archives and their usefulness in society."[18] What gets remembered and what gets forgotten may not be completely in the hands of archivists, but certainly archivists have prominent roles to play in those decisions.

In her 2006 expansive analysis of the relationship between archives and memory, Laura Millar determined that archives were "touchstones" of memory and "vehicles of memory."[19] Earlier, in 2002, her fellow Canadians Terry Cook and Joan Schwartz had noted that, "archives—as records—wield power over the shape and direction of historical scholarship, collective memory, and national identity, over how we know ourselves as individuals, groups and societies."[20]

At a conference in Dundee, Scotland, in 2010, Terry Cook outlined the evolving role of archivists, declaring, "beyond evidence, archives also preserve memory. And they create memory."[21] He further noted that "evidence and memory have evolved, then, in archival discourse in a kind of creative tension, each worthless without the other despite the contrary implications they seemingly have for the archival endeavour."[22] Cook named evidence as the first archival paradigm shift and memory as the second, when archivists asserted themselves as proactive managers of their collections. Identity, in which the archivist becomes mediator, and Community, the democratization of archives, were the third and fourth paradigms. He unites these paradigms by suggesting that evidence and memory working together support and encourage identity and community, and "by anchoring its increasingly diverse activities and approaches through an engagement with lived communities and their evidence-memory-identity practices, archival practice (and identity) can itself remain plural and diverse."[23]

Although the archives/memory relationship has in the past tended toward memory as a subject that archivists need to understand, rather than as a framework that uses memory itself as a lens through which archival material can be understood, appraised, and described, there are many indications that archivists are engaging with memory on a more complex level. A 2010 study at the University of Michigan examined the archives/memory relationship as expressed in the archival literature published between 1980 and 2010 in four leading English-language archives journals,[24] finding that the articles indicated the high degree to which archivists saw the need to engage memory as an essential feature of archival work,[25] Archivists increasingly recognized that the substance of memory in giving particular meanings to the past required that memory not only be treated as archival but as a strategy toward uncovering forgotten or deliberately misplaced pasts.

Technologies of Memory—An Archival Strategy

In her book *Tangled Memories: The Vietnam War, the AIDS Epidemic, and the Politics of Remembering,* in which she examines the American collective memory of the Vietnam War and the AIDS epidemic, communications scholar Marita Sturken uses the term "technologies of memory" to refer to the vast array of cultural products and texts, including photographs, films, artifacts and documents that "embody and generate memory and are thus implicated in the power dynamics of memory's production."[26] In the same volume, Sturken also suggests several roles for the archives, noting that the cultural narratives of history are as much evidence of events as the textual narratives and asserting that "memory is a narrative rather than a replica of an experience that can be retrieved and relived."[27] She points out that,

> when personal memories of public events [individual possessions left at the Vietnam Wall and collected by the National Park Service] are shared, their meaning changes . . . they become a part of cultural memory. When they are then placed in a government archive, they acquire both aesthetic and historical meaning.[28]

Sturken suggests that one of the tasks of archivists is to turn cultural memory into national narrative. She writes that,

> personal memory, cultural memory and history do not exist within neatly defined borders. Rather, memory and memory objects can move from one realm to another, shifting meaning and context. Thus personal memories can sometimes be subsumed into history, and elements of cultural history can exist in concert with historical narratives.[29]

Broadening the archival narrative through "technologies of memory" speaks not only to documenting those groups whose community expressions are difficult to capture through individual documents and whose collective characterizations tend toward the nontextual but also speaks to continually adding to that toolkit. Digital technologies, as suggested in the Tahir Square example, bring a whole new set of tools to the archives/memory construct, as explored in the following sections.

Memory = Archives

As demonstrated by the smartphones in Tahir Square, the abilities of digital technologies to disrupt sequentialities have helped to move memory closer to the events themselves. This time compression creates a dynamic archives where memory and records seem to occur almost simultaneously. This shifting sequencing can also create different archival constructs that offer a way to overcome the often seemingly static quality of records. For example, in his 2015 book *Performing Digital: Multiple Perspectives on a Living Archive,* digital humanist David Carlin reflects on his experiences creating an archives for Circus Oz, an Australian performing arts company and pioneering animal-free circus founded in 1978. The Circus Oz website includes this description of the troupe's beginnings:

> The founding members of Circus Oz loved the skills and tricks of traditional circus but wanted to make a new sort of show that a contemporary audience could relate to, adding elements of rock'n'roll, popular theatre and satire. They wanted it to be funny, irreverent and spectacular, a celebration of the group as a bunch of multi-skilled individual women and men, rather than a hierarchy of stars. Above all, they didn't want to take themselves too seriously. They sewed and welded together their own circus tent, got together a collection of old trucks and caravans and went on the road. Circus Oz was a fresh and original voice in circus and the company was immediately popular with Australian audiences. Within a few years, the company began to tour internationally, with visits to New Guinea and Europe.[30]

The challenge of the project was how to document this circus through a "living archive," and the challenge was met by the creation of an interactive dynamic website featuring current and past acts and readers' posts of memories of the acts. As Carlin writes, "the Living Archive presents not a history, but annals, a navigable set of microstories, memories and information rather than a comprehensive unified story of Circus Oz, by drawing on specific tricks computers can do."[31] He sees the archive as a potentially democratic distributed phenomenon as opposed to the fixed and static "classical archive" of "state power." Through the affordances of technology, specifically the digital media, he suggests the possibility of considering how "live performance excperiences [are] to be remembered."[32]

A similar attempt to create a "living archive" that brings together memory and record in a dynamic interplay is "John Cage Unbound: A Living Archive," a permanent exhibit on the New York Public Library's website that celebrates the work of twentieth-century composer John Cage. Described as "an online record of John Cage's work and its evolving impact on music and performance," the website includes ongoing space for videos of current interpretations of Cage's music as well as commentary about the effects of his work on other musicians. The website asks members of the public to post their own videos, explaining "most important, contribute your own video showing how you interpret Cage's music. Videos will appear on this homepage as the Living Archive grows. Cage believed that, following his detailed directions, anyone could make music from any kind of instrument—and so we welcome your interpretations of his music."[33]

Contemporary renditions of Cage's music in a wide and broad variety of interpretations recognize and attempt to realize his enduring vision of his music that lives on in multiple and continual translations. In this living performance archive, as with Circus Oz, the memory and the record are one—continually interacting and evolving, indistinguishable from one another, the memory is the archive.

The concerns that the creators of the videos express about their sustainability as memories—essentially the reason for their creation—also points to the effect that technology has on the act of archiving itself. Media scholar Abigail De Kosnik, drawing from performance scholar Diane Taylor's binary of the archives (scribal) and the repertoire (physical performance) in the production of memory, asserts that in a digital environment, "archival labor consists of a repertoire."[34] That is, the physical efforts required to preserve digital memories through migration, preservation, coding, and so on, mean that although the traditional memory work of archivists has moved to the digital, that work requires a certain performance. Taylor contends that "embodied and performed acts generate, record and transmit knowledge."[35] De

Kosnik writes, "For every actual and virtual archive in the digital age depends heavily on repertoire and can even be said to rely more on repertoire—by which I mean physical, bodily acts of repetition, of human performance—than seems readily apparent."[36] If true, then, this means that in a digital environment, archivists act continually in the "living archive," where memories are remembered or forgotten as part of an evolving digital performance.

Archives Are Everywhere

Responding to the digital memory turn does not mean that archivists must forsake their memory roots. On the contrary, records can memorialize as well as trigger, can be the recognition as well as the touchstone, the living archive as well as the vehicle of remembrance.

What has changed is the memory-creation process, the space (or lack of) between the record and the memory, and the immediacy of the memory itself. Thomas Mallon's father's checks were factors in his daily life, and years later, his son imbued them with personal memory while also recognizing them as a social collective memory of an era. But the Tahir Square protesters were not looking back in order to remember; they themselves were intent on creating the memory of the events unfolding around them. And their efforts toward remembering were primarily focused on not being forgotten.

This deliberate effort to conflate the record and the memory in the drive to be remembered is illustrated by archivists Dima Saber and Paul Long, who describe an archive of digital videos taken by citizens in Darra, Syria, at the beginning of the Syrian uprising in 2011. The authors ask, "So does a citizen-generated capturing of the first public declaration of the Syrian uprising constitute a record or an archive? Who gets to decide? And is it enough that its author sees it as an archive, for us to accept the definition and consider the Daraa material as a new social memory of the Syrian war?[37] In this combination of witnessing and documenting, memory is being created in real time, constituting another type of "living archive," one in which the immediacy of both the event and its memory are captured together. When the authors interviewed the creators of the videos, it became apparent that, similarly to the Tahir Square records, the archive not only serves as both evidence and memory of a series of events, but, as they write, "it is apparent from our interviews that one of the main motivations behind compiling the Daraa archive was preservation: to counter forgetfulness, and to safeguard the memory of the people and places from the destructive chaos of the war."[38]

Cox has also suggested that "the effort to destroy or create archives is part of a process of destroying group identity by eradicating its memory or generating sources to create identity and cohesion of a group."[39] Nowhere is that truer than in the growing Community Archives movement, which is often as much about preventing forgetting as it is about supporting remembering and preserving community heritage and values. Michelle Caswell uses the term "symbolic annihilation" to describe what happens to marginalized groups when they are ignored and underrepresented in the archives. She sees community archives and a distributed web presence as ways to reverse that process: "In this way, community archives are responses not only to the omissions of history as the official story written by a guild of professional historians, but the omissions of memory institutions writ large, and can thus be read as a direct challenge to the failure of mainstream repositories to collect a more accurate and robust representation of society."[40] The drive toward social justice can become a battle between remembering and forgetting, identity and annihilation, where memory is the contested entity to be fought over, disputed, and defended.

A recent book, *Archive Everything, Mapping the Everyday* by Gabriella Giannachi, supports and explicates the increasingly interdependent and immediate archives/memory relationship in our technological climate. Not an archivist but a media scholar, Giannachi takes a broad look at the archival discipline, tracing its history from the ancient Greeks to the digital era, attempting to bring together traditional archival theory with the more ubiquitous academic "archival turn" in order to demonstrate why "the archive has become the apparatus through which we map the everyday."[41] She describes the development of archives in phases from Archives 0.0 to Archives 4.0. Expanding on a model developed by media scholar Michael Shanks who theorized Archives 1.0 as "bureaucracy in the early state," Archives 2.0 as "digitization of archival data bases, with an aim of fast, easy access," and Archives 3.0 as "architectures for the production and sharing of archival resources—the animated archive,"[42] Giannachi adds Archives 0.0 and 0.4. Archives 0.0 might be characterized as "pre-archival" or ancient archives, while in Archives 4.0, the user has become fully engaged within the archives and the archives has "become our environment."[43] Giannachi writes, "there is, in principle, no more delay between the present and the creation of its memory in the archive but rather the technical option of immediate feedback, particularly visible through the use of social media, turns all present data into instantly accessible archival entries and vice versa."[44]

Conclusion

How do archivists traverse the memory spectrum when questions of remembering and forgetting are critical both to society and individual lives? There may be no one way to "do" memory, but nonetheless the memory stakes are high. Archivists, those foot soldiers of memory, need to get it right or at least do no harm.

Leveraging memory by recognizing and utilizing all the tools and technologies at our disposal, acknowledging the variety of roles that memory can play in relation to records, and capturing those tools and content that are the meaningful components of a particular situation may be ways in which archivists keep their options open and themselves remain open to all possibilities. From triggers to vehicles to paradigms to living archives, memory and records work together in multiple complex ways that all have their own values: A Canadian archivist seeks memory to help validate his family genealogy;[45] an archivist from the Caribbean island of Montserrat creates a micro-history of a sugar worker in the colonial era through combining an oral history with official records;[46] Indigenous peoples in Australia combine stories, language, history, and images on their website in an effort to sustain the memory of their people;[47] a translator and media scholar connects memories of donors about their own materials in order to enrich and deepen the meanings of their archival collections;[48] and the members of a diasporic community creates an archive as a way of affirming their identity.[49] And the examples go on. Memory is ubiquitous; it cannot be harnessed, but it is also a central component in how we think about, represent, and share archives. Perhaps the best we can do is to recognize memory as both a process and a product in the archiving endeavor, utilize all the memory tools at our disposal, and understand that both memory and forgetting are ultimately about people and their survival.

Notes

1   I am indebted to Richard Cox for introducing me to this article when I was his
    doctoral student.

2   Thomas Mallon, "Memories Held in Check: Perusing a Lifetime of My Father's
    Expenditures," *Harper's Magazine* 287 (October 1993).

3   Amir-Hussein Radjy, "How to Save the Memories of the Egyptian Revolution,"
    Atlantic, January 25, 2018, https://www.theatlantic.com/international/archive
    /2018/01/an-internet-archive-rekindles-the-egyptian-revolutions-spirit/551489/,
    captured at https://perma.cc/8WVA-ZKH3.

4   The archive is available at https://858.ma/grid/title/keywords==sky&topic==Tahrir
    _Protests.

5   Radjy, "How to Save the Memories."

6   Annette Wieviorka, *The Era of the Witness* (Ithaca: Cornell University Press, 2006),
    xii.

7   Abigail De Kosnik, *Rogue Archives: Digital Cultural Memory and Media Fandom*
    (Cambridge, MA: MIT Press, 2016): 3.

8   Richard J. Cox, *No Innocent Deposits: Forming Archives by Rethinking Appraisal*
    (Lanham, MD: Scarecrow Press, 2004), 234.

9   Maurice Halbwachs, *On Collective Memory*, ed. and trans. Lewis A. Coser
    (Chicago: University of Chicago Press), 22.

10 Jeffrey K. Olick, Vered Vinitzky-Seroussi, and Daniel Levy, eds., *The Collective
    Memory Reader* (London: Oxford University Press, 2012), 17.

11 Adam D. Brown, Yifat Gutman, Lindsey Freeman, Amy Sodaro, and Alin
    Coman, "Introduction: Is an Interdisciplinary Field of Memory Studies Possible?,"
    International Journal of Politics, Culture, and Society 22, no. 2 (June 2009): 118.

12 A number of surveys of archives/memory scholarship have appeared over the past
    decade. See, for example, Anthea Josias, "Toward an Understanding of Archives
    as a Feature of Collective Memory," *Archival Science* 11 (March 2011): 95–112;
    and Trond Jacobsen, Ricardo L. Punzalan, and Margaret L. Hedstrom, "Invoking
    'Collective Memory': Mapping the Emergence of a Concept in Archival Science,"
    Archival Science 13 (April 2013): 217–251.

13 Michael Piggott, "Archives and Memory," in *Archives: Recordkeeping in Society*,
    ed. Sue McKemmish, Michael Piggott, Barbara Reed, and Frank Upward (Wagga
    Wagga, New South Wales, Australia: Charles Sturt University Press, 2005), 301.

14 Sir Hilary Jenkinson, *A Manual of Archive Administration* (London: Percy Lund,
    Humphries & Co., 1937), 23, quoted in Piggott, "Archives and Memory," 301
    (emphasis in original).

15 National Archives of Australia, "Welcome to the National Archives," http://www.naa
    .gov.au/about-us/, captured at https://perma.cc/BJ6H-G2L3.

[16] Library of Congress, American Memory, "Mission and History," http://memory.loc
.gov/ammem/about/index.html, captured at https://perma.cc/4TWR-D34W.

[17] Jean-Pierre Wallot, "Building a Living Memory for the History of Our Present:
New Perspectives on Archival Appraisal," *Journal of the Canadian Historical
Association* 2 (1991): 282. For further discussion of Wallot's meaning, see Terry
Cook, "What Is Past Is Prologue: A History of Archival Ideas Since 1898, and the
Future Paradigm Shift," *Archivaria* 43 (Spring 1997): 18.

[18] Richard Cox, *No Innocent Deposits*, 243.

[19] Laura Millar, "Considering the Relationship Between Memory and Archives,"
Archivaria 61 (Spring 2006): 119, 121.

[20] Joan M. Schwartz and Terry Cook, "Archives, Records, and Power: The Making of
Modern Memory," *Archival Science* 2 (2002): 2.

[21] Terry Cook, "Evidence, Memory, Identity, and Community: Four Shifting
Archival Paradigms," *Archival Science* 13, no. 2–3 (June 2013): 101. The papers
from the Dundee conference, "Memory, Identity and the Archival Paradigm: An
Interdisciplinary Approach," were published in a special issue of *Archival Science* in
June 2013.

[22] Cook, "Evidence," 102.

[23] Cook, "Evidence," 117.

[24] Trond Jacobsen, Ricardo L. Punzalan, and Margaret L. Hedstrom, "Invoking
'Collective Memory': Mapping the Emergence of a Concept in Archival Science,"
Archival Science 13 (April 2013), 217–251, https://doi.org/10.1007/s10502-013
-9199-4.

[25] See, for example, Anthea Josias, "Towards an Understanding of Archives as a
Feature of Collective Memory," *Archival Science* 11 (2011): 95–112; Joanna
Sassoon, "Phantoms of Remembrance: Libraries and Archives as 'the Collective
Memory,'" *Public History Review* 10 (2003): 45; and Ricardo L. Punzalen, "'All
the Things We Cannot Articulate': Colonial Leprosy Archives and Community
Commemoration," in *Community Archives: The Shaping of Memory*, ed. Jeannette
A. Bastian and Ben Alexander (London: Facet, 2009), 199.

[26] Marita Sturken, *Tangled Memories: The Vietnam War, the AIDS Epidemic, and the
Politics of Remembering* (Berkeley: University of California Press, 1997), 10.

[27] Sturken, *Tangled Memories*, 7.

[28] Sturken, *Tangled Memories*, 3.

[29] Sturken, *Tangled Memories*, 7–8.

[30] "The History of Circus Oz," Circus Oz, https://www.circusoz.com/about-circus
-oz/history.html.

[31] David Carlin, ed., *Performing Digital: Multiple Perspectives on a Living Archive*
(Surrey, England: Ashgate, 2015), 13.

[32] Carlin, *Performing Digital*, 18.

[33] John Cage Unbound: A Living Archive, New York Public Library, http://exhibitions .nypl.org/johncage/.

[34] De Kosnik, *Rogue Archives*, 7.

[35] Diane Taylor, *The Archive and the Repertoire: Performing Cultural Memory in the Americas* (Durham, NC: Duke University Press, 2003), 21.

[36] De Kosnik, *Rogue Archives*, 6.

[37] Dima Saber and Paul Long, "'I Will Not Leave, My Freedom Is More Precious Than My Blood': From Affect to Precarity: Crowd-Sourced Citizen Archives as Memories of the Syrian War," *Archives and Records*, 38 (2017): 84.

[38] Saber and Long, "I Will Not Leave," 94.

[39] Richard Cox, "Archives, War, and Memory: Building a Framework," *Library & Archival Security* 25 (2012): 23.

[40] Michele Caswell, "Seeing Yourself in History: Community Archives and the Fight Against Symbolic Annihilation," *Public Historian* 36 (November 2014): 32.

[41] Gabriella Giannachi, *Archive Everything: Mapping the Everyday* (Boston: MIT Press, 2016), xv.

[42] Giannachi, *Archive Everything*, 1.

[43] Giannachi, *Archive Everything*, 23.

[44] Giannachi, *Archive Everything*, 23.

[45] Robert C. Fisher, "'The Grandmother's Story': Oral Tradition, Family Memory and a Mysterious Manuscript," *Archivaria* 57 (Spring 2004): 107–130.

[46] Gracelyn Cassell, "Capturing Personal Stories, Oral Histories of Microhistories. A Case Study from Monserrat," *Decolonizing the Caribbean Record, An Archives Reader*, ed. J. Bastian, J. Aaron, and S. Griffin (Sacramento, CA: Litwin Books, 2018), 461–474.

[47] Juluwarlu Group Aboriginal Corporation, https://www.juluwarlu.com.au.

[48] Carmen Ruschiensky, "Meaning-making and Memory-making in the Archives: Oral History Interviews with Archives Donors," *Archivaria* 84 (Fall 2017): 103–126.

[49] "Black Cultural Archives," Community Archives and Heritage Group, updated June 2, 2015, http://www.communityarchives.org.uk/content/organisation/black -cultural-archives, captured at https://perma.cc/VD75-7XYC.

17

Commentary
Memory

Joel A. Blanco-Rivera

On May 29, 2018, the *New England Journal of Medicine* published "Mortality in Puerto Rico after Hurricane María,"[1] a joint study between Harvard University and the Carlos Albizu University in Puerto Rico that estimated 4,645 possible deaths related to the impact of Hurricane María between September 20 and December 31, 2017. This estimate was in stark contrast to the Puerto Rican government's official number, which at the time stood at 64 deaths.[2] Although the study was explicit in that the number should not be considered as exact and final,[3] many in Puerto Rico used it as a symbol to remember those who lost their lives and to protest both the federal and local government's handling of the post-María recovery efforts. On June 1, in front of Puerto Rico's capitol building, Puerto Ricans reacted to the study by establishing an impromptu memorial where people placed the shoes of the relatives they had lost, with names, pictures, and messages.[4] By June 3, 2,760 pairs of shoes were part of the memorial.[5]

This story encapsulates the power of individual memories to construct a collective memory and how artifacts and documents become part of this process of memorialization. It also evokes some of the main themes from the three essays from this section. For instance, the memorial in Puerto Rico became a space, although temporary, to construct and transmit personal narratives as is also seen in the invocation of spaces in each of these essays.

Photographs and videos were shared through social media, providing an opportunity for Puerto Ricans living in the United States to become part of this memorializing process, similar to how religious fiesta videos from La Plaza del Limón help preserve memories and transmit them to the immigrant communities in the United States, as explored by Janet Ceja Alcalá. The memorial itself, and what was shared through the internet, became a performance, a repertoire, as investigated by Jeannette Bastian. Finally, the lack of a clear process of acquisition and preservation of the artifacts and documents that were part of the memorial echoes Tonia Sutherland's imperative message about the "need for archivists to liberate narratives, support accountability, and document and preserve subaltern histories and cultures."[6]

The themes covered in the three essays illustrate the evolution of memory studies from an archival perspective. As Bastian explains, traditionally the literature has seen the role of archives as evokers, or triggers of memory. Through archives, individuals and communities can evoke and construct their memories. Yet, if we recognize this power of archives in relation to memory-making, then we need to extend the view of what archives are. In this regard, Sutherland offers a powerful argument when discussing the significant role of oral traditions in the understanding of African and African American history. If archivists maintain a fixed view of archives and records, we are marginalizing "embodied experiences such as live performances, rituals, festivals, and oral traditions that produce embodied records which remain outside the archival corpus, and so, too, do the communities and cultural practices they represent."[7] But this goes beyond understanding history; it is, perhaps more important, about accountability and justice as Sutherland's pointed analysis of African American land ownership and retention demonstrates. And although there are issues that go beyond the archivist's role, there are things archivists can do, including activism and advocacy promoting changes to federal and state laws in the United States, such as the recognition of oral testimonies as records.

Ceja Alcalá's essay about La Plaza del Limón underlines the importance of reconceptualizing archival concepts. Reconceptualization is needed not only because of the active role of oral traditions in rural communities like La Plaza but also because of the lack of a physical libraries or archives in that small town. Both oral traditions and personal videos attempt to fill gaps in historical documentation, and thus personal archives become triggers of memories for the residents of La Plaza and those from the diasporic community. Yet, those videos are still a representation of the fiesta in La Plaza. The testimony of Oscar Nieto on his process of video editing, and how he negotiates with people from the town about what to include and what not to include, echoes the work of the archivist in regards to selection and appraisal in that through these processes archivists select what will become part of the archival record and, thus, evokers of memories.

The memory–technology relationship is present in the three essays. Ceja Alcalá explores how smartphones and tablets significantly changed the dynamics of recording and sharing the Fiesta of Our Lady of Guadalupe in La Plaza, leading "to a transition from a handful of videographers having a monopoly on recording technology to a stronger democratization of means in recording one's own experiences."[8] Similarly, Bastian discusses the crowd-sourced videos documenting the protests in Tahir Square and the creation of the virtual "resistance archive" by the media group Mosireen. The immediacy of recording and sharing those instances, Bastian argues, "has changed our relationship with memory," and therefore the records are "no longer merely triggers and touchstones, our records have become our memories, our memories have become our records."[9] Yet, I contend that these records, regardless of how instantly they are shared, are still triggers and evokers of individual and collective memories. Although there is an immediacy in the process of creation and transmission, those new records still need to be viewed, used, and re-shared to become part of the collective memory-making process. The most significant change, demonstrated by both Bastian and Ceja Alcalá in their examples about the use of technologies, is that more people become active records creators, significantly increasing the volume of information, which is shared through complex systems.

In "Digital Curation and the Citizen Archivist," Richard Cox reflects about ways archivists can address significant waves of personal digital archiving. Focusing primarily on advocacy and activism, Cox urges archivists to engage in "developing new mechanisms for educating the public about how to care for their personal and family archives."[10] These three essays take us a step further, advocating for the importance of individual and communal documentation, in all forms, and therefore inviting archivists to embrace a more diverse view of archives.

Notes

[1] Nishant Kishore et al., "Mortality in Puerto Rico after Hurricane Maria," *New England Journal of Medicine* 379, no. 2 (2018): 162–170, https://www.nejm.org/doi/full/10.1056/NEJMsa1803972.

[2] In a July 2018 report, the Puerto Rican government presented a new estimate of 1,427 lives lost. See Frances Robles, "Puerto Rican Government Acknowledges Hurricane Death Toll of 1,427," *New York Times,* August 9, 2018, https://www.nytimes.com/2018/08/09/us/puerto-rico-death-toll-maria.html, captured at https://perma.cc/XZK8-KRMD.

[3] The study was based on household surveys; therefore, it had a wide margin of error, something that is indicated in the article.

[4] Adrian Florido, "An Impromptu Memorial to Demand That Puerto Rico's Hurricane Dead Be Counted," *NPR,* June 1, 2018, https://www.npr.org/2018/06/01/616216225/an-impromptu-memorial-to-demand-puerto-ricos-hurricane-dead-be-counted, captured at https://perma.cc/9SXX-ABEP.

[5] Eric de León Soto, "Víctimas de María transcendieron de un listado a un calzado," *Noticel,* June 3, 2018, https://www.noticel.com/la-calle/victimas-de-maria-trascendieron-de-un-listado-a-un-calzado/749032973, captured at https://perma.cc/83VD-HFH8.

[6] Tonia Sutherland, "Where There's a Will: On Heir Property, African American Land Stories, and the Value of Oral Records in American Archives," 238.

[7] Sutherland, "Where There's a Will," 241.

[8] Janet Ceja Alcalá, "Fiesta Videos: Living and Producing Social Memory of El rancho," 234.

[9] Jeannette A. Bastian, "The Road to Memory: Beyond Touchstones and Triggers," 258.

[10] Richard J. Cox, "Digital Curation and the Citizen Archivist," in *Digital Curation: Practice, Promises and Prospects,* eds. Helen Tibbo et al. (Chapel Hill, NC: School of Information and Library Science, 2009), 107.

18

Richard Cox and the 1950 Generation

James M. O'Toole

At some point in the 1990s, probably during an informal conversation in the bar at a professional meeting, a group of archivists discovered that they had all been born in 1950. As they talked, they added names of other colleagues, who were not present, to the roster of coincidence. This seemed a suitably historic year, dead center in the twentieth century, as a starting point in life, particularly for people whose work caused them to spend much of their mental time in the past. Having entered the profession in their twenties, the participants sharing this accident of birth were, as they reached middle age, heavily involved in its activities. Most had responsible positions in their own employing institutions—in governments, universities, and businesses, and in religious, charitable, cultural, and other organizations—and collectively they represented a broad cross section of archives in North America. They also held office in the many associations of archivists, librarians, and records managers, serving on committees and as officers, attending and regularly making presentations at meetings, sometimes contributing to journals and other publications. Some had doubled as instructors in workshops that sought to impart basic professional skills to newcomers beginning the work of care for original materials, and a few were teaching in the more formal master's degree programs that were then emerging, designed to define a comprehensive archival curriculum and to convey its contents to a rising generation of practitioners. Together with others of more or less the same vintage, born a few years on either side of the mid-century marker, this group constituted a professional generation with some distinct characteristics.

None of the members of this group had grown up wanting to become an archivist, but they had all found their way into this sort of work and, with time, that is what they became. Observance of the bicentennial of the American Revolution, just as they were embarking on careers, had created a favorable climate of interest and, despite inevitable ups and downs, they were fortunate to be part of a profession that was expanding. The number of institutions devoting sustained attention to their own records—often for the first time— was growing. These newly established archives were demonstrating that records had practical, administrative uses in addition to commemorative appeal. At the same time, collecting and organizing sources of more purely historical interest were benefiting from new energy. For their part, academic historians were widening the circles of their interest, extending their studies beyond the doings of "great white men" to those of previously overlooked, but no less important, historical actors and events. Membership in the national professional society of archivists, about half a century old by then, was increasing steadily, spurred by this generation's influx, and the scope of its programs was expanding. A number of smaller archival associations on the regional, state, and even municipal levels had also proliferated, multiplying the possibilities for regular encounters with like-minded colleagues with whom one could share ideas, problems, and solutions, while also promoting a sense of professional solidarity. Perhaps few of these practitioners had as much support from their supervisory organizations as they might have wished for—there was always more that could be done—but it was nonetheless a good time to be an archivist, a time when new thoughts and approaches seemed possible and maybe even necessary. Someone with drive and appropriate ambitions, both professional and intellectual, could make a mark.

Richard Cox was and is a "1950 baby" (full disclosure: so am I). Like others in this generational cohort, though he may have come to his career unexpectedly, he discovered in it many satisfactions. Born and raised in Baltimore, his love of history was nurtured early, helped by family visits to the Colonial Williamsburg restoration and other sites. After graduation from Towson State University in 1972 with a degree in history, unforeseen circumstances led him to a job at the Maryland Historical Society, preparing collections for microfilming; in short order, other unforeseen circumstances promoted him to the position of curator of manuscripts there. Though at the outset he felt, he says, that he was "probably the most ignorant and inexperienced archivist in North America," he soon learned that others were in much the same boat, working their way toward a sense of professionalism, and he found himself "becoming more interested in the nature of archival work."[1] While at Maryland, Cox pursued a master's degree in history at the University of Maryland, where he came under the tutelage of Walter Rundell, whose monumental survey of the use of original sources in graduate history education encouraged him to continue in archives as a career.[2] A succession of increasingly responsible positions followed: archivist and records manager for the city of Baltimore; head of the archives and records division of the Alabama Department of Archives and History; associate archivist at the New York State Archives and Records Administration; and, finally, a member of the faculty of the School of Information at the University of Pittsburgh, where he had also earned a PhD. At each step, while fulfilling the demands of his job, Cox also pursued wider interests and, in the process, emerged as one of the leading archival thinkers and writers in the United States. His concerns paralleled those of the swiftly developing field, and at the same time his work played a significant part in shaping that development. A full review of his influence, especially as expressed in a prodigious volume of published work, would be an impossible task, but several themes stand out as important for identifying his role in defining this professional generation.

He became well known initially through his work on the subject of archival appraisal, a topic that had suddenly attracted pressing interest. If, as Thomas Aquinas insisted, theology had been the "queen of the sciences" in medieval universities, with that discipline understood as holding the key to all others, by the 1980s appraisal had become the queen of the archival sciences. The exponential growth of modern records, compounded by technologies that were supposed to reduce "paperwork" but instead always increased it, gave urgency to the matter. Archivists, no matter their setting, simply could not keep everything that came their way. Were they to attempt to do so, they would run out of space almost overnight, and the forest of meaning would disappear amid the overgrowth of trees. How to decide which records were crucial to retain (and, even more important, which were not) thus became essential in a way that it had not previously been. In the past, archivists might have kept pretty much whatever had managed to survive; those records had value simply because they had endured and something else had not. But now a condition of records abundance, rather than records scarcity, prevailed, and the archivist was put more clearly in the position of having to make selective decisions, actively shaping the contents of their archives. Previous writers, most notably legendary British archivist Sir Hilary Jenkinson, had foreclosed that possibility for the profession: someone else decided what records were worthy of preservation, and once that happened the archivist simply kept them. The reality of abundance rendered such a passive approach obsolete. The archivist had a responsibility— it might even be considered the archivist's "first responsibility"—to shape the historical record.[3]

Along with others, such as Canadian Terry Cook, Cox was a strong and persistent voice in these discussions, and much of his early published work focused on the need for better approaches to the subject of appraisal. Too many archivists—and perhaps especially those with more seniority in the profession—still relied on vague criteria for selection. "I know the good stuff when I see it" was a common refrain. Given the challenges of contemporary records, such idiosyncratic methods were obviously inadequate. A more thoughtful process was needed. One particular approach of which Cox became a proponent was that of the documentation strategy: a planned, deliberate effort to understand the contexts that produced records in the first place, to analyze what information they contained and therefore what it was possible for users to learn from them and then to shape their appraisal and selection for archival preservation. Such a program could be profitably employed by an individual institution, but it would also benefit measurably from cooperation among archives. No one repository could hope to collect everything that might be relevant to the study of a given topic, and the quality of the collective documentary heritage could be improved by institutions working together. Cox published a case study showing how the "doc-strat" approach might be applied to preserving the records of local history in the state of New York and, together with Helen Samuels of the Massachusetts Institute of Technology, he offered workshops that encouraged others to apply the same methods in their own settings.[4] The discussion of documentation strategies at meetings and otherwise proved surprisingly passionate, with some rejecting the idea as more complicated than it needed to be. Cox and his colleagues agreed that no mechanistic, one-size-fits-all approach could be articulated, and indeed that was never the intent. But the nature of the profession's conversation about appraisal had changed nonetheless, and archivists accepted their responsibility to approach the building of their collections more thoughtfully than had often been the case in the past.

A second critical issue throughout Cox's years as a working archivist was the rapid advance of technology, and nothing affected the work of his professional generation more than this. The changing nature of records themselves and of any effort to manage them successfully, all under the influence of spreading access to electronic technologies, were matters of daily concern. In the 1960s, libraries had hesitantly begun using computers (to assist in the work of cataloging, for instance), but the archival world lagged behind. As computers became more and more generally available, however—why, by the early 1990s, they were no longer room-sized machines full of tubes but were small enough to fit on your lap—archivists discovered that, like their library colleagues, they could now accomplish certain tasks more easily. Archives could produce more sophisticated guides to their holdings, and they could share information about those holdings far and wide. Inevitably, an even more serious challenge to traditional archival thinking and practice emerged: records that were themselves created and used only in electronic formats, bypassing the step to paper altogether, records that would later be described as having been "born digital." How could archivists realistically deal with these records and carry out their fundamental duty to preserve those with lasting value, especially since the technology (both hardware and software) required to make them intelligible was itself constantly changing, with obsolescence always a prospect? What did archivists need to know about all this? Were there examples of archival programs that were successfully addressing the issue, and could that knowledge be shared with others who would, probably sooner rather than later, have to face it, too?

These were the questions that Cox began to explore as he moved into teaching at the University of Pittsburgh, and they provided the basis for his 1992 doctoral dissertation. Some archives—particularly those of state governments, where the impact of the "information age" was felt most insistently—were beginning to address the problem by redefining the qualifications that employees would need for the management of electronic records. At the same time, some of the emerging university-based programs of archival education at the master's level were also seeking to prepare students to live and work in this new world, no matter where they might wind up after graduation. In his thesis, subsequently published as a monograph, Cox concluded that, in both realms, the professional glass was at best half full.[5] Clear-eyed assessments, both positive and negative, marked his conclusions, and he also described an effort, in which he himself was a principal, to try to fill the glass a little higher. Between 1989 and 1992, the university joined forces with an association of government archivists to run a summer institute that would provide continuing education for archivists already working with such materials in their own settings. Known familiarly as "Camp Pitt," the institute attracted about a hundred participants who studied both the general principles of institutional strategic planning and the specific concerns of planning in an electronic environment. The technological details were never far away, but increasingly important was the nature of the underlying information policy and how it could address the extent and pace of change. Cox left the development of specific technical standards and programs to others, but he was a leader in helping his professional generation of archivists come to terms with the problems of electronic records. Not to do so guaranteed irrelevance.

The issues of appraisal and of electronic records were both matters of immediate moment to archivists of the 1950 generation as they entered into the most active time of their careers, and at that point Cox's interest took a turn to the larger question of professionalism itself. Long considered by many to be mere "handmaidens" to historians—the Library of Congress classification system places books about archives among the "auxiliary sciences" of history, together with heraldry and numismatics—archivists were coming to see themselves as members of a distinct professional group, still in the process of formation, perhaps, but requiring all the more deliberation because of that. Though he and his peers had mostly come to archives through their interest in history, they were now thinking of themselves as part of a field that was related to that discipline but nonetheless different from it. Their work made history possible, of course, but historians were not archivists' only—and perhaps not even their most important—clients. An archivist in state or national government, for instance, served the larger goal of holding public officials accountable for their actions by preserving and making available the records of those transactions. The archivist of a business organization provided support for the company's legal team and even its advertising department. The archivist of a religious body helped it fulfill its otherworldly spiritual mission but also assisted in the group's works of charity and education in this world. The archivist in a state or local historical society spent more time with amateur genealogists than with tweedy professors embarked on a study that only other specialists might read; work with the local elementary school to instill in children a sense of community was as important as helping graduate dissertation writers. What were the attitudes, values, and skills that all of these archivists shared? How might these attitudes, values, and skills be developed among archivists already in the profession and, even more critically, imparted to those who were just entering into their work?

Cox's seminal contribution to this emerging discussion came in his study of the very idea of professionalism as applied to archivists. The product of a summer fellowship at the Bentley Historical Library at the University of Michigan—extending over fifteen years, this fellowship program was crucial in promoting the idea that archives, like other disciplines, benefited from serious, extended research about its own concerns—the essay began with a survey of the sociological literature that described the characteristics of a true profession. Then, Cox proposed actions that would help archivists approach those standards, including efforts to demonstrate the social utility of their work and development of a stronger national voice on archives and records issues. Later, he provided a defense of the profession when it would come under criticism from those who fundamentally misunderstand it. His response to novelist Nicholson Baker's argumentative but naïve assertion that archivists could (and should) save in hard copy every newspaper ever printed was a scholarly rarity—a book-length riposte to a book-length attack—but it effectively described and defended what archivists did and why.[6] In doing all this, Cox was helping to make a larger case for the substantive intellectual content of archival work. The profession was not just a trade, a collection of specific skills that practitioners could learn through apprenticeship (as he and the others of his generation had) and thereafter apply to a set of familiar, recurring problems. Rather, there actually were things to think and theorize about. Yes, archivists had practical duties that had to be accomplished. But they could perform those duties better if they paused and asked larger questions about context and meaning: Where had archival records come from in the first place? What purposes, individual and collective, did records accomplish initially, and how did their usefulness change with time? How did information of all kinds move around in society, and what was distinctive (or not) about the archival portion of that information ecology? How did the forms that information took affect its usefulness and meaning?

To this extent, Cox became a significant figure in what might be considered a kind of intellectual revolution in archives at the end of the twentieth century. To those (and there were some) who insisted that there was nothing for archivists to theorize about—"Just shut up and shuffle the papers," they seemed to say—he and others insisted that stepping back from the demands of the day-to-day work was always healthy. He helped make the case for identifying archival research agendas—the very idea that there were such things was new—outlining the specific areas that would benefit from focused study. Appraisal was the most obvious example, but there were others, including the history of archives and the archival profession. Like everyone else, archivists could profit from knowing their own history, and Cox produced a number of case studies of particular settings and recordkeeping practices. He edited a collection of the writings of Lester Cappon, an important American historian, archivist, documentary editor, and historical administrator, and he produced a series of essays (originally intended as a monograph) on various aspects of Cappon's career. Cox's research for this project in Cappon's personal papers at Colonial Williamsburg was an occasion for him to return to the historical research skills he had acquired long before. More generally, he argued for the value of archival history, encouraged studies of it during his tenure as editor of the *American Archivist*, and pointed out opportunities for its further study.[7]

These larger enduring interests provided the basis for Cox's transition from archival practitioner to archival educator. He was fortunate in being present at the creation of a new system for the education of archivists in the United States, a system he helped define. Just as he and others of his generation were advancing their careers, there was renewed discussion of how best to prepare those seeking to enter the profession and how to assure employers that a potential archivist had the knowledge and skills that would be required. Most of the 1950 cohort seemed to agree that their own backdoor entrance into the field was not the best, but the dimensions of a better approach were as yet unclear. Some thought that a procedure to certify professional qualifications through study and examination (as with accountants, for example) was the right approach; indeed, Cox was a member of the governing council of the Society of American Archivists that approved a process for the certification of individual archivists, a decision he later regretted. More promising was the emergence of university-based, graduate-level programs of archival education, with coursework and research overseen by PhD-level faculty, whether in history departments, library and information science schools, or, in some cases, in dual-degree programs. (The Canadian model of a distinct master's degree in archives was discussed but never implemented in the United States.) When Cox joined the University of Pittsburgh faculty in 1988, he became part of another generation, the first of those with full-time responsibilities for these graduate programs, which quickly became the principal means of entry for new professionals.[8]

In this capacity, he had the opportunity to mark out both the extent and the content of a full archival curriculum. Where university-based archival education programs had existed previously, usually taught by adjunct faculty, an introductory course was usually followed by ill-defined seminars and successive internship experiences; the intellectual content of these was thin. At Pittsburgh, Cox moved beyond this model, offering courses that gave detailed consideration to substantive subject matter, including ethics, in addition to his well-established interests in appraisal and archival history. His classes, all of which had extensive reading lists, quickly gained a reputation for rigor. He continued to engage actively in his own research and writing, and he also demanded it of his students, especially those completing doctorates under his direction, thereby positioning them to be leaders of a second cohort of archival faculty at universities elsewhere. By developing the elements essential to any legitimate program of graduate study, he made the curriculum at Pitt one of the leading programs in the country.

If the archival field as a whole was changing just when he had entered it in the 1970s, so too the field of archival education was now expanding in the 1990s and after, and Cox became a leader among his fellow academics from around the country. He played a role in organizing a forum for educators (most of them, like him, articulating programs for the first time) to be held in advance of the annual meeting of the Society of American Archivists. These were opportunities to discuss concerns that were peculiar to them: the design of coursework, the integration of research, the problems of student recruitment and placement, and the organizational setting of archival study within the larger framework of a university. Similarly, he was active in the meetings of the Association of Library and Information Science Education, bringing the particular concerns of archival education to that group. Increasingly, he turned his attention to issues surrounding the preparation of future archival faculty, and in this he played a central role in establishing the Archival Education and Research Institute in 2008. These annual gatherings provided the opportunity for junior faculty and those seeking to secure faculty appointments to present their own research, as well as the chance for informal exchanges with their more senior colleagues. More important, they helped embed in the educators themselves—and by extension in the archival profession at large—a belief that rigorous graduate programs, conducted by faculty who were expected to do all the things that faculty in other disciplines did, were essential to continued intellectual vitality.

Every generation in every profession faces its own challenges. Changes, both expected and unexpected, present a variety of demands, and a healthy profession learns how to respond to them. Moreover, it devises effective means for preparing the next generation of practitioners to face its own, as yet unimagined, challenges. So it has been with the 1950 generation of archivists in general, and so it has been in particular with Richard Cox, a representative and a shaper of that professional generation. The "most ignorant and inexperienced archivist in North America" was not that when he thought it in 1972, and he is certainly not that today. Rather, he is someone who measurably affected the course of archives throughout his own career and who, through his writings and his students, will continue to do so in the future. No professional could ask for more.

Notes

[1] Richard J. Cox, *American Archival Analysis: The Recent Development of the Archival Profession in the United States* (Metuchen, NJ: Scarecrow Press, 1990), viii–ix.

[2] Walter Rundell Jr., *In Pursuit of American History: Research and Training in the United States* (Norman: University of Oklahoma Press, 1970).

[3] Richard J. Cox and Helen W. Samuels, "The Archivist's First Responsibility: A Research Agenda to Improve the Identification and Retention of Records of Enduring Value," *American Archivist* 51 (Winter/Spring 1988): 28–42.

[4] Richard J. Cox, "A Documentation Strategy Case Study: Western New York," *American Archivist* 52 (Spring 1989): 192–200.

[3] Richard J. Cox, *The First Generation of Electronic Records Archivists in the United States: A Study in Professionalization* (New York: Haworth Press, 1994).

[6] Richard J. Cox, "Professionalism and Archivists in the United States," *American Archivist* 49 (Summer 1986): 229–247; Richard J. Cox, *Vandals in the Stacks? A Response to Nicholson Baker's Assault on Libraries* (Westport, CT: Greenwood Press, 2002). See also Nicholson Baker, *Double Fold: Libraries and the Assault on Paper* (New York: Random House, 2001).

[7] Richard J. Cox, ed., *Lester J. Cappon and the Relationship of History, Archives, and Scholarship in the Golden Age of Archival Theory* (Chicago: Society of American Archivists, 2004). See also Richard J. Cox, "American Archival History: Its Development, Needs, and Opportunities," *American Archivist* 46 (Winter 1983): 31–41; Richard J. Cox, "On the Value of Archival History in the United States," *Libraries and Culture* 23 (Spring 1988): 135–151; and Richard J. Cox, *Closing an Era: Historical Perspectives on Modern Archives and Records Management* (Westport, CT: Greenwood Press, 2000).

[8] For a useful overview of the development of archival education, see Alison Langmead, "The History of Archival Education in America: What's Next?," *Archival Research and Education: Selected Papers from the 2014 AERI Conference*, ed. Richard J. Cox, Alison Langmead, and Eleanor Mattern (Sacramento, CA: Litwin Books, 2015), 273–314.

About the Authors

Janet Ceja Alcalá is an assistant professor in Archival Studies and Library and Information Science at Simmons University. Her research and teaching are in the area of archives, specializing in audiovisual archives, oral history, and cultural heritage archives in Latinx communities. She earned a BA in Film Studies from the University of California, Santa Barbara, an MA in Film and Media Preservation from the University of Rochester, and a PhD in Library and Information Science from the University of Pittsburgh. She has also worked as a moving image archivist in Los Angeles.

Jeannette A. Bastian is a Professor Emerita in the School of Library and Information Science at Simmons University. A former territorial librarian of the US Virgin Islands, she holds a PhD from the University of Pittsburgh. Her books include *West Indian Literature, A Critical Index, 1930–1975* (as Jeannette B. Allis; G. K. Hall, 1981); *Owning*

Memory: How a Caribbean Community Lost Its Archives and Found Its History (Libraries Unlimited, 2003); *Community Archives: The Shaping of Memory* (co-editor with Ben Alexander; Facet Publishing, 2009); *Archives in Libraries; What Librarians and Archivists Need to Know to Work Together* (co-author with Megan Sniffin-Maranoff and Donna Webber; Society of American Archivists, 2015); and *Decolonizing the Caribbean Record, An Archives Reader*, editor (co-editor with John A. Aarons and Stanley H. Griffin; Litwin Books, 2018). She was elected a Fellow of the Society of American Archivists in 2019.

Joel A. Blanco-Rivera is a professor in the National School of Conservation, Restoration, and Museography "Manuel del Castillo Negrete" in Mexico City. He holds a PhD from the University of Pittsburgh and an MSI from the University of Michigan. His research interests are archives and transitional justice in Latin America and the Caribbean, collective memory and community archives, and social media archives.

Gracen Brilmyer is a PhD candidate in Information Studies at the University of California, Los Angeles. Their research lies at the intersection of disability studies and archival studies, where they investigate disability, coloniality, and affect primarily in natural history museums. Their work at this intersection has been published in *Archival Science*, and their research on entomological collections and digital archives has been published in various journals. They have also published a poster, "Dismantling White Supremacy in Archives," with Michelle Caswell, in *Library Quarterly*. They earned their master's in information management and systems from the University of California, Berkeley.

Kathy Carbone is a postdoctoral scholar and lecturer in the Department of Information Studies at the University of California, Los Angeles, and a researcher with the Refugees Rights in Records (R3) Project team. Before this, she was the Institute Archivist and Performing Arts Librarian at the California Institute of the Arts for more than a decade. Her research interests focus on the intersection of archives, broadly conceived, with contemporary art practices, memory and identity productions, migration, social justice, and human rights.

Michelle Caswell, PhD, is associate professor of Archival Studies in the Department of Information Studies at the University of California, Los Angeles, where she directs the UCLA Community Archives Lab (https://communityarchiveslab.ucla .edu/). She is the co-founder of the South Asian American Digital Archive (http://www.saada.org), an online repository that documents and provides access to the stories of South Asian Americans. She is also the author of *Archiving the Unspeakable: Silence, Memory and the Photographic Record in Cambodia* (University of Wisconsin Press, 2014), as well as more than three dozen peer-reviewed articles on archives, memory, and communities.

Wendy Duff is a professor and dean in the University of Toronto's Faculty of Information, where she teaches courses in the areas of archival access and community archives. Her research and publications focus on the archival users, the impact of archives on social justice, and archival access. In her most current research she explores the impact of the creation of a digital archives as well as different methodologies for studying the impact of community archives and the emotional impact of working with records of violence.

Luciana Duranti is a professor of archival theory, diplomatics, and the preservation of digital records in the master's and doctoral archival studies programs of the School of Library, Archival and Information Studies of the University of British Columbia. She is director of the Centre for the International Study of Contemporary Records and Archives (CISCRA; www.ciscra.org) and of the InterPARES research project on the long-term preservation of authentic electronic records (1998–2019; www.interpares.org).

Joyce Gabiola earned an MSLIS in archives management at Simmons University. Most recently, they worked as a doctoral student researcher at the University of California, Los Angeles, and is currently a steering member of the AAPI LGBTQ+ Archiving Collective in Los Angeles; the program committee co-chair for the 2019 SAA/CoSA Annual Meeting; and member of the #WeHere Collective, which serves and supports Black, Indigenous, and People of Color in efforts to navigate the systems of power that control archives and libraries. Joyce's archival research/praxis requires being perpetually mindful of power structures that control the interconnected lives of archives, archivists, academics, and communities.

Patricia Galloway joined the University of Texas at Austin's School of Information's archival program in 2000. Now a professor there, she teaches courses in digital archives, archival appraisal, and historical museums. From 1979 to 2000, she worked at the Mississippi Department of Archives and History, where she was manager of archival information systems, directing a project to create an electronic records program for Mississippi. Her recent publications include articles in *American Archivist*, *Archivaria*, *D-Lib*, *Library Trends*, *Information and Culture*, and *IEEE Annals of the History of Computing*.

Anne J. Gilliland is associate dean for Information Studies in UCLA's Graduate School of Education & Information Studies and professor and director of the Center for Information as Evidence, Department of Information Studies. She is the director of the Archival Education and Research Initiative (AERI) and a Fellow of the Society of American Archivists. Her research and teaching relate broadly to the history, nature, human impact and technologies associated with archives, recordkeeping, and memory, particularly in translocal and international contexts.

Alison Langmead currently holds a joint faculty appointment at the University of Pittsburgh in the Dietrich School of Arts and Sciences and the School of Computing and Information. She serves as the director of the Visual Media Workshop (VMW), a humanities lab located in the Department of the History of Art and Architecture that focuses on the investigation of material and visual culture in an environment that encourages technological experimentation. Alison is also the principal contact for the DHRX: Digital Humanities Research at Pitt initiative.

Heather MacNeil is a professor in the Faculty of Information at the University of Toronto, where she teaches courses on archival history, theory, and methods. In her research she explores cross-disciplinary perspectives on archival concepts and methods and the history of representational practices across archives, museums, and libraries. She is a founding organizer, with Barbara Craig and Philip Eppard, of the International Conference on the History of Records and Archives (I-CHORA); the author of *Without Consent: The Ethics of Disclosing Personal Information in Public Archives* (Scarecrow Press, 1992) and *Trusting Records: Legal, Historical, and Diplomatic Perspectives* (Kluwer Academic Publishers, 2000); and co-editor, with Terry Eastwood, of *Currents of Archival Thinking* (Libraries Unlimited, 2010; 2017).

Eleanor "Nora" Mattern is an assistant teaching professor at the University of Pittsburgh's School of Computing and Information. She earned her PhD in Library and Information Sciences from the University of Pittsburgh in 2014, where she studied with Dr. Richard J. Cox. Before beginning her current role, Nora was a librarian at the University of Chicago and held a visiting joint position with the University Library System and the School of Computing and Information at the University of Pittsburgh. Her research interests are in the areas of information policy, government information practices and systems, and digital curation.

Lindsay Kistler Mattock is an assistant professor at the University of Iowa's School of Library and Information Science. Her work focuses on the archival practices of noninstitutional archival spaces, such as media collectives and community archives. Her ongoing digital project, *Mapping the Independent Media Community*, builds from archival resources and traces the historical social networks emerging between independent film and video makers, distributors, media arts centers, and cultural heritage institutions to offer understandings of how the historical conditions of the independent and avant-garde have influenced contemporary archival praxis.

James M. O'Toole is the Clough Millennium Professor of History at Boston College. Most recently, he authored *The Faithful: A History of Catholics in America* (Belknap Press, 2008). He wrote the first edition of *Understanding Archives and Manuscripts* (Society of American Archivists, 1990) and prepared the second edition with Richard Cox in 2006.

Robert B. Riter works in the University of Alabama's School of Library & Information Studies, where he holds the Marie Drolet Bristol-EBSCO Endowed Professorship and coordinates the Program in Archival Studies. He holds appointments in library and information studies and book arts, teaching courses in archival studies, book history, and analytical bibliography. His research examines historical questions regarding the history of archival ideas and concepts, materiality, archival production, and the publication of original sources. Locally, he serves on the advisory boards of the Birmingham Black Radio Museum (BBRM) and the Invisible Histories Project (iHP).

Donghee Sinn, PhD, is an associate professor in Information Science, College of Emergency Preparedness, Homeland Security, and Cyber-security, University at Albany. Her current research interests include personal digital archiving, information management and literacy within the personal domain, digital presence of archival materials for historical events, and archival documentation and appraisal in government contexts. She received her PhD degree in library and information science at the University of Pittsburgh. Previously, she worked in the National Archives of Korea.

Heather Soyka is an assistant professor at the Kent State University iSchool teaching in the areas of archival studies and research data management. Her recent research examines community engagement and recordkeeping factors relevant to capacity building, sustainability, and reuse. She earned a PhD from the University of Pittsburgh iSchool.

 **Jefferson Sporn** is a recent graduate of the University of Toronto's Master of Information program, where he specialized in archives and records management. He holds a BA in anthropology from Emory University. He is passionate about politics, film, and the intersection of community archives and representation. He currently works at an antiracism and race relations education organization in Toronto.

 **Tonia Sutherland,** PhD, is assistant professor in the Department of Information and Computer Sciences at the University of Hawai'i at Mānoa. Global in scope, Sutherland's critical and liberatory scholarship in the fields of archival studies, digital studies, and science and technology studies (STS) examines analog histories of modern information and communication technologies; interrogates entanglements of technology and culture; and engages the latest work at the intersections of national infrastructures and community informatics. Sutherland is a faculty affiliate of the Center for Race and Digital Studies at New York University and the author of *Digital Remains: Race and the Digital Afterlife* (forthcoming).

 **David A. Wallace,** PhD, is a clinical associate professor at the University of Michigan School of Information (UMSI). He took the first class that Richard Cox taught on archives at SUNY Albany in 1987 and later wrote his dissertation under Richard's guidance at the University of Pittsburgh from 1992 to 1997. In 2002 he and Richard co-edited *Archives and the Public Good: Accountability and Records in Modern Society* (Quorum Books). In 2015 he relocated to Cape Town, South Africa, to co-manage UMSI's Global Information Engagement Program, which partners graduate students with nongovernmental organizations to address pressing information challenges.

Elizabeth Yakel, PhD, is a professor and associate dean for Academic Affairs at the University of Michigan School of Information. Throughout her career, she has researched how users discover, analyze, and use primary sources and investigated how metrics can be used to better serve both researchers and the repositories that serve them. Her research has been funded by the Andrew W. Mellon Foundation and the Institute for Museum and Library Services (IMLS). She is active in the Society of American Archivists (SAA), where she served on the governing council and was elected a Fellow in 1999.

Jimmy Zavala is the project coordinator librarian for *Transforming Knowledge, Transforming Libraries,* a three-year Institute of Museum and Library Services–funded research project analyzing the intersection of ethnic studies theory and community archives at the University of California, Irvine. Jimmy received his MLIS from the University of California, Los Angeles.

Index